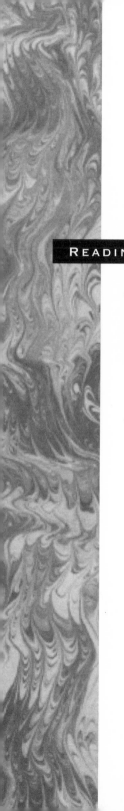

THE GREAT GATSBY

OTHER TITLES IN THE GREENHAVEN PRESS LITERARY COMPANION SERIES:

AMERICAN AUTHORS

Maya Angelou
Stephen Crane
Emily Dickinson
William Faulkner
F. Scott Fitzgerald
Nathaniel Hawthorne
Ernest Hemingway
Herman Melville
Arthur Miller
Eugene O'Neill
Edgar Allan Poe
John Steinbeck
Mark Twain

BRITISH AUTHORS

Jane Austen
Joseph Conrad
Charles Dickens

WORLD AUTHORS

Fyodor Dostoyevsky
Homer
Sophocles

AMERICAN LITERATURE

Of Mice and Men
The Scarlet Letter

BRITISH LITERATURE

Animal Farm
The Canterbury Tales
Lord of the Flies
Romeo and Juliet
Shakespeare: The Comedies
Shakespeare: The Sonnets
Shakespeare: The Tragedies
A Tale of Two Cities

WORLD LITERATURE

Diary of a Young Girl

THE GREENHAVEN PRESS
Literary Companion
TO AMERICAN LITERATURE

THE GREAT GATSBY

David Bender, *Publisher*
Bruno Leone, *Executive Editor*
Brenda Stalcup, *Managing Editor*
Bonnie Szumski, *Series Editor*
Katie de Koster, *Book Editor*

Greenhaven Press, San Diego, CA

Library of Congress Cataloging-in-Publication Data

Readings on the Great Gatsby / Katie de Koster, book editor.
    p.   cm. — (The Greenhaven Press literary
companion to American literature)
    Includes bibliographical references and index.
    ISBN 1-56510-645-8 (lib. : alk. paper). —
ISBN 1-56510-644-X (pbk. : alk. paper)
    1. Fitzgerald, F. Scott (Francis Scott), 1896–1940.
Great Gatsby. I. de Koster, Katie, 1948–   . II. Series.
PS3511.I9G88   1998
813'.52–dc21   97-12901
                                                CIP

Every effort has been made to trace the owners of copyrighted material. The articles in this volume may have been edited for content, length, and/or reading level. The titles have been changed to enhance the editorial purpose of the Opposing Viewpoints® concept. Those interested in locating the original source will find the complete citation on the first page of each article.

Cover photo: Archive Photos

Copyright ©1998 by Greenhaven Press, Inc.
PO Box 289009
San Diego, CA 92198-9009
Printed in the U.S.A.

"A writer can spin on about his adventures after thirty, after forty, after fifty, but the criteria by which these adventures are weighed and valued are irrevocably settled at the age of twenty-five."

F. Scott Fitzgerald,
"Ring"

Contents

Foreword   11

Introduction   13

F. Scott Fitzgerald: A Biography   15

Chapter 1: Who Is Jay Gatsby?

1. Gatsby Is a Classic Romantic *by Robert Ornstein*   33
The Great Gatsby is Fitzgerald's fable of the unending quest of the romantic dream. But in shifting the "frontier" of unlimited possibilities from the West to Wall Street, Gatsby is traveling in the wrong direction both in time and in space. His romantic dream is an attempt to recapture something lost in the past, not a future possibility; yet he is "great" because his dream is a grand illusion.

2. Gatsby Is a Sinister Gangster *by Thomas H. Pauly*   41
When Jay Gatsby replaces the perception of a gangster as a lowlife with an image of an upscale, stylish, wealthy figure, he is faithfully reflecting the gamblers, bootleggers, and bond thieves of the 1920s. Under his genial front, Gatsby was undoubtedly a more cunning criminal than Nick Carraway realizes.

3. Gatsby Is a Profoundly Comic Character
by Brian Way   52
The Great Gatsby is a social comedy. Fitzgerald's greatest success in this comic venture is the character of Gatsby himself, who has what Way calls the "power to arouse wild incredulous laughter."

4. Gatsby Is a Pathological Narcissist *by Giles Mitchell*   61
A clinical analysis of Jay Gatsby's personality shows that he is a pathological narcissist. His desires for perfection and omnipotence are classic symptoms of narcissism, in which the "ego-ideal" has become inflated and destructive. Gatsby's grandiose lies, poor sense of reality, sense of entitlement, and exploitive treatment of others—particularly women—confirm the diagnosis.

5. Gatsby Is a Fairy-Tale Hero for the Middle Class
   by Robert Emmet Long   68
   Gatsby's middle-class dream is a fairy tale, the product of a
   middle-class imagination. Fitzgerald draws from the resources and energies of the fairy tale to evoke the enchanted horror of a world in which the good prince is put
   to death and evil survives.

Chapter 2: Reflections of America in *The Great Gatsby*

1. The Cynical Views of an American Literary
   Generation *by William Goldhurst*   73
   Many authors of the 1920s were unified in their reaction
   against the popular aspirations and values of post–World
   War I Americans. In Fitzgerald's case, that reaction led to a
   suggestion that religious belief had degenerated into just
   another business, while business had attained the status of
   a new religion.

2. The American Dream: All Gush and Twinkle
   by Louis Auchincloss   83
   In creating a hero out of a monster, Fitzgerald creates an
   illusion of an illusion. "Dreadful Daisy"—who is both
   Gatsby's dream and the American dream—is able to transform Gatsby into a romantic hero through the spell of her
   superficial charm. By investing a shallow, dull, drab world
   with a romantic glow, Fitzgerald catches the folly as well
   as the magic of the dream, and illuminates the lonely business of living.

3. Delusions of American Idealism *by Joyce A. Rowe*   87
   In *The Great Gatsby*, Fitzgerald illustrates the tension between America's idealized, spiritual image of itself and its
   true exploitive nature. Reflecting and manifesting this national blindness, the materialistic Gatsby sees himself as
   on a heroic quest, but he is pursuing a grail of wealth and
   power.

4. The True Heir of the American Dream
   by Marius Bewley   96
   The Great Gatsby offers close and severe criticism of the
   deficiencies of American values in the 1920s. Gatsby,
   whom Bewley calls a mythical incarnation of "the aspiration and the ordeal of his race," is pitted against Tom
   Buchanan, who not only virtually murders Gatsby but
   tries to destroy his vision. Since, in the end, Buchanan
   fails, *Gatsby* is an affirmation of the American spirit in a
   world that denies the soul.

5. **The Grotesque End Product of the American Dream** *by Richard Lehan* 104

Jay Gatsby marks the logical end of the Horatio Alger rags-to-riches tradition. Although the former poor farm boy has acquired considerable wealth, Gatsby's idealism crashes against the brute strength and power of Tom Buchanan and his materialistic world. Gatsby never learns that his dream is dead, but that realization is Nick's nightmare.

6. **Ethics in *Gatsby:* An Examination of American Values** *by Tony McAdams* 111

Since *The Great Gatsby* expresses Fitzgerald's doubts about America's moral direction, it offers an excellent ground for an examination of American ethics. Among the subjects for study: the individual characters (liars all); Nick's moral growth; and why Gatsby—a boorish fraud who uses others—is likable. On a broader scale, *Gatsby* is a good basis for an analysis of the values of wealth, class, and the American dream of gleaming possibilities.

7. **Corruption and Anti-Immigrant Sentiments Skew a Traditional American Tale** *by Jeffrey Louis Decker* 121

The Great Gatsby mirrors American uneasiness about the loss of white supremacy in the United States. Fitzgerald takes a traditional self-made-man tale as told by Horatio Alger and guided by Ben Franklin's precepts, but distorts the standard elements to reflect the fears, negative perceptions, and loss of faith of the early 1920s. Although the resulting story has been called *the* novel of the American dream, the term "American dream" was created in the 1930s to offer a way to deal with the problems of the Great Depression; it is inappropriately used when applied to *The Great Gatsby*.

8. **A Farewell to Flappers** *by Edwin Clark* 133

A conflict between spirituality and commercial life animates *The Great Gatsby*. Despite what Clark calls its "whimsical magic," the book portrays a tragic decay of souls with insight and keen psychological observation. The characters, mean of spirit, careless, and disloyal, are more to be pitied than despised because they are unaware of their flaws.

Chapter 3: The Art of *The Great Gatsby*

1. **An Introduction to *Gatsby*** *by F. Scott Fitzgerald* 137

In 1934 Random House asked Fitzgerald to write an introduction to their Modern Library edition of *The Great Gatsby*. Fitzgerald took the opportunity to disparage the current crop of literary critics as being worse than useless and to defend his efforts at keeping his "artistic conscience" pure while he wrote the book. After reexamining his work, he decides that, while there might be some room for improvement in the novel, he has nothing to be embarrassed about.

2. The High Cost of Immersion *by Malcolm Bradbury*   141
Although some critics believe Fitzgerald was little more than a chronicler of American life during the 1920s, his true gift was the discovery of and immersion in the psychic forces that drove life during that frenzied decade. As in *Tender Is the Night* and *The Last Tycoon,* Fitzgerald's exploration of the society and psychology of the times in *The Great Gatsby* required a deep personal involvement that was reflected in his life, from the euphoria of the beginning of the decade to the deep depression that ended it.

3. Using a Dramatic Narrator to Present a Bifocal View *by Douglas Taylor*   147
Using Nick Carraway to present a filtered image of Jay Gatsby, Fitzgerald created a work artistically worthy of the intense moral and social passions of its time. The somewhat detached narrator allows Fitzgerald to explore the tale from both sentimental and self-critical angles, revealing the subtle ironies of the tension between inner feeling and outer form. While the tawdry images of the world are presented to the reader through Nick's eyes, at the same time Nick embraces and chooses to validate Gatsby's romantic vision, sympathetically presenting the sadness and magic of unfulfilled youthful dreams.

4. Creating a Creator *by David H. Lynn*   154
In *The Great Gatsby,* it is impossible to know a character's essential qualities because each character is seen through the eyes of another character. For example, the reader sees Nick's private attempt to add flesh to the skeleton of Gatsby's public gestures; the portrait that emerges is Nick's interpretation, and as such illuminates him even more than it does Gatsby. Using the traditions of both realism and romanticism, Nick synthesizes these different views into his ironic but affectionate vision of Gatsby as an exotic, romantic dreamer.

5. Fitzgerald's Remarkable Narrative Art *by R.W. Lid*   163
By using Nick Carraway as narrator, Fitzgerald is able to create ingenious solutions to the problems of tying together a compressed, episodic narrative. Such solutions constitute much of the technical brilliance of the novel. Married to these technical turns of artistry is Fitzgerald's strong narrative sense, which allows him to rearrange time and orchestrate two threads of the story so that the threads continually complement each other as they develop toward a mutual, horrific climax.

6. Transforming Old Values into New Art

by Robert Sklar   172

Before he wrote *The Great Gatsby*, Fitzgerald had worked with a variety of themes and ideas. For example, he wrote variations on the genteel romantic formula in which the flapper heroine, rather than the hero, wields the ultimate power. He struggled with issues of wealth and class, especially the acquisition of sudden wealth, often "punishing" his characters for both their faults and their good fortune. It is possible to trace the maturation of Fitzgerald's ideas through his early novels and short stories to the turning point of his career, *The Great Gatsby*.

Chronology   180

For Further Research   184

Works by F. Scott Fitzgerald   188

Index   189

FOREWORD

"'Tis the good reader that
makes the good book."

Ralph Waldo Emerson

The story's bare facts are simple: The captain, an old and scarred seafarer, walks with a peg leg made of whale ivory. He relentlessly drives his crew to hunt the world's oceans for the great white whale that crippled him. After a long search, the ship encounters the whale and a fierce battle ensues. Finally the captain drives his harpoon into the whale, but the harpoon line catches the captain about the neck and drags him to his death.

A simple story, a straightforward plot—yet, since the 1851 publication of Herman Melville's *Moby-Dick*, readers and critics have found many meanings in the struggle between Captain Ahab and the whale. To some, the novel is a cautionary tale that depicts how Ahab's obsession with revenge leads to his insanity and death. Others believe that the whale represents the unknowable secrets of the universe and that Ahab is a tragic hero who dares to challenge fate by attempting to discover this knowledge. Perhaps Melville intended Ahab as a criticism of Americans' tendency to become involved in well-intentioned but irrational causes. Or did Melville model Ahab after himself, letting his fictional character express his anger at what he perceived as a cruel and distant god?

Although literary critics disagree over the meaning of *Moby-Dick*, readers do not need to choose one particular interpretation in order to gain an understanding of Melville's novel. Instead, by examining various analyses, they can gain numerous insights into the issues that lie under the surface of the basic plot. Studying the writings of literary critics can also aid readers in making their own assessments of *Moby-Dick* and other literary works and in developing analytical thinking skills.

The Greenhaven Literary Companion Series was created with these goals in mind. Designed for young adults, this unique anthology series provides an engaging and comprehensive introduction to literary analysis and criticism. The essays included in the Literary Companion Series are chosen for their accessibility to a young adult audience and are expertly edited in consideration of both the reading and comprehension levels of this audience. In addition, each essay is introduced by a concise summation that presents the contributing writer's main themes and insights. Every anthology in the Literary Companion Series contains a varied selection of critical essays that cover a wide time span and express diverse views. Wherever possible, primary sources are represented through excerpts from authors' notebooks, letters, and journals and through contemporary criticism.

Each title in the Literary Companion Series pays careful consideration to the historical context of the particular author or literary work. In-depth biographies and detailed chronologies reveal important aspects of authors' lives and emphasize the historical events and social milieu that influenced their writings. To facilitate further research, every anthology includes primary and secondary source bibliographies of articles and/or books selected for their suitability for young adults. These engaging features make the Greenhaven Literary Companion series ideal for introducing students to literary analysis in the classroom or as a library resource for young adults researching the world's great authors and literature.

Exceptional in its focus on young adults, the Greenhaven Literary Companion Series strives to present literary criticism in a compelling and accessible format. Every title in the series is intended to spark readers' interest in leading American and world authors, to help them broaden their understanding of literature, and to encourage them to formulate their own analyses of the literary works that they read. It is the editors' hope that young adult readers will find these anthologies to be true companions in their study of literature.

INTRODUCTION

For a relatively short novel, *The Great Gatsby* has inspired a mountain of books and essays that seek to explore and explain it. The plot is not in itself complex; many critics have admitted that the tale could have been told as a short story. Yet the writing is so rich that students and scholars have found it worthwhile to study and ponder every scene—indeed nearly every line and image. The book is satisfying as entertainment, thought provoking as a study, and increasingly rewarding the more closely it is examined. And after every nuance has been deciphered, every contemporary reference explained, every one of each character's thoughts and actions understood, every bit of narrative magic revealed, it still repays the attentive reader with revelations about the author, society—and the reader.

One set of revelations concerns the American dream: Is honest hard work reliably rewarded with material success? *Can* a person obtain anything, become everything he or she wants to be, transcend class barriers? San Diego State University English professor Don Gervais notes that "when young people first read Fitzgerald, they are fascinated. Fitzgerald was a superior writer with a poetic touch. One of his themes is universal: He often wrote about the poor boy who tries to win the rich girl. That was one version of the American dream."

Jay Gatsby's life is modeled on such uplifting classic American rags-to-riches tales as those told by Horatio Alger and Benjamin Franklin. But somewhere along the way Gatsby's life (and, by extension, American society) took a very different turn than those of the wholesome heroes who were his literary forebears. Fitzgerald and his disillusioned contemporaries of the so-called Lost Generation, casting a cynical eye on those tales they had grown up hearing, rejected the hearty picture of American society they presented. As Gervais points out, the period of the 1920s "was the first time that youth established its own culture." Fitzgerald both reflected and helped form that new and dissident culture.

One of the cultural themes he expresses so eloquently is the distortion of the American dream through a variety of lenses: a heavy emphasis on self-indulgent materialism; fears that whites might lose their supremacy in American society, and that the rich and powerful might thus lose their preeminence; a loss of religious faith and values, replaced by the siren lure of new and seductive forms of advertising.

These are all issues society is—again? still?—dealing with at the beginning of the twenty-first century. Comparing today's conflicts to those of Fitzgerald's era helps to explain their roots, and viewing them through the telescope of time grants a perspective that is obscured by focusing only on the current.

The Greenhaven Press Literary Companion to *The Great Gatsby*, like all other books in the series, also includes a biography of the author that helps illuminate the connections and cross-fertilization between life and work; a chronology that combines the major events in the author's life and concurrent major events in history; a listing of the author's works; and a gateway to further research, in this case through both other books and the Internet.

F. Scott Fitzgerald:
A Biography

*"There never was a good biography of
a novelist. There couldn't be. He is too
many people, if he's any good."*

F. Scott Fitzgerald

F. Scott Fitzgerald's early works showed great promise, but most critics find them flawed; his later works strived for a depth and breadth that he never quite achieved to his own satisfaction. But in-between, written when he was less than thirty years old, was *The Great Gatsby*. In *Gatsby* Fitzgerald achieved a balance none of his other novels was able to maintain—a balance between comedy and tragedy, between buoyancy and weight, between analysis and blind faith.

The form of the novel, narrated by one of the characters, helped him sustain that delicate equilibrium, in large part because the two main characters personified warring aspects of himself. As Fitzgerald biographer Arthur Mizener writes, "The events of his stories are nearly always events in which Fitzgerald has himself participated with all his emotional energy." And yet, as one of his Princeton friends, author John Peale Bishop, noted, Scott had "the rare faculty of being able to experience romantic and ingenuous emotions and half an hour later regard them with satiric detachment."

In some ways, F. Scott Fitzgerald was Jay Gatsby: poor dreamer become financially successful, vitally attached to a romantic dream. He was also Nick Carraway, the participating yet detached observer of life, who admired the dreamer's intensity but regretted his fatal flaws. In fact, many of the characters in *The Great Gatsby* reflect aspects of their creator's life.

A CODDLED CHILD

Like his main characters in *Gatsby*, Scott Fitzgerald was from the Midwest. Scott, the only son and third child of Edward and Mary McQuillan Fitzgerald, was born on September 24, 1896, at 481 Laurel Avenue in St. Paul, Minnesota. (Fitzgerald scholar Matthew J. Bruccoli deduces that the author of *Gatsby* "is almost certainly locating Nick's home in St. Paul"; Jay's father sent a telegram from his home in "a small town in Minnesota.") Francis Scott Key Fitzgerald was named for a distant relative of his father, Francis Scott Key, who wrote the poem later set to music as "The Star-Spangled Banner."

Edward Fitzgerald was of English heritage, his background the genteel southern grace of Maryland. Fitzgerald biographer Jeffrey Meyers describes him as "a small, ineffectual man with well-cut clothes and fine Southern manners." Scott's legacy from his father included a sense of gentility and southern standards of gentlemanly behavior. To his son, Edward seemed a man in the wrong time, an eighteenth-century soul who lived into the twentieth century: "He was of the generation of the colony and the revolution." His memories of helping Confederate snipers and spies enlivened his son's early years and gave him a taste both for adventure and for a well-told tale.

Mary ("Mollie") McQuillan, Scott's mother, came from Irish stock; her grandparents had come to America to escape desperate poverty in Ireland. They were not genteel, but they were financially successful, which Edward was not. Mollie was never conventionally pretty (her husband said, with southern gallantry, that she "just missed being beautiful"), but after financial reverses left the Fitzgeralds dependent on her inheritance from her father and support from the rest of her family, she abandoned the attempt to keep up her personal appearance, which embarrassed her fastidious son. In "An Author's Mother" he described her as "a halting old lady in a black silk dress and a rather preposterously high-crowned hat that some milliner had foisted upon her declining sight." According to Jeffrey Meyers:

> A voracious but indiscriminate reader of sentimental poetry
> and popular fiction, she was often seen carrying piles of

books from the local library. She toted an umbrella even in fine weather and wore mismatched shoes of different colors [she liked to break in a new pair of shoes "one at a time"]. Mollie was also accustomed to blurting out embarrassingly frank remarks without realizing their effect on her acquaintances. She once stared at a woman whose husband was dying and said: "I'm trying to decide how you'll look in mourning."

Scott's two older sisters died at ages one and three while his mother was pregnant with him. Having lost two children (another, born four years later, lived only an hour), Mollie coddled her son, worrying constantly about his health and catering to his whims. Oddly, her attempts to spoil him strengthened his distaste for her. And, as he wrote later to his daughter, Scottie, the spoiling had its ill effects: "I didn't know till 15 that there was anyone in the world except me, and it cost me *plenty*."

Edward Fitzgerald tried to counteract the effects of his wife's coddling Scott, but he was preoccupied with his own problems. He headed a firm called the American Rattan and Willow Works, which produced wicker furniture in St. Paul; the business failed in 1898. In April of that year the Fitzgeralds moved to Buffalo, New York, where Edward became a soap salesman for Proctor and Gamble. They stayed there for most of the next ten years, except for a temporary move to Syracuse from January 1901 to September 1903, where Scott's only sibling to survive, Annabel, was born in July 1901. Back in Buffalo in time for his seventh birthday, Scott invited his old friends to his birthday party. It rained, and no one came. His mother allowed him to eat the entire birthday cake—candles included—as consolation.

In March 1908, Edward Fitzgerald lost his job with Proctor and Gamble. Scott recalled, "That morning he had gone out a comparatively young man, a man full of strength, full of confidence. He came home that evening, an old man, a completely broken man. He had lost his essential drive, his immaculateness of purpose. He was a failure the rest of his days." Mollie retreated into hysteria, and frequently remarked to Scott that the family would be lost but for support from the McQuillans. The force of this blow is echoed in Jeffrey Meyers's judgment that "Fitzgerald inherited his elegance and propensity to failure from his father, his social insecurity and absurd behavior from his mother."

Returning to St. Paul in defeat, Edward took up the

McQuillan trade of wholesale grocery sales, working from a desk in his brother-in-law's real estate office. For several months the children lived with their grandmother McQuillan while Edward and Mollie moved in with a friend. But the move did have its bright side: In New York, the family had changed residences nearly every year, so the children had developed no long-term friendships. In St. Paul, although the family continued to move often, they stayed in the same general neighborhood, often on or near Summit Avenue. Summit Avenue was the home of many of the wealthiest families in St. Paul, although the Fitzgeralds lived just beyond the ritziest area of the street. (The real James J. Hill, the wealthy railroad tycoon to whom the fictional Jay Gatsby's father compares his son, lived on Summit Avenue—although in a more expensive section.)

With McQuillan backing, the Fitzgeralds had a place in society, and with McQuillan money, they managed to attend the right schools and maintain a respectable social status. Yet Edward's business failures and the family's attempts to keep up a standard of living they could barely afford gave Scott a permanent sense of being an outsider. His mother embarrassed him, and he was embarrassed for his father.

A STORYTELLER, NOT A SCHOLAR

Scott had always been an excellent storyteller; at the same time, he was an indulged and indifferent scholar. When he first went off to school, he made such a fuss that he was told he need only attend half a day—which half was up to him. By the time he entered St. Paul Academy at the age of twelve, Scott had launched himself into a literary career at the expense of his other studies. "I wrote all through every class in school in the back of my geography book and first year Latin and on the margins of themes and declensions and mathematics problems," he later recalled. In addition to adventure stories for the school newspaper, he penned melodramatic plays for the Elizabethan Dramatic Club, named not for the queen of Shakespeare's time but for the club's founder, Elizabeth Magoffin.

Scott's poor academic performance disappointed his parents, who hoped a strict boarding school would help. He eagerly set off for the Newman School in Hackensack, New Jersey, believing that his attractive appearance, social graces, and intelligence would make him popular. He was sadly disappointed; this was when he learned, as he later wrote to Scottie, that the world did not revolve around him. Although he tried to curry favor with his classmates by writing their English papers for them, the strategy won him no permanent friends. Fitzgerald biographer Arthur Mizener quotes his roommate, Martin Amorous, as saying Scott had "the most impenetrable egotism I've ever seen"; yet Scott was constantly aware, Amorous added, that "he was one of the poorest boys in a rich boys' school."

Still academically indifferent, Scott was receiving encouragement for his creative efforts. During the summers, when he was home from Newman, the Elizabethan Dramatic Club performed his plays, turning a small profit for the charitable causes it benefited. And while he was at Newman he developed a strong rapport with a worldly priest who was a school trustee, Father Sigourney Webster Fay. Father Fay, who frequently invited Scott to his Washington home, encouraged Scott to develop his talent. Fay introduced Fitzgerald to his friends among the intellectual and social elite, including writer and historian Henry Adams and the wealthy and well-connected Shane Leslie, who later recommended Scott's first novel to Scribner's publishing company and wrote a favorable review of it.

Such encouragement notwithstanding, Scott's academic performance continued to suffer, and when he decided to attend Princeton University, he was told that his grades were inadequate for admission. He took an entrance exam, failed it, spent the summer studying, then went to New Jersey to take the makeup entrance exam—and again failed to make the grade. It says something for his powers of persuasiveness that he managed to talk the school authorities into granting him a probationary acceptance.

PRINCETON

Sergio Perosa, in *The Art of F. Scott Fitzgerald*, describes Fitzgerald's adjustments to the "rich and unprejudiced" East after having been raised in the "closed and conservative" Middle West.

> These years at Princeton were the most intense and determinant phase of Fitzgerald's development. They were years of exultation and depression, of intellectual awakening, as well as of misdirected energy. His athletic ambitions were shattered, he suffered repeated humiliations from companions

richer than he; but at Princeton he found his way to literary achievement. Quickly, after an initial moment of ostracism, Fitzgerald became a member of the Triangle Club and of the editorial board of the *Daily Princetonian*, contributed to the *Nassau Lit.* and *The Tiger*, and was admitted to one of the best eating clubs. There is something impressive in the lucid perception with which the young outsider discovered the subtle secrets of the place, and in the iron will with which he pursued his social and cultural aims under a pretense of aristocratic detachment.

Although Scott was once again a poor boy in a rich man's environment, he did make some lifelong friends at Princeton. John Peale Bishop and Edmund ("Bunny") Wilson both made literary names for themselves, and both helped Scott develop and find his focus as a writer. Their opinions of his works were important to him for the rest of his life.

UNREQUITED LOVE

The Princeton Triangle Club wrote, composed, and produced musical comedies; during Christmas vacations the club members presented their productions at college campuses across the country. Not surprisingly, this is where Scott's energies were focused, again at the expense of his academic studies. When one of his professors protested his frequent tardiness, he exclaimed, "Sir—it's absurd to expect me to be on time. I'm a genius!"

Genius or no, failing grades could keep Scott from fulfilling his campus ambitions. He later recalled, "I spent my entire freshman year writing an operetta for the Triangle Club. I failed in algebra, trigonometry, coordinate geometry and hygiene, but the Triangle Club accepted my show, and by tutoring all through a stuffy August I managed to come back a sophomore and act in it as a chorus girl." And a stunningly beautiful showgirl he was, too. Although he was forbidden to travel with the company during the Christmas break because of his poor grades, his photograph as a sexy chorine appeared in newspapers in many of the towns where the company toured.

Instead of being on the road playing a beautiful woman at Christmas during his sophomore year, Scott went home to St. Paul and met a beautiful young woman—Ginevra King—and fell in love. The sophisticated sixteen-year-old came from Lake Forest, "a [Chicago] suburb which epitomized the zenith of upper-class Midwestern society," according to Jeffrey Meyers. (Lake Forest was apparently a home base of Tom Buchanan, Daisy's husband in *Gatsby:* "Now he'd left Chicago and come east in a fashion that rather took your breath away: for instance he'd brought down a string of polo ponies from Lake Forest.") Fitzgerald scholar Matthew J. Bruccoli notes that Ginevra "matched his dreams of the perfect girl: beautiful, rich, socially secure, and sought after. The last qualification was important. His ideal girl had to be one pursued by many men; there had to be an element of competition." His romantic standards are ambitiously echoed by Jay Gatsby, who fell permanently in love with Daisy Fay, "by far the most popular of all the young girls in Louisville."

Scott's two-year pursuit of Ginevra gave him literary material rather than romantic satisfaction (she provided the model for the heroine, Rosalind, in *This Side of Paradise*, as well as for women in other stories). That she was not impressed with his potential future may be judged by the fact that in 1917 she destroyed the hundreds of letters he had sent her. Although he had begun to feel the relationship was doomed in 1916 when he overheard someone say that "poor boys should not think of marrying rich girls," he kept her letters for many years after they broke up. Some Fitzgerald scholars find in Gatsby's perpetual pursuit of Daisy Fay an indication that the author never really got over his rejection by Ginevra King.

One of Ginevra's first literary appearances was as the female lead in a story Fitzgerald wrote for the *Nassau Lit.*, Princeton's literary magazine. Matthew Bruccoli describes "The Pierian Springs and the Last Straw":

> The story develops a major theme in Fitzgerald's fiction: the gifted man ruined by a selfish woman. The hero is a scandalous middle-aged novelist who lost his Ginevra as a young man and never got over it. When he marries her after she is widowed, he stops writing. Much of Fitzgerald's fiction would take the form of self-warnings or self-judgments, and this story is the first in which he analyzed the conflicting pulls of love and literature. The girl is the writer's inspiration, but only when she is unattained. The satisfied artist is unproductive.

TRYING TO GO TO WAR

By 1917 Scott's romance with Ginevra was not the only thing falling apart. While the Triangle Club was the second-most important organization on campus (after the football team), success there did not impress the academic authorities. During his entire Princeton career, Fitzgerald struggled with makeup studies while failing current courses. Finally, on the verge of failing completely, he contracted malaria (a common ailment then on the marshy campus) and chose to leave "because of illness" during November of his junior year (1915). He had hoped to become president of the Triangle Club, and the dashing of that hope was a bitterness he carried for the rest of his life. It seemed unreasonable to him that the university should fail to recognize and make allowances for an artist—specifically, for him.

Several of Fitzgerald's Princeton classmates had already died during the war being waged in Europe. He repeated his junior year (1916–1917), then decided to enlist in the army. In July 1917 he took the examinations for a provisional appointment as a second lieutenant in the regular army (he could not become an officer until he reached twenty-one in September), and he received his commission that October. He immediately went to Brooks Brothers in New York to order tailored uniforms.

Fitzgerald trained at various locations around the country for the next few months. At Fort Leavenworth, Kansas, leading the provisional officers in calisthenics and bayonet drills was a young, blue-eyed captain named Dwight David Eisenhower, who would follow his success as a general in the *next* world war with a two-term stint as president of the United States. Fitzgerald was not much interested in drills, though; once again, his studies were ignored as he scribbled through his classes and hid his writing pad behind his copy of *Small Problems for Infantry* (apparently unaware of the fact that lives would depend on his military knowledge were he to lead men into battle). He was working on "The Romantic Egoist" (which would eventually be published as *This Side of Paradise*), rushing to finish it and find a publisher before he went off to war, where he was sure he would be killed. After Scott was caught writing during evening study periods, he shifted to spending his entire weekend writing: "I wrote a one hundred and twenty thousand word novel on the consecutive weekends of three months," he reported.

Writing was somewhat complicated by frequent transfers around the country; by March 1918 he was at Camp Zachary Taylor, near Louisville, Kentucky (home of Daisy Fay); in

April he was in Augusta, Georgia, at Camp Gordon; in June he became part of the Ninth Division at Camp Sheridan, near Montgomery, Alabama. His regiment was just about to leave for France—it had even boarded the ship, then disembarked—when the war ended on November 11, 1918. Although he regretted for the rest of his life that "I Never Got Over" (as he titled a later short story), the men who might have fought under him were probably fortunate. He had already seriously endangered another company when he mistakenly ordered his men to fire on it; he went to visit Princeton when he was supposed to be supervising the unloading of equipment in Hoboken, New Jersey, and thousands of dollars' worth of matériel was stolen; and, although his companions generally liked him, one who had served with him during most of his military "career," Alonzo Myers, gently phrased the prevailing opinion: "As an Army officer, Fitzgerald was unusually dispensable."

ZELDA SAYRE FITZGERALD

From June 1918 to February 1919, Scott spent most of his time stationed in Montgomery, Alabama. It was there in July 1918 that he met Zelda Sayre, daughter of a prominent though not wealthy family (her father was an associate justice of the Alabama Supreme Court). Zelda had just graduated from high school and turned eighteen the month they met. According to Jeffrey Meyers, "Protected by the respectability and prestige of her family, Zelda was known for her striking beauty, her unconventional behavior and her sexual promiscuity." (Some biographers believe her flirtations did not lead to sexual activity, suggesting more than was delivered.) Virginia Foster Durr, who knew her in Montgomery, told Meyers:

> Zelda was like a vision of beauty dancing by. She was funny, amusing, the most popular girl, envied by all the others, worshipped and adored, besieged by all the boys. She *did* try to shock. At a dance she pinned mistletoe on the back of her skirt, as if to challenge the young men to kiss her bottom.
>
> In the South women were not supposed to *do* anything. It was sufficient to be beautiful and charming. Zelda, a spoiled baby just out of high school, never even learned to read or sew. She was always treated like a visiting film star: radiant, glowing, desired by all. Since she had absolutely nothing to do and no personal resources to draw on, she later bothered Scott when he was trying to write. She had no ability to suffer adversity, and was unprepared for it when it came.

When Scott first saw Zelda, she was surrounded by young men—with an army base nearby, she had plenty of admirers. The spirit of competition kicked in, and Scott became determined to win her for himself. Throughout their lives together, the admiration of other men for Zelda would both gratify and torment Scott: gratify, because she married him; torment, because she continued to respond to other men to make him jealous.

Unlike Ginevra King, Zelda wanted something Scott could provide: an escape from the provincial life of an Alabama town. By the time he was discharged from his unit in February 1919 (so dispensable, he was one of the first of his unit to be let go), he thought he might join his friend Edmund Wilson, who was leading a comfortable life in the literary circle of New York. He would soon, he hoped, be settled in a lucrative and congenial position and be able to afford to marry and have a cozy apartment, like Wilson's, in Greenwich Village in Manhattan.

Instead he found work writing advertising slogans for signs on streetcars. He moved into a dingy, depressing room far uptown, which he decorated with the rejection slips he received for the stories and sketches he was unable to sell. He visited Zelda in Montgomery three times in the spring of 1919 and tried to persuade her to marry him. Although she said she loved him, she refused to consider marriage until he was better able to support a wife. Her family also objected, feeling, as Meyers puts it, "that she needed a strong, reliable husband who could control rather than encourage her wild behavior. In their view, he was an unstable Irish Catholic who had not graduated from college, had no career and drank too much."

Impatient with Scott's failures, Zelda broke off their engagement that June. Although she would later agree to marry Scott when *This Side of Paradise* was published, the fact that she would not marry him before he had proved himself, and was even willing to give him up if he did not, took much of the sparkle out of the relationship for him when it resumed. Then again, perhaps the sparkle could not have survived anyway: Once Zelda said yes, she was no longer the unattainable ideal he had found in Ginevra King.

Scott and Zelda looked enough alike to be taken for brother and sister, and they seemed to bring out in each other a wild need to run amok. Although there were good times, it was to prove an odd, twisted relationship that eventually led, inexorably it seemed, to Zelda's schizophrenia. In the end they were unable to live together, but they never divorced.

AFTER SEVERAL TRIES, OVERNIGHT SUCCESS

Zelda's refusal to marry him drove Scott to find success in writing. He quit his job in New York and returned to his parents' home in St. Paul, where he devoted himself to work on *This Side of Paradise.* Maxwell Perkins, a young editor at Scribner's, had responded encouragingly to the second draft and suggested improvements. Scott finished the revision in early September 1919 and shipped it off to Perkins. With a speed unheard-of today, especially for a first novelist, Perkins wrote Scott on September 16: "I am very glad, personally, to be able to write to you that we are all for publishing your book, *This Side of Paradise.* . . . It abounds in energy and life. . . . The book is so different that it is hard to prophesy how it will sell but we are all for taking a chance and supporting it with vigor."

Scott was so excited that he ran up and down the street, stopping friends and strangers alike to tell them of his good fortune. Then he returned to New York to accept what he expected would be the accolades of an adoring world.

That summer he seemed to have found the key to his power as a professional writer. Now his stories began to sell, too. Not only did his first story in a mass circulation magazine ("Head and Shoulders," published in the February 1920 *Saturday Evening Post*) earn $400 for the serial (magazine) rights, but he sold the movie rights for the very generous sum of $2,500. Now he was a success; now Zelda would marry him. *This Side of Paradise* came out on March 26, 1920; Scott and Zelda were married on April 3. A year later, Zelda was pregnant; their only child, Frances Scott ("Scottie") Fitzgerald, was born on October 26, 1921.

THE JAZZ AGE

On one hand, it was naïve for Fitzgerald to expect fame and fortune to follow on the publication of a first novel. On the other hand, that's what happened.

Burton Rascoe wrote in the *Chicago Daily Tribune* (dated on Scott's wedding day):

If you have not already done so, make a note of the name, F. Scott Fitzgerald. It is borne by a 23-year-old novelist who will, unless I am much mistaken, be much heard of hereafter. His first novel *This Side of Paradise* gives him, I think, a fair claim to membership in that small squad of contemporary American fictionists who are producing literature. It is sincere, it is honest, it is intelligent, it is handled in an individual manner, it bears the impress, it seems to me, of genius. It is the only adequate study that we have had of the contemporary American in adolescence and young manhood. . . .

It is a novel which is, curiously, important largely through its apparent defects—its bland egotism, its conceited extravagance, its immaturity of thoughts. The hero is frequently a prig, a snob, an ass, and—may I whisper it?—something of a cad; but a youth is all these things.

How should a genius, who months before had briefly taken a job repairing train roofs in Minnesota, deal with such praise? The Fitzgerald of 1932 looked back at the Fitzgerald who had fled the city in 1919 and recalled:

When I returned six months later the offices of editors and publishers were open to me, impresarios begged plays, the movies panted for screen material. To my bewilderment, I was adopted, not as a Middle Westerner, not even as a detached observer, but as the arch type of what New York wanted. . . .

For just a moment, the "younger generation" idea became a fusion of many elements in New York life. . . . The blending of the bright, gay, vigorous elements began then and for the first time there appeared a society a little livelier than the solid mahogany dinner parties of Emily Price Post.

For the Fitzgeralds, that "livelier" society meant a constant round of parties, carousing, drinking, such antics as climbing into fountains fully dressed, and causing commotions that landed Scott in jail for a night on occasion.

The constant partying made writing difficult, especially writing a novel. Fortunately for Scott, it was a time when short stories were widely and eagerly read, and the short story market was lucrative. In fact, until the last few years of his life, short stories supported Scott and Zelda in the style to which they wished to become accustomed; he earned more for them than he did from books, and he could whip them out much more easily than novels (which he considered his true work) whenever the coffers were empty. Fitzgerald published a book of short stories after each novel; the one that followed *This Side of Paradise* was *Flappers and Philosophers*. His next novel, *The Beautiful and Damned*, was published in April 1922; that September, *Tales of the Jazz Age* established Fitzgerald as proprietor of the name of the era.

By then their New York City life had become too frenzied to get much work done, so in October 1922 they moved to Long Island; but their friends—and parties—just followed them to their new home in Great Neck. (The images of the lavish parties at Gatsby's house more closely resemble the Fitzgeralds' life in those days than do the more sedate meals at the Buchanans'.) The Fitzgeralds were in Long Island when Scott's play *The Vegetable* closed during out-of-town tryouts, a blow that put a disturbing cramp in their enjoyment of celebrity.

By now the frantic pace of their lives was becoming less fun and more destructive: Scott would disappear on three-day benders, finally showing up asleep on the front lawn; they spent money as if it were a challenge; their New York friends were, Scott said, turning their home into "a roadhouse." In April he wrote to his editor, Max Perkins, about the novel he was working on:

> Much of what I wrote last summer was good but it was so interrupted that it was ragged + in approaching it from a new angle I've had to discard a lot of it. . . . It is only in the last four months that I've realized how much I've—well, almost *deteriorated* in the three years since I finished *The Beautiful and Damned.* The last four months of course I've worked but in the two years—over two years—before that, I produced exactly *one* play, *half a dozen* short stories and three or four articles—an average of about *one hundred* words a day. If I'd spent this time reading or travelling or doing anything—even staying healthy—it'd be different but I spent it uselessly, neither in study nor in contemplation but only in drinking and raising hell generally.

Although Great Neck provided the background for the novel-in-progress that would become, after several major revisions of plot, style, and character, *The Great Gatsby*, it was not conducive to finishing the book. In May 1924 the Fitzgeralds set sail for Europe. Scott said they would stay away until he had accomplished some great thing.

THE GREAT GATSBY

For the next two and a half years, the Fitzgeralds spent most of their time in Paris or on the Riviera. Unlike most of their contemporary expatriates, Scott did not attempt to immerse himself in the culture of Europe. While Ernest Hemingway, for example, was in Europe turning his experiences there into *The Sun Also Rises* (1926), Fitzgerald had, as he had said he would, carried the atmosphere of Long Island with him to Europe. Away from the United States, Scott wrote the very American *Great Gatsby*, accomplishing the "great thing" he had promised.

In July 1924, while they were at St. Raphaël in France, "Zelda and a handsome French aviator named Edouard Josanne fell very much in love," reports Arthur Mizener. Although she had always been flirtatious—her biographer Nancy Milford writes of her "necking with young men because she liked the shapes of their noses or the cut of their dinner jackets"—this seemed more serious. According to Milford, Fitzgerald later reported that Zelda had asked for a divorce so that she could marry Josanne. Scott blew up, Zelda acquiesced to his demand that she give up her lover, and the aviator departed.

Zelda seemed to enjoy living dangerously; friends noted, for example, that when she was driving she liked to turn to Scott at a particularly dangerous spot on the road and ask him to light her cigarette. Dorothy Parker remembered their first meeting: Zelda was riding the hood of a taxi (with Scott perched on the roof). But it was around this time that Zelda took an overdose of sleeping pills, one of several unsuccessful attempts to take her own life. Many people found Scott and Zelda incredibly attractive and charming, but those who spent time with Zelda often remarked that she seemed frantic, desperate, and strange. She would become more so over the years, until her actions were no longer simply the outrageous antics of a flapper but the uncontrollable behavior of a mentally ill woman. In time, Zelda would be diagnosed as incurably schizophrenic.

Scott had often seemed to match Zelda's erratic behavior; indeed, outrageousness was their trademark as a couple. But the affair with the aviator had damaged the relationship; Scott wrote later, "That September 1924 I knew something had happened that could never be repaired." That sense of betrayal found its way into the novel he was working on: Nick clearly saw that Daisy had betrayed Gatsby; Gatsby the romantic apparently refused to recognize or acknowledge her betrayal, and he died still in love with his idealized version of Daisy.

The emotional crisis did not keep Scott from working on *Gatsby*, though. Perhaps it sharpened his focus, supplying emotional intensity he could draw on while he wrote. In any case, he went on the wagon in August and by early November he sent the manuscript off to Max Perkins at Scribner's.

FITZGERALD AND HEMINGWAY

Gatsby was published in April 1925; in May, Fitzgerald met Hemingway, and he soon began helping the younger author, recommending Ernest's work to Perkins and to others who might help his career. This was the beginning of an odd, wary, on-again-off-again relationship that lasted until Fitzgerald's death. In many ways, the men were polar opposites, and it sometimes seemed that all they had in common was enormous talent. Hemingway had a habit of turning on his friends, and Fitzgerald could be self-pitying and, especially when drunk (which was often), either outrageous and annoying or blindly inconsiderate. Fitzgerald once said that Hemingway spoke with the authority of success, while he (Fitzgerald) spoke with the authority of failure. At least one biographer, André Le Vot, has characterized them as sadist and masochist, with all the uneasy nuances that can lend to a relationship between two highly talented, artistic men.

Hemingway's literary life was largely ahead of him at this point; his first major novel, *The Sun Also Rises*, would be published the year after *The Great Gatsby* (by Scribner's; Max Perkins had agreed with Fitzgerald's assessment of Hemingway). He would go on to win the Nobel and Pulitzer prizes. As for Fitzgerald, on the other hand, *The Great Gatsby* would represent his highest critical acclaim; nothing he published afterward would receive the same enthusiastic reception.

THE LONG SLIDE DOWNHILL

Gatsby did not sell as well as Fitzgerald would have liked, but as a stage adaptation it was a hit both on Broadway in February 1926 and later on tour. This success helped take some of the sting out of the failure of *The Vegetable*, and the income from sale of the stage rights helped Fitzgerald pay off the debts he and Zelda kept running up. For the first time he had a financial cushion, which Hemingway warned him posed a danger: Both men needed a financial incentive to force themselves to write their best work.

After *Gatsby* (and the short-story collection that followed, *All the Sad Young Men*), Fitzgerald did not publish another book for eight years. *Tender Is the Night* came out in 1934, but by then the nation was nearly half a decade into the Great Depression. It seemed that Scott had outlived his time; the new novel seemed out of step, a bit old-fashioned. Scott thought perhaps it needed a major rewriting, and he proposed massive changes. He never followed up on those ideas, but after his death, Malcolm Cowley edited a new edition, published "with the author's final revisions," so the novel now exists in two very different published forms.

Fitzgerald had tried to keep up with the times—he had even taken a couple of stabs at writing for Hollywood, with an occasional minor success—but it seemed his personal fortunes had waned with those of the previous decade, which ended with the Crash of October 1929, the beginning of the Great Depression. Zelda was by this time seriously ill. Her schizophrenia had finally been diagnosed, and she was spending long periods of time in mental hospitals. During intervals when she was well enough to be released, she began going home to her mother rather than to Scott; although she and Scott still wrote each other and remained affectionate, being together seemed to make them both irrational.

Trying to attend to Zelda, take care of their daughter, Scottie, and write dozens of short stories to pay the bills for all three of them had undoubtedly taken a toll of both time and concentration. Worse, after about 1932 Scott found that he no longer had the facility to dash off the lucrative stories that had been supporting them for years. Whether he or the editors had changed or the times simply no longer suited his stories (he remarked that editors all wanted stories with happy endings now, and few of his stories were sufficiently upbeat anymore), he was no longer able to command top dollar, automatic publication of whatever he submitted, or even advances against future work, as he had long been accustomed to. (Nor were his books selling well: The last royalty check to arrive before he died, in August 1940, was for $13.13.)

He turned once again to Hollywood, landing a contract with MGM in mid-1937. But Fitzgerald was not a good team player when it came to literary collaboration, and he did not bother to hide his unhappiness when his work was rewritten. By the end of 1938, MGM declined to renew his contract. He was putting his time in California to use, though: He began a new novel, one he envisioned as his masterpiece, about Hollywood. Based loosely on the life of producer Irving Thalberg, he called it *The Last Tycoon*. Ill health, including cardiac problems and at least one heart attack, slowed him somewhat, but he was hoping to finish the book by mid-January 1941. On December 21, 1940, while he was relaxing and eating a chocolate bar, waiting for his physician to come by, he suddenly stood, reached for the chimney, and then slid to the floor. He had had another heart attack, and died quickly. He was buried six days later in Rockville, Maryland.

TOGETHER AGAIN

Zelda and Scott Fitzgerald had been apart for years before his death; their last time together was a disastrous trip to Cuba in 1939, where he drank heavily and was beaten by spectators at a cockfight he tried to stop. After that Zelda lived with her mother when she was well and returned to the hospital when schizophrenia threatened to overwhelm her. In March 1948 she had been hospitalized for four months and was looking forward to returning home. On the night of March 10 a fire broke out in the hospital; Zelda and eight other women were trapped and died in the flames. On March 17 she was laid to rest next to Scott.

LOOKING BACK

In 1931, at the age of thirty-five, Fitzgerald looked back nostalgically at the Jazz Age, a brief period between the First World War and the Great Depression, an era of which he was both chronicler and, to many, personification. "It is too soon to write about the Jazz Age with perspective," he wrote:

> It is as dead as were the Yellow Nineties in 1902. Yet the present writer already looks back to it with nostalgia. It bore him up, flattered him and gave him more money than he had dreamed of, simply for telling people that he felt as they did, that something had to be done with all the nervous energy stored up and unexpended in the War.

CHAPTER 1

Who Is Jay Gatsby?

Gatsby Is a Classic Romantic

Robert Ornstein

Unlike the many critics who see in *The Great Gatsby* Fitzgerald's treatment of modern materialism and moral anarchy, Shakespearean scholar Robert Ornstein sees it as a fable about the unending quest of the romantic dream. But in shifting the "frontier" of unlimited possibilities from the West to Wall Street, Fitzgerald finds a displacement of the historic romantic pilgrimage from East to West; Gatsby is traveling in the wrong direction both in time and in space. His romantic dream is an attempt to recapture something lost in the past, not a future possibility; yet he is "great" because his dream is a grand illusion of the kind that keeps people from becoming, as Ornstein puts it, "too old or too wise or too cynical."

> He felt then that if the pilgrimage eastward of the rare poisonous flower of his race was the end of the adventure which had started westward three hundred years ago, if the long serpent of the curiosity had turned too sharp upon itself, cramping its bowels, bursting its shining skin, at least there had been a journey; like to the satisfaction of a man coming to die—one of those human things that one can never understand unless one has made such a journey and heard the man give thanks with the husbanded breath. The frontiers were gone—there were no more barbarians. The short gallop of the last great race, the polyglot, the hated and the despised, the crass and scorned, had gone—at least it was not a meaningless extinction up an alley. (*The Crack-Up*)

After a brief revival, the novels of Scott Fitzgerald seem destined again for obscurity, labeled this time, by their most recent critics, as darkly pessimistic studies of America's spiritual and ideological failures. *The Great Gatsby*, we are now told, is not simply a chronicle of the Jazz Age but rather a dramatization of the betrayal of the naive American dream

From Robert Ornstein, "Scott Fitzgerald's Fable of East and West," *College English*, vol. 18, no. 3, December 1956.

in a corrupt society. I would agree that in *Gatsby* Fitzgerald did create a myth with the imaginative sweep of America's historical adventure across an untamed continent. But his fable of East and West is little concerned with twentieth century materialism and moral anarchy, for its theme is the unending quest of the romantic dream, which is forever betrayed in fact and yet redeemed in men's minds.

FITZGERALD'S DREAM OF ROMANCE

From the start, Fitzgerald's personal dreams of romance contained the seeds of their own destruction. In his earliest works, his optimistic sense of the value of experience is overshadowed by a personal intuition of tragedy; his capacity for naive wonder is chastened by satiric and ironic insights which make surrender to the romantic impulse incomplete. Though able to idealize the sensuous excitement of an exclusive party or a lovely face, Fitzgerald could not ignore the speciosity inherent in the romantic stimuli of his social world—in the unhurried gracious poise that money can buy. Invariably he studied what fascinated him so acutely that he could give at times a clinical report on the very rich, whose world seemed to hold the promise of a life devoid of the vulgar and commonplace. A literalist of his own imagination (and therefore incapable of self-deception), he peopled extravagant phantasy with superbly real "denizens of Broadway." The result in the earlier novels is not so much an uncertainty of tone as a curious alternation of satiric and romantic moments—a breathless adoration of flapper heroines whose passionate kisses are tinged with frigidity and whose daring freedom masks an adolescent desire for the reputation rather than the reality of experience.

The haunting tone of *Gatsby* is more than a skilful fusion of Fitzgerald's satiric and romantic contrarieties. Nick Carraway, simultaneously enchanted and repelled by the variety of life, attains Fitzgerald's mature realization that the protective enchantment of the romantic ideal lies in its remoteness from actuality. He knows the fascination of yellow windows high above the city streets even as he looks down from Myrtle Wilson's gaudy, smoke-filled apartment. He still remembers the initial wonder of Gatsby's parties long after he is sickened by familiarity with Gatsby's uninvited guests. In one summer Nick discovers a profoundly melancholy esthetic truth: that romance belongs not to the present but to a past transfigured by imagined memory and to the illusory promise of an unrealizable future. Gatsby, less wise than Nick, destroys himself in an attempt to seize the green light in his own fingers.

THE VERY RICH

At the same time that Fitzgerald perceived the melancholy nature of romantic illusion, his attitude towards the very rich crystallized. In *Gatsby* we see that the charming irresponsibility of the flapper has developed into the criminal amorality of Daisy Buchanan, and that the smug conceit of the Rich Boy has hardened into Tom Buchanan's arrogant cruelty. We know in retrospect that Anthony Patch's tragedy was not his "poverty," but his possession of the weakness and purposelessness of the very rich without their protective armor of wealth [in *The Beautiful and Damned*].

The thirst for money is a crucial motive in *Gatsby* as in Fitzgerald's other novels, and yet none of his major characters are materialists, for money is never their final goal. The rich are too accustomed to money to covet it. It is simply the badge of their "superiority" and the justification of their consuming snobberies. For those who are not very rich—for the Myrtle Wilsons as well as the Jay Gatsbys—it is the alchemic reagent that transmutes the ordinary worthlessness of life. Money is the demiurgos of Jimmy Gatz's Platonic universe, and the proof, in [Fitzgerald's story] "Babylon Revisited," of the unreality of reality (". . . the snow of twenty-nine wasn't real snow. If you didn't want it to be snow, you just paid some money"). Even before *Gatsby,* in "The Rich Boy," Fitzgerald had defined the original sin of the very rich: They do not worship material gods, but they "possess and enjoy early, and it does something to them, makes them soft where we are hard, and cynical where we are trustful." Surrounded from childhood by the artificial security of wealth, accustomed to owning rather than wanting, they lack anxiety or illusion, frustration or fulfillment. Their romantic dreams are rooted in the adolescence from which they never completely escape—in the excitement of the prom or petting party, the reputation of being fast on the college gridiron or the college weekend.

Inevitably, then, Fitzgerald saw his romantic dream threaded by a double irony. Those who possess the necessary means lack the will, motive, or capacity to pursue a dream. Those with the heightened sensitivity to the promises of life have it because they are the disinherited, forever barred from the white palace where "the king's daughter, the golden girl" awaits "safe and proud above the struggles of the poor." Amory Blaine loses his girl writing advertising copy at ninety a month [in *This Side of Paradise*]. Anthony Patch loses his mind after an abortive attempt to recoup his fortune peddling bonds. Jay Gatsby loses his life even though he makes his millions because they are not the kind of safe, respectable money that echoes in Daisy's lovely voice. The successful entrepreneurs of Gatsby's age are the panderers to vulgar tastes, the high pressure salesmen, and, of course, the bootleggers. Yet once, Fitzgerald suggests, there had been opportunity commensurate with aspiration, an unexplored and unexploited frontier where great fortunes had been made or at least romantically stolen. And out of the shifting of opportunities from the West to Wall Street, he creates an American fable which redeems as well as explains romantic failure.

EAST VS. WEST

But how is one to accept, even in fable, a West characterized by the dull rectitude of Minnesota villages and an East epitomized by the sophisticated dissipation of Long Island society? The answer is perhaps that Fitzgerald's dichotomy of East and West has the poetic truth of Henry James's antithesis of provincial American virtue and refined European sensibility. Like *The Portrait of a Lady* and *The Ambassadors, Gatsby* is a story of "displaced persons" who have journeyed eastward in search of a larger experience of life. To James this reverse migration from the New to the Old World has in itself no special significance. To Fitzgerald, however, the lure of the East represents a profound displacement of the American dream, a turning back upon itself of the historic pilgrimage towards the frontier which had, in fact, created and sustained that dream. In *Gatsby* the once limitless western horizon is circumscribed by the "bored, sprawling, swollen towns beyond the Ohio, with their interminable inquisitions which spared only the children and the very old." The virgin territories of the frontiersman have been appropriated by the immigrant families, the diligent Swedes—the unimaginative, impoverished German farmers like Henry Gatz. Thus after a restless nomadic existence, the Buchanans settle "permanently" on Long Island because Tom would be "a God damned fool to live anywhere else." Thus Nick comes to New York with a dozen volumes on finance which promise "to unfold the shining secrets that only Midas, Morgan and Maecenas knew." Gatsby's green light, of course, shines in only one direction—from the East across the Continent to Minnesota, from the East across the bay to his imitation mansion in West Egg.

Lying in the moonlight on Gatsby's deserted beach, Nick realizes at the close just how lost a pilgrimage Gatsby's had been:

> I became aware of the old island here that had flowered once for Dutch sailors' eyes—a fresh, green breast of the new world. Its vanished trees, the trees that had made way for Gatsby's house, had once pandered in whispers to the last and greatest of all human dreams; for a transitory moment man must have held his breath in the presence of this continent, compelled into an aesthetic contemplation he neither understood nor desired, face to face for the last time in history with something commensurate to his capacity for wonder.

Gatsby is the spiritual descendant of these Dutch sailors. Like them, he set out for gold and stumbled on a dream. But he journeys in the wrong direction in time as well as space. The transitory enchanted moment has come and gone for him and for the others, making the romantic promise of the future an illusory reflection of the past. Nick still carries with him a restlessness born of the war's excitement; Daisy silently mourns the romantic adventure of her "white" girlhood; Tom seeks the thrill of a vanished football game. Gatsby devotes his life to recapturing a love lost five years before. When the present offers nothing commensurate with man's capacity for wonder, the romantic credo is the belief—Gatsby's belief—in the ability to repeat the disembodied past. Each step towards the green light, however, shadows some part of Gatsby's grandiose achievement. With Daisy's disapproval the spectroscopic parties cease. To preserve her reputation Gatsby empties his mansion of lights and servants. And finally only darkness and ghostly memories tenant the deserted house as Gatsby relives his romantic past for Nick after the accident.

Like his romantic dream Jay Gatsby belongs to a vanished past. His career began when he met Dan Cody, a debauched relic of an earlier America who made his millions in the copper strikes. From Cody he received an education in ruthlessness which he applied when the accident of the war brought him to the beautiful house of Daisy Fay. In the tradition of Cody's frontier, he "took what he could get, ravenously and unscrupulously," but in taking Daisy he fell in love with her. "She vanished into her rich house, into her rich full life, leaving Gatsby—nothing. He felt married to her, that was all."

"He felt married to her"—here is the reaction of bourgeois conscience, not of calculating ambition. But then Gatsby is not really Cody's protégé. Jimmy Gatz inherited an attenuated version of the American dream of success, a more moral and genteel dream suited to a nation arriving at the respectability of established wealth and class. Respectability demands that avarice be masked with virtue, that personal aggrandisement pose as self-improvement. Success is no longer to the cutthroat or the ruthless but to the diligent and the industrious, to the boy who scribbles naive resolves on the flyleaf of *Hopalong Cassidy.* Fabricated of pulp fiction clichés (the impoverished materials of an extraordinary imagination), Gatsby's dream of self-improvement blossoms into a preposterous tale of ancestral wealth and culture. And his dream is incorruptible because his great enterprise is not sidestreet "drugstores," or stolen bonds, but himself, his fictional past, his mansion and his gaudy entertainments. Through it all he moves alone and untouched; he is the impresario, the creator, not the enjoyer of a riotous venture dedicated to an impossible goal.

It may seem ironic that Gatsby's dream of self-improvement is realized through partnership with Meyer Wolfsheim, but Wolfsheim is merely the post-war successor to Dan Cody and to the ruthlessness and greed that once exploited a virgin West. He is the fabulous manipulator of bootleg gin rather than of copper, the modern man of legendary accomplishment "who fixed the World's Series back in 1919." The racketeer, Fitzgerald suggests, is the last great folk hero, the Paul Bunyan of an age in which romantic wonder surrounds underworld "gonnegtions" instead of raw courage or physical strength. And actually Gatsby is destroyed not by Wolfsheim, or association with him, but by the provincial squeamishness which makes all the Westerners in the novel unadaptable to life in the East.

Despite her facile cynicism and claim to sophistication, Daisy is still the "nice" girl who grew up in Louisville in a beautiful house with a wicker settee on the porch. She remains "spotless," still immaculately dressed in white and capable of a hundred whimsical, vaporous enthusiasms. She has assimilated the urbane ethic of the East which allows a bored wife a casual discreet affair. But she cannot, like Gatsby's uninvited guests, wink at the illegal and the criminal. When Tom begins to unfold the sordid details of Gatsby's career, she shrinks away; she never intended to leave her husband, but now even an affair is impossible. Tom's provinciality is more boorish than genteel. He has assumed the role of Long Island country gentleman who keeps a mistress in a midtown apartment. But with Myrtle Wilson by his side he turns the role into a ludicrous travesty. By nature a libertine, by upbringing a prig, Tom shatters Gatsby's façade in order to preserve his "gentleman's" conception of womanly virtue and of the sanctity of his marriage.

Ultimately, however, Gatsby is the victim of his own small-town notions of virtue and chivalry. "He would never so much as look at a friend's wife"—or at least he would never try to steal her in her husband's house. He wants Daisy to say that she never loved Tom because only in this way can the sacrament of Gatsby's "marriage" to her in Louisville—his prior claim—be recognized. Not content merely to repeat the past, he must also eradicate the years in which his dream lost its reality. But the dream, like the vanished frontier which it almost comes to represent, is lost forever "somewhere back in that vast obscurity beyond the city, where the dark field of the republic rolled on under the night."

After Gatsby's death Nick prepares to return to his Minnesota home, a place of warmth and enduring stability, carrying with him a surrealistic night vision of the debauchery of the East. Yet his return is not a positive rediscovery of the wellsprings of American life. Instead it seems a melancholy retreat from the ruined promise of the East, from the empty present to the childhood memory of the past. Indeed, it is this childhood memory, not the reality of the West which Nick cherishes. For he still thinks the East, despite its nightmarish aspect, superior to the stultifying small-town dullness from which he fled. And by the close of *Gatsby* it is unmistakably clear that the East does not symbolize contemporary decadence and the West the pristine virtues of an earlier America. Fitzgerald does not contrast Gatsby's criminality with his father's unspoiled rustic strength and dignity. He contrasts rather Henry Gatz's dull, grey, almost insentient existence, "a meaningless extinction up an alley," with Gatsby's pilgrimage Eastward, which, though hopeless and corrupting, was at least a journey of life and hope—an escape from the "vast obscurity" of the West that once spawned and then swallowed the American dream. Into this vast obscurity the Buchanans finally disappear. They are not Westerners any longer, or Easterners, but merely two of the very rich, who in the end represent nothing but themselves. They are careless people, Tom and Daisy, selfish, destructive, capable of anything except human sympathy, and yet not sophisticated enough to be really decadent. Their irresponsibility, Nick realizes, is that of pampered children, who smash up "things and creatures . . . and let other people clean up the mess." They live in the eternal moral adolescence which only wealth can produce and protect.

GATSBY: THE GREAT ROMANTIC

By ignoring its context one can perhaps make much of Nick's indictment of the Buchanans. One can even say that in *The Great Gatsby* Fitzgerald adumbrated the coming tragedy of a nation grown decadent without achieving maturity—a nation that possessed and enjoyed early, and in its arrogant assumption of superiority lost sight of the dream that had created it. But is it not absurd to interpret Gatsby as a mythic Spenglerian anti-hero? Gatsby *is* great, because his dream, however naive, gaudy, and unattainable, is one of the grand illusions of the race which keep men from becoming too old or too wise or too cynical of their human limitations. Scott Fitzgerald's fable of East and West does not lament the decline of American civilization. It mourns the eternal lateness of the present hour suspended between the past of romantic memory and the future of romantic promise which ever recedes before us.

Gatsby Is a Sinister Gangster

Thomas H. Pauly

Jay Gatsby replaced the perception of a gangster as a lowlife with an image of an upscale, stylish, wealthy figure, reports Thomas H. Pauly, author of *An American Odyssey: Elia Kazan and American Culture.* In so doing, he is faithfully reflecting the gamblers, bootleggers, and bond thieves who were making handsome profits during Prohibition, with its contradictory conservative law and liberal disregard for that law. Pauly compares Gatsby to real criminals of the era, particularly Arnold Rothstein, "the most important underworld figure in New York City" during the 1920s, and concludes that under his genial front, Gatsby was undoubtedly a more cunning criminal than Nick Carraway realizes.

In an article entitled "The Passing of the Gangster," published in the March 1925 issue of *American Mercury,* Herbert Asbury confidently offered the remarkable assertion: "There are now no more gangs in New York and no gangsters in the sense that the newspapers use the word." The surprising disparity between this contemporary evaluation of the crime scene and our perception of the 1920s as the heyday of gangsters hinges upon Asbury's belief that the gangsters of his age owed their notoriety to ambitious journalists, novelists, playwrights, and scriptwriters fiercely competing for audiences and paychecks. Asbury viewed these accounts as distortions of truth in support of a threadbare stereotype. "The moving picture and the stage," he pointed out, "have always portrayed the gangster as a low-browed person with an evilly glinting eye, a plaid cap drawn down over beetling brows and a swagger that in itself is enough to inform the world that here is a man bent on devilment." With obvious

Excerpted from Thomas H. Pauly, "Gatsby as Gangster," *Studies in American Fiction,* vol. 21, no. 2, Autumn 1993; © by Northeastern University. Reprinted by permission of *Studies in American Fiction.*

contempt, he counters: "In the main, the really dangerous gangster, the killer, was apt to be something of a dandy."[1] Asbury invoked his stylish gangster to return enthusiasts for these fictions to the hard fact that truly successful gangsters didn't make brazen displays of their intent.

A "DANDY" NEW TYPE OF GANGSTER

Even though his article shrewdly appealed to the same interest in gangsters he was criticizing, Asbury little suspected that his revisionist proposal would be quickly embraced. Unwittingly his "dandy" anticipated the innovative gangster which F. Scott Fitzgerald introduced a few weeks later with the publication of *The Great Gatsby*. Jay Gatsby effectively overturned the dated assumption that gangsters were lowlifes from the Bowery and replaced it with an upscale figure who was enviably wealthy and fashionably stylish. Significantly, this portrayal was an outgrowth of actual changes in existing criminal conditions. Fitzgerald understood better than Asbury that since the advent of Prohibition, gangsters were, in fact, on the rise; not only were they gaining more wealth and power, but they were presuming to status and respectability as well. If Fitzgerald's Gatsby was solidly grounded in these historical developments, he too came perilously close to being an implausible gangster and a distortion of fact. Though readers still find Gatsby too romantic, too idealistic, and too naive to be a criminal success, Fitzgerald counteracted this impression by cloaking his gangster in mystery, then frustrating Nick's efforts to penetrate it, and finally suggesting that Gatsby, like Asbury's dandy, may be more dangerous than Nick realizes. If this elusive figure involved a significant modification of the actual gangsters on which Fitzgerald was drawing, he was not the specious fabrication that Asbury was decrying. To characterize Gatsby as a "dandy" might seem inappropriate since clothing is rather incidental to his depiction. This quality is communicated to Nick more by his other possessions than by his white suit, silver shirt, and gold tie—his palatial house, his grand parties, his fancy automobile, his hydroplane, and his library of real books. His flourish of expensive shirts late in the novel merely embellishes this image. This Gatsby is an ideal consumer in his expenditure of so much on the nonessential. He

1. Herbert Asbury, "The Passing of the Gangster," *American Mercury,* 4 (1925), 358, 362

is a dandy who buys expensive merchandise to take on its desirability and to convince Daisy of his worthiness. These traits confirm the potency of a consumer culture and illuminate the social instability generated by the age's myriad products and aggressive advertising. The new credit economy of the 1920s accelerated social mobility and empowered a new ethos whereby merchandise rivaled background, profession, and merit as a determinant of status.[2]

All around him Fitzgerald beheld people who had risen from commonplace backgrounds to affluence and prominence.[3] His own success as a writer validated this new upward mobility. Still, the advances of gangsters were truly extraordinary. In 1920 George Remus was a small-time criminal lawyer who purchased a distillery for medicinal spirits in order to circumvent the recently passed Volstead Act. Though today's readers are often confused by the connection between Gatsby's bootlegging and his drugstores, Fitzgerald was merely registering the widespread exploitation of pharmacies' exemption from Prohibition law due to the large quantities of alcohol used in their prescriptions. Remus' success was to make drug stores as well known for alcohol as speakeasies. Within four years, he controlled fourteen distilleries, a sprawling network of pharmacies and some 3,000 employees. He had cornered one-seventh of the national market for medicinal alcohol and realized a gross income of some $25 million. His accumulated holdings were estimated at $40 million.[4] . . .

ARNOLD ROTHSTEIN

Arnold Rothstein afforded another example of gangster wealth with a stronger, more direct influence upon Fitzgerald's novel. In a letter written in 1937, in which he reflected on *The Great Gatsby,* Fitzgerald wrote: "I selected the stuff to fit a given mood or 'hauntedness' or whatever you might call it, rejecting in advance in Gatsby, for instance, all of the ordinary material for Long Island, bit crooks, adultery theme and always starting from the small focal point that impressed me—my own meeting with Arnold Rothstein

2. William E. Leuchtenburg, *The Perils of Prosperity* (Chicago: Univ. of Chicago Press, 1958), pp. 178–203, and Roland Marchand, *Advertising the American Dream: Making Way for Modernity 1920–40* (Berkeley: Univ. of California Press, 1985) 3. Henry Dan Piper, *F. Scott Fitzgerald: A Critical Portrait* (New York: Holt, Rinehart & Winston, 1965), pp. 114–15 4. John Kobler, *Ardent Spirits: The Rise and Fall of Prohibition* (New York: Putnam, 1973), pp. 315–16

for instance."⁵ Just prior to World War I, Rothstein was a small-time gambler whose livelihood was jeopardized by the reckless actions of his hot-headed friend Herman Rosenthal. This crucial turning point in Rothstein's career is referred to in the initial conversation between Nick and Meyer Wolfsheim:

> "What place is that?" I asked.
> "The old Metropole."
> "The old Metropole," brooded Mr. Wolfsheim gloomily.
> "Filled with faces dead and gone. Filled with friends gone now forever. I can't forget so long as I live the night they shot Rosy Rosenthal there. It was six of us at the table, and Rosy had eat and drunk a lot all evening. When it was almost morning the waiter came up to him with a funny look and says somebody wants to speak to him outside. 'All right,' says Rosy. . . . He turned around in the door and says: 'Don't let that waiter take away my coffee!' Then he went out on the sidewalk, and they shot him three times in his full belly and drove away."
> "Four of them were electrocuted," I said, remembering.
> "Five, with Becker." His nostrils turned to me in an interested way.⁶

The wave of reform set off by these events propelled Rothstein to close his modest gambling parlor and initiate a system of floating games like those memorialized in [the musical and movie] *Guys and Dolls*. When Rothstein returned to a permanent facility several years later, he relocated outside the city, first with an elegant casino created from a Long Island estate and then with the "Brook" in Saratoga, which, at the time of its opening in 1919, was the most luxurious gaming house in the country.⁷ Meanwhile Rothstein's diversification into sports betting climaxed with his reputed fixing of the 1919 World Series.⁸ For Fitzgerald and most Americans at the time, this was a breathtaking exemplification of Rothstein's power. As Nick explains:

> The idea staggered me. I remembered, of course, that the World's Series had been fixed in 1919, but if I had thought of it at all I would have thought of it as a thing that merely *happened*, the end of some inevitable chain. It never occurred to me that one man could start to play with the faith of fifty million people—with the single-mindedness of a burglar blowing a safe.

5. *The Letters of F. Scott Fitzgerald*, ed. Andrew Turnbull (New York: Scribners, 1963), p. 551 6. *The Great Gatsby* (New York: Scribners, 1925). Despite some minor factual errors, this account confirms Fitzgerald's extensive knowledge about Rothstein. For a thorough discussion of this episode see Leo Katcher, *The Big Bankroll: The Life and Times of Arnold Rothstein* (New York: Harper, 1959), pp. 72–97. 7. Katcher, pp. 109–12 8. Rothstein was approached during the planning, but refused to participate and therefore was not involved in the actual fix. However, he used his knowledge to profit handsomely in the betting. See Katcher, pp. 138–48.

Though Rothstein was to reap handsome profits from Prohibition, his emergence during the 1920s as the most important underworld figure in New York City owed more to an involvement with stolen bonds like the ones Gatsby is peddling at the time of his death. During the same year as the World Series fix, Jules "Nicky" Arnstein, a long-time gambling friend of Rothstein's, stole some $5 million worth of Liberty bonds from vulnerable errand boys relaying them between brokerage houses and banks. Since these losses were covered by surety companies and Rothstein's experience with bail bonding provided him with an insider's knowledge of these companies, Rothstein may have provided Arnstein with confidential knowledge about these transfers. Whether or not he actually alerted Arnstein to this prospect, he quickly sprang to Arnstein's defense when a minor criminal fingered him as the one responsible for these thefts. Significantly, these bonds were never recovered; meanwhile Liberty bonds played a role in several important Rothstein deals.[9] Rothstein's take from these bonds vastly exceeded his return from the fixed Series and was perhaps his single most lucrative venture.[10] Indeed, Tom Buchanan's sources appear most reliable in his characterization of Gatsby's drug store chain as "just small change" compared to his stolen bonds. . . .

GATSBY: A FINE FRONT

Readers are led to believe that Gatsby's wealth derives from serving as a front of respectability for Meyer Wolfsheim, a "man bent on devilment" who badly needs someone to mask his blatant criminality. . . . Unlike the Waspish Gatsby, whose smile of greeting warmly acknowledges Nick, this "small flat-nosed Jew . . . with two fine growths of hair which luxuriated in either nostril" ignores him and continues with his account of a recent payoff. He only responds to Nick when he shows knowledge of the Rosenthal affair. Wolfsheim's one effort to engage Nick consists of calling attention to himself and pointing out how his cuff links are made of human mo-

---

9. Scholars have never tracked Fitzgerald's idea for the stolen bonds beyond his interest in the Fuller-McGee case. However, the main issue of this case was the fact that Fuller & Co. was a "bucket shop," a brokerage house that pocketed customer money without actually buying the intended securities. Bonds figured into this case only peripherally but sensationally, when it was revealed that Arnold Rothstein owed Fuller $187,000 and that liberty bonds worth $58,925 that he had posted as collateral were missing. See *New York Times*, January 26, 1923, p. 1.   10. Katcher, pp. 98–99, 170–79

lars. His ensuing characterization of Gatsby as "a perfect gentleman," a "man of fine breeding" who went to "Oggsford
College," suggests the propriety Wolfsheim seeks from
Gatsby while simultaneously establishing his distance from
it. Nick's account implies that Wolfsheim owes his success
more to a brazen disregard for the law than any perceptive
reading of character or subtle scheming.

A BUSINESSMAN WHOSE BUSINESS IS CRIME

It is not really enough to say, as so many critics have with
Nick, that Gatsby's ingenuous faith redeems his criminal
nature, or that his is merely the immorality of the law, not the
heart. . . . To sanctify Gatsby's divided nature in this manner
is to give oneself to the same kind of self-delusion he does—
and in doing so to ignore those very complexities that raise
the book far above the level of naïve culture myth. . . . Gatsby
is a businessman (hence the comic irony in Wolfsheim's cele-
bration of his "Oggsford" appearance; it makes a respectable
front) whose business is crime—and this means whatever illegal enterprise comes to hand. Today he would be dealing in
narcotics and selling arms to terrorists.

Joyce A. Rowe, *Equivocal Endings in Classic American Novels*, 1988.

The implication of Wolfsheim's example—that most gangsters are obtuse, intractable lowlifes—is further reinforced
by the phone call that Nick intercepts following Gatsby's
death. Without ever confirming that he is speaking to
Gatsby, the caller blurts out how his disposal of the stolen
bonds has miscarried. His characterization of Chicago as a
"hick town" by way of justification only confirms his ignorance and incompetence.

Alongside these figures, Gatsby almost succeeds at being
the possessor of manners and refinement he strives to appear, so much so that he comes across as a rather implausible gangster. Those same qualities which differentiate Gatsby
from his criminal associates threaten his believability as the
effective gangster he is supposed to be—unless, of course,
there is more to Gatsby than his ungangsterish appearance
and manner. Critics usually assume that Fitzgerald chan-
neled the model of Arnold Rothstein into his characterization
of Meyer Wolfsheim. While it is true that Wolfsheim is identified as the man who fixed the 1919 World Series, it is also

true that Gatsby was associated with the stolen bonds that were more crucial to Rothstein's successful career. The presumed linkage of Wolfsheim and Rothstein also disregards the significant fact that the crude Wolfsheim was nothing like the actual Rothstein, who was something of a Gatsby to those who knew him. Ironically, Rothstein's skills at engineering social mobility so far surpassed those of Gatsby that he would have had no need for him.

When he served as Fitzgerald's inspiration, Rothstein was a man of enormous experience and sophistication. His early success at high-stakes gambling came from considerable intelligence and chameleon-like adjustment to the conditions of his profession. Well before he opened his own gambling parlor, he acquired the dress and demeanor of a man about town and successfully won the confidence of the well-to-do who made his games profitable. If the decidedly conservative cast of Rothstein's dress, deportment, and choice of residences belied his aggressive pursuit of money and useful connections, it was cultivated not just to suggest well-heeled respectability but even more to avoid the kind of attention that . . . Remus so hungrily sought.[11] . . .

THE PARADOXICAL HEART OF GATSBY'S CHARACTER

Although Rothstein differed from Gatsby in his metropolitan background, his more refined tastes, his vast network of criminal associates, and his calloused selfishness, he was that paradoxical blend of gentleman "dandy" and criminal success at the heart of Gatsby's characterization. This aspect of Rothstein draws attention to a frequently overlooked aspect of Fitzgerald's presentation, Gatsby's evasiveness. Given all the confusion created by Gatsby's "old sport" affectation, his indirect mode of communication, alongside all that is not known about him, Gatsby probably practices the same deception which made Rothstein so successful. At issue here is the central question of Gatsby's function as a front. Many

11. Craig Thompson and Allen Raymond, *Gang Rule in New York* (New York: Dial, 1940), pp. 53–55, 59. See also Katcher, pp. 41, 53, 106, 115, 166. 12. As one of the few fronts whom Rothstein did employ, Dapper Dan Collins (Robert Tourbillon) offers some compelling reasons to suspect Nick's perception of Gatsby. Collins was a tall man whose striking good looks owed much to his well-barbered, peroxide blond hair. As a lifelong con artist and legendary womanizer, Collins invested enormous care in his grooming and attire in order to deceive and exploit his victims. He actively preyed on women, robbing some of their money and turning others into prostitutes. In sharp contrast to Gatsby and his unselfish devotion to Daisy, Collins sought what he wanted from his prey. He was a particularly good front because he was so adept at exploiting those taken in by his attractiveness; Katcher, pp. 241–42.

readers, like Nick, tend to assume that Gatsby's wealth derives from facilitating a necessary liaison between the crude
Wolfsheim and the proprieties of respectable society. Presumably Gatsby handles all public relations for the alcohol
and stolen bonds that Wolfsheim supplies. This unexamined
assumption never considers that behind his shaky facade of
Waspish gentility Gatsby would have needed to be a more
cunning criminal than Nick allows to have amassed so much
wealth. Obviously a good front doesn't just look impressive—
he capitalizes on his impressiveness to gain the confidence of
his victims and to mask his crafty maneuvering.[12]

Artist that he was, Fitzgerald was sufficiently concerned
about Gatsby's implausibility as a gangster and his own limited knowledge of underworld operations that he made a
concerted effort to obscure the course of events that transformed his innocent product of midwestern morality into a
big time metropolitan gangster. Throughout the first half of
the book, much of what the reader learns about Gatsby's
background is a crazy-quilt collection of rumors whose sum
result is confusion and unbelievability. Gatsby is said to have
been a German spy, to have gone to Oxford, and to have
killed a man. His house and parties establish that he is very
rich and cause him to be known by people from every level
of society. However, few have actually met him and fewer
have any reliable knowledge about the sources of his vast
wealth. None of the many guests at his party can identify
him. Significantly, the dust cover of the original edition of
the novel accentuated this obscurity: "It is the story of Jay
Gatsby who came so mysteriously to West Egg."[13] Reviewers
of the novel noticed as well; the *Saturday Review,* for example, noted "all the cleverness of his [Gatsby's] hinted nefari-
ous proceedings" and suggested that "the mystery of Gatsby
is a mystery saliently characteristic of this age in America."[14]

NICK'S TAKE ON GATSBY

Much of the success of these jumbled suggestions derives
from Fitzgerald's use of Nick Carraway as a narrator who
struggles to make sense of his confusing neighbor. Fitzgerald adds to the mystery surrounding Gatsby by first making

13. Matthew J. Bruccoli, *F. Scott Fitzgerald: A Descriptive Bibliography* (Pittsburgh:
Univ. of Pittsburgh Press, 1987), p. 66 14. *Saturday Review* (May 9, 1925), 740. See also
New York Times, April 19, 1925, p. 9; *Dial* 79 (August 25, 1920), 163; and *International
Book Review* (May 25, 1925), 426.

Nick an outsider who learns about Gatsby as he is generally known (or not known). As he registers these baffling shreds of information, he naturally struggles to make sense of them. Meanwhile Fitzgerald teases his curiosity, along with that of the reader, by allowing him limited contact with Gatsby. The result of these suspect bits of information and brief glimpses is at best an impression.

Fitzgerald characterizes Nick as a person more intent upon learning than deciding. As he says in the novel's introductory paragraphs, accentuating his mediation in our understanding of Gatsby, "I'm inclined to reserve all judgements." . . . In sharp contrast to Gatsby, Nick comes from a very proper background that has carried him from Yale to the respectable but unprofitable career of a bond salesman. His inside knowledge of Eastern society and its mores enables him to see Gatsby for the "roughneck" he is. At the same time, his growing reservations about this society set off a reaction that invests Gatsby with greater significance and greater worth. "I wanted the world to be in uniform and at a sort of moral attention forever," he admits in a frequently cited comment. Not unsurprisingly, this longing for a world that is pure and decent makes him acutely aware of the ways in which it isn't. Troubled by his age's award of respectability to the Buchanans and wealth to gangsters, Nick can't help admiring Gatsby's resolute commitment to success, love, and dreams. This Gatsby evidences traits which Nick deeply respects but finds sorely lacking in everyone else around him. Measured by this bias, Gatsby's excesses and unbelievability validate his reassuring uniqueness.

Ultimately Nick does pass judgement without ever reckoning with these biases. In spite of Gatsby's extensive involvement with crime, Nick arrives at the startling conclusion that he is essentially an innocent victim of other people's heartlessness, a true believer destroyed by the cynicism of his age. "You're worth the whole damn bunch put together," Nick tells Gatsby at his last meeting, in a comment that vents his mounting disillusionment with his own social circle. Later he stamps out the obscene desecration scrawled on the steps of Gatsby's empty house and offers his final association of Gatsby with the original beholder of the new world he imagines. Even though Gatsby's loss of Daisy and ensuing death confirm Nick's worst fears, he concludes that Gatsby "turned out all right at the end" because his death saved him from the demoralizing disillusionment that haunts Nick's consciousness.

HINTS ABOUT GATSBY'S SINISTER SIDE

Because Nick's estimate of Gatsby stems from such limited understanding of Gatsby and absorbs so many concerns peculiar to himself, one cannot help wondering if the man at the center of the mystery is really the one he finds. The novel offers at least one telling suggestion that Nick may have overlooked qualities that would make Gatsby more sinister than he has allowed. Nick shows surprisingly little reaction to Tom's revelation of Gatsby's involvement with stolen bonds and to the phone call following Gatsby's death that reveals how his plans for disposing of them have miscarried. To the extent that he makes anything of these revelations, they reinforce his belief that Gatsby's death saved him from having to face his across-the-board defeat.

True as this may be, Nick never suspects that Gatsby's elaborate plans may have involved using him as an agent for his bonds. After all, Nick is a bond salesman. Moreover, he is too trusting and uncritical to question Gatsby's persistent offers of help. "I'm going to make a big request of you today," Gatsby explains before he takes Nick to meet Wolfsheim, "so I thought you ought to know something about me. I didn't want you to think I was just some nobody." Nick decides that Gatsby's objective will be fulfilled when he later learns about the undisclosed "matter" from Jordan. Consequently, he is confused by Wolfsheim's assumption that he is seeking "a business gonnegtion." It never occurs to him that Gatsby, like the reader, might have perceived Nick's uneasiness with Wolfsheim and thus squelched part of his plan with his hurried dismissal of Wolfsheim's comment as a "mistake." That Gatsby may have been cultivating Nick as a possible outlet for his bonds is made even more likely in his later remarks on the eve of his meeting with Daisy.

> "Why, I thought—why, look here, old sport, you don't make much money, do you?"
> "Not very much."
> This seemed to reassure him and he continued more confidently.
> "I thought you didn't, if you'll pardon my—you see, I carry on a little business on the side, a sort of side line, you understand. And I thought that if you don't make very much— You're selling bonds, aren't you, old sport?"

"Trying to."

"Well, this would interest you. It wouldn't take up much of your time and you might pick up a nice bit of money. It happens to be a rather confidential sort of thing."

For the reader bothered by Nick's retreat from his ingrained skepticism in the case of Gatsby, this man of mystery seems more scheming and duplicitous than Nick acknowledges, if only because Gatsby's extravagant possessions attest so eloquently to his success with crime. Nick simply cannot conceive that Gatsby would exploit others to achieve his objectives—nor that Nick's own innocence and propriety might have carried Gatsby elsewhere to dispose of his bonds. *The Great Gatsby* poses a central question: Is Gatsby, as Nick assumes, one of the last romantics wholly dedicated to the love of his life, or is he perhaps, as Nick never really considers, a devious criminal who pursues his business with the same evasion and intrigue shown in his plotted reunion with Daisy? Of course, it is quite possible that he could be both. To see Gatsby as both lover and gangster would demand that this figure be recognized as having more in common with both the criminal Meyer Wolfsheim and the conniving Arnold Rothstein than Nick ever allows. Fitzgerald encourages his reader to consider this possibility. Although this Gatsby is as obsessed with the girl of his dreams as Nick believes, he also appears to be someone who is more intent upon his own objectives and more manipulative than Nick comprehends. This Gatsby is at once more sinister and more believably unbelievable, a true product of Prohibition's criminal conditions.

Gatsby Is a Profoundly Comic Character

Brian Way

In form, *The Great Gatsby* is a dramatic novel, constructed in scenes; in type, it is a social comedy, declares Brian Way, senior lecturer in English at University College, Swansea, England. Fitzgerald's greatest success in this comic venture is the character of Gatsby himself. As simply recorded—not interpreted—by Nick, Gatsby has the "power to arouse wild incredulous laughter," according to Way. Gatsby's parties resemble one of the great comic scenes of classic literature, Trimalchio's banquet in Petronius's *Satyricon*, but Fitzgerald's comic sense is entirely his own.

The most striking formal characteristic of *The Great Gatsby* is its scenic construction, and Scott Fitzgerald himself . . . spoke of it as a 'dramatic' novel. In this respect, it shows extraordinarily close affinities with the theory and practice of Henry James's later fiction. James's vivid account of the little diagram he drew in order to explain the structure of *The Awkward Age* to his publisher corresponds exactly with what we find in *Gatsby:*

> I drew on a sheet of paper . . . the neat figure of a circle consisting of a number of small rounds disposed at equal distance about a central object. The central object was my situation, my subject in itself, to which the thing would owe its title, and the small rounds represented so many distinct lamps, as I liked to call them, the function of each of which would be to light with all due intensity one of its aspects. . . . Each of my 'lamps' would be the light of a single 'social occasion' in the history and intercourse of the characters concerned, and would bring out to the full the latent colour of the scene in question and cause it to illuminate, to the last drop, its bearing on my theme. I revelled in this notion of the Occasion as a thing by itself, really and completely a scenic thing.[1]

1. Henry James, *The Art of the Novel*, edited by R.P. Blackmur, New York, 1934, p. 110

The 'central object' of *The Great Gatsby* is clearly Gatsby himself, and the chapters of the novel are in the main a series of dramatic scenes, each illuminating some new aspect of his character and situation. The scenes are invariably 'social occasions'; often they are parties, in that special sense which is so fundamental to Fitzgerald's understanding of the 1920s. Chapter I is built around the dinner party at the Buchanans' at which Nick Carraway discovers the subtle charm and the inner corruption of Daisy and of the American rich—the woman and the class which Gatsby has made the object of his dreams. Chapter II presents the 'foul dust' that floats in the wake of his dreams. It opens with a poetic and atmospheric evocation of the valley of ashes, but its main source of energy is once again dramatic—the raucous Prohibition-style party in Myrtle Wilson's apartment. In Chapter III, Nick visits one of Gatsby's own parties for the first time, and begins to understand the equivocal nature of the latter's creative powers—his capacity to mix the beautiful with the vulgar, the magical with the absurd. Chapter IV functions like an act in two scenes, each revealing a contrasted aspect of Gatsby's identity: the lunch in New York, at which Nick meets Meyer Wolfsheim and has a glimpse of Gatsby's underworld connections; and the tea during which Jordan Baker tells him the story of Gatsby's wartime affair with Daisy. The dramatic focus of Chapter V is the tea party at Nick's house, when Gatsby and Daisy are reunited; and in Chapter VI Nick attends a second party at Gatsby's, at which Daisy herself is present. Chapter VII, like Chapter IV, is an act in two scenes: the lunch party at the Buchanans' where Tom realizes for the first time that Daisy and Gatsby are lovers; and the abortive cocktail party at the Plaza Hotel in New York, where Tom not only ends the affair, but succeeds in destroying Gatsby's 'platonic conception' of himself. Only in the last two chapters does Fitzgerald largely abandon the dramatic method, and, even here, some of the most vivid moments depend on effects which are scenic in character— Mr Gatz's arrival at Gatsby's house, Nick's second meeting with Meyer Wolfsheim in New York, and Gatsby's funeral. . . .

This principle of construction affects every aspect of Fitzgerald's artistry: in particular, the language of *The Great Gatsby* often rises at moments of intensity to the level of dramatic poetry; and the element of social comedy, which gives the novel its predominant tone and colouring, always finds expression through specifically theatrical effects of action and spectacle. The structure of a dramatic novel, however, is not an end in itself: each scene, to use James's metaphor, is a lamp illuminating a central object, and it is this object which must remain the reader's primary concern. For this reason, a scene-by-scene analysis is by no means the best way to approach *The Great Gatsby,* and a thematic treatment is far more likely to bring out the true nature of Gatsby himself: . . . his dramatic identity—his essentially comic nature. . . .

An Overwhelmingly Comic Character

It is easier to discuss Gatsby's significance and the nature of his experience . . . than to say what kind of fictional character he is. A number of early readers of the novel, including Edith Wharton and H.L. Mencken, felt that as a character he virtually didn't exist. Most later critics have evaded the problem altogether by elevating him to the status of a mythic figure. Approached in this way he becomes a symbolic abstraction, the vehicle for a few school-book platitudes about American history, and the question of whether or not he is a tangible dramatic and human presence conveniently disappears. If one simply reads the novel, however, his dramatic and human presence obstinately and delightfully remains:

> Gatsby, his hands still in his pockets, was reclining against the mantelpiece in a strained counterfeit of perfect ease, even of boredom. His head leaned back so far that it rested against the face of a defunct mantelpiece clock, and from this position his distraught eyes stared down at Daisy, who was sitting, frightened but graceful, on the edge of a stiff chair.
>
> 'We've met before', muttered Gatsby. His eyes glanced momentarily at me, and his lips parted with an abortive attempt at a laugh. Luckily the clock took this moment to tilt dangerously at the pressure of his head, whereupon he turned and caught it with trembling fingers and set it back in place. Then he sat down, rigidly, his elbow on the arm of the sofa and his chin in his hand.
>
> 'I'm sorry about the clock', he said.
>
> My own face had now assumed a deep tropical burn. I couldn't muster up a single commonplace out of the thousand in my head.
>
> 'It's an old clock', I told them idiotically.
>
> I think we all believed for a moment that it had smashed in pieces on the floor.

The reality of Gatsby's character here is, overwhelmingly, comic, and it is this comic Gatsby—not a shadowy abstraction—who dominates the novel.

The Great Gatsby itself is best regarded as a social comedy, but the phrase doesn't perhaps sufficiently convey the extent to which the comic is the vital creative element in Fitzgerald's achievement. The term social comedy usually implies a mode of writing which is satirical and moral, and this is certainly true of his treatment of a number of characters and episodes—in particular of Tom Buchanan. But frequently his writing rises to a level of rich absurdity where comedy is not subordinated to a satirical or moral point, but is itself the point—the truly creative thing. Such a moment occurs in the episode in which Myrtle Wilson buys a dog:

> We backed up to a grey old man who bore an absurd resemblance to John D. Rockefeller. In a basket swung from his neck cowered a dozen very recent puppies of an indeterminate breed.
>
> 'What kind are they?' asked Mrs. Wilson eagerly, as he came to the taxi-window.
>
> 'All kinds. What kind do you want, lady?'
>
> 'I'd like to get one of those police dogs; I don't suppose you got that kind?'
>
> The man peered doubtfully into the basket, plunged in his hand and drew one up, wriggling, by the back of the neck.
>
> 'That's no police dog', said Tom.
>
> 'No, it's not exactly a police dog', said the man with disappointment in his voice. 'It's more of an Airedale'. He passed his hand over the brown washrag of a back. 'Look at that coat. Some coat. That's a dog that'll never bother you with catching cold.'
>
> 'I think it's cute', said Mrs. Wilson enthusiastically. 'How much is it?'
>
> 'That dog?' He looked at it admiringly. 'That dog will cost you ten dollars'.
>
> The Airedale—undoubtedly there was an Airedale concerned in it somewhere, though its feet were startlingly white—changed hands and settled down into Mrs. Wilson's lap, where she fondled the weatherproof coat with rapture.
>
> 'Is it a boy or a girl?' she asked delicately.
>
> 'That dog? That dog's a boy'.
>
> 'It's a bitch', said Tom decisively. 'Here's your money. Go and buy ten more dogs with it'.

To say that this incident illustrates the false gentility of Myrtle Wilson or the crudeness of Tom Buchanan's desires would be true but inessential. What really matters is the irresistibly joyous and liberating sense of the ridiculous which Fitzgerald conveys—that quality in literature which we call, not loosely but precisely, Dickensian. As Grahame Smith admirably expresses it in his study of Charles Dickens à propos of Mrs. Gamp—'we recognize that we are enclosed in a magic circle of pure comedy from which it is impossible to break out with explanations of satirical intent or didactic purpose'.[2] The whole ensuing scene of the party at Myrtle Wilson's apartment is conceived on the same level of pure comedy. Nick Carraway's two encounters with Meyer Wolfsheim have the same quality. Wolfsheim isn't in the novel to give us tangible proof of Gatsby's underworld connections—the cryptic telephone calls the latter occasionally receives are enough to do that. Wolfsheim's monstrous absurdity—his nostrils, his cuff buttons, his sentimentality and his philosophy of life—is an end in itself. It is significant that Edith Wharton considered him ('your wonderful Jew') the best thing in the novel.[3]

A NONSTOP THEATRICAL PERFORMANCE

Fitzgerald's greatest success by far in this mode of comedy, however, is the character of Gatsby himself. It is the comic element in Gatsby which makes him seem credibly alive—which gives him an independent existence as a fictional character. We depend on Nick Carraway's testimony for much of what we believe about him. Without the benefit of Nick's wide privilege of interpretation, and the assurance of his sober integrity, we should not be able to guess at the stupendous imaginative life that lies beneath Gatsby's trivial aspirations. But we don't need Nick to tell us how funny Gatsby is—we see it for ourselves. Here, Nick no longer interprets and guarantees, he merely records—he might almost as well not be there. We should probably be less ready to take his word even for Gatsby's imagination, if Gatsby were less comic. His sole creative talent—it is one of which he is entirely unconscious—is his power to arouse wild incredulous laughter. His life has the aspect of a nonstop theatrical performance—an 'unbroken series of successful gestures'; even his name, Jay Gatsby, is a farcical stunt. He does not provoke the superficial kind of laughter which is a mere brief contortion of the facial muscles; he appeals to a profound comic sense which makes life seem richer and fuller than it normally is. When one laughs at his car, his clothes, his parties, his manner, his autobiographical confidences, one is not merely amused, one is responding, through him, to the fertile, creative ludicrousness of life itself. . . .

2. Grahame Smith, *Dickens, Money, Society*, Berkeley and Cambridge, 1968, see chapter 1 throughout, and especially p. 5 3. In a letter to Fitzgerald reprinted by Edmund Wilson in *The Crack-Up*, New York, 1945, p. 309

The most successful of Gatsby's theatrical gestures are his parties. At the simple level they are fun, an aspect of the novel's meaning which is as true and as important as Nick Carraway's moral disapproval of Gatsby's guests. We are reminded once again of what Henry James and Henry Adams were forced to concede, however reluctantly—that the charm, the success, of American life is in democratic manners, even in social chaos. The corresponding failure of the aristocratic experiment—the stuffy, boorish, hypocritical life of the Buchanans—is clear enough, and throws Gatsby's achievement into sharp relief. Daisy finds—and this is perhaps the sole basis of her love for Gatsby—that there are romantic possibilities in the disorderly riot of his world totally absent from her own. Even the dissipations he offers, or condones, at his house are frank, lively and diverting—very different from Tom Buchanan's crude and furtive relaxations.

Gatsby's parties, too, are virtually his only genuine acts of creation. His dream of Daisy and the way of life she represents, whatever imaginative intensity he puts into it, is an absurd and vulgar illusion. His 'platonic conception' of himself does not differ very significantly from the pattern of Dan Cody's career—the robber baron turned playboy. But his parties are triumphant expressions of that 'vast, vulgar and meretricious beauty' which . . . is one of the most characteristic manifestations of American life. When Nick tells Gatsby that his house looks like the World's Fair, and reflects that his guests 'conducted themselves according to the rules of behaviour associated with an amusement park'; or when Tom Buchanan calls Gatsby's car a 'circus-wagon', the implications are clearly unfavourable. And yet, taken in relation to the parties themselves, these gibes help to direct our attention to something very different: 'There was music from my neighbour's house through the summer nights. In his blue gardens men and girls came and went like moths among the whisperings and the champagne and the stars.'

> The lights grow brighter as the earth lurches away from the sun, and now the orchestra is playing yellow cocktail music, and the opera of voices pitches a key higher. Laughter is easier minute by minute, spilled with prodigality, tipped out at a cheerful word. The groups change more swiftly, swell with new arrivals, dissolve and form in the same breath; already there are wanderers, confident girls who move here and there among the stouter and more stable, become for a sharp, joyous moment the centre of a group, and then, excited with

triumph, glide on through the sea-change of faces and voices and colours under the constantly changing light.

That Gatsby should have brought to life all this miraculous shimmering ephemeral beauty and excitement places him among the great artist-showmen of America—the architects who designed the World's Fairs and Expositions; the circus ringmasters, and the gifted mountebanks of the state and county fairs; the directors of Hollywood epics and musicals; and the scientists, astronauts and media men who, between them, turned the Apollo moon-shots into the best television entertainment ever made.

TRIMALCHIO'S RELIABLE STORYTELLER

Among the titles Fitzgerald proposed for Gatsby *were* Trimalchio *and* Trimalchio in West Egg, *an indication to scholars that they should examine the Trimalchio section of* The Satyricon *by Petronius for its influences on the novel.*

Midway through the dinner party that Petronius details, Trimalchio, surrounded by drunken guests, demands that a story be told. His immediate choice for a narrator is one Niceros: "Trimalchio now turned to his old friend Niceros. 'You used to be better company, my friend,' he said, 'but now you're solemn and glum, and I don't know why. But if you'd like to make your host happy, why not tell us the story of your famous adventure?'" . . .

Like Niceros, Nick appears to grow increasingly "solemn and glum"—or at least disillusioned and rigid—during his association with Gatsby and his circle. And . . . both narrators are concerned with the question of reliability. Trimalchio leaps to Niceros's defense in this regard: "'I, for one, . . . wouldn't dream of doubting you. . . . I know old Niceros and he's no liar. Nope, he's truth itself and never exaggerates.'"

To these creative gifts, Gatsby adds the gift of comedy. His parties always seem about to bubble over into a burst of irresistible laughter. Even the mechanical housekeeping arrangements have a comic effect: the servants who toil 'with mops and scrubbing-brushes and hammers and garden-shears, repairing the ravages of the night before'; the caterers who, with tempting foods, yards of canvas, and hundreds of coloured lights, turn Gatsby's gardens into an enormous Christmas tree; the crates of oranges and lemons which arrive like expected guests from New York, have their juice extracted, and leave his back door in a 'pyramid of pulpless halves.' When, a little later in the evening, Nick Carraway speaks of 'the premature moon, produced like the supper, no doubt, out of a caterer's basket', the whole scene seems to hover between the magical and the absurd. . . .

As Nick's evocation of the atmosphere of Gatsby's parties gradually modulates into his account of the first one he actually attended, the comic element becomes more explicit. At the beginning, it is like a ripple of suppressed laughter half-heard in the general concert of sounds, but soon, like the mounting hilarity of the guests themselves, it becomes unmistakably the dominant note. It is at this phase of the evening that Nick and Jordan find the owl-eyed man admiring Gatsby's library. Then the rhythm of the party changes again—from hilarity to comic uproar: a drunken soprano performs with tears of black mascara streaming down her face, and, in the riotous finale, the owl-eyed man reappears—as the uncomprehending passenger of a car which has lost one of its wheels. The presiding genius at this scene of comic revelry is Gatsby: he surveys his departing guests from the steps of his house, his hand raised, amid the din of motor-horns in a formal gesture of farewell.

TRIMALCHIO

It is in this respect that he most resembles Trimalchio, a character who was very much in Fitzgerald's mind while he was writing *The Great Gatsby.* When Gatsby abruptly stops giving his parties, Nick remarks that 'his career as Trimalchio was over'; and at one stage Fitzgerald actually considered *Trimalchio* and *Trimalchio in West Egg* as possible titles for the novel.[4] Trimalchio's banquet, the longest episode in the *Satyricon* of Petronius, is one of the great comic scenes of classical literature, and has certain obvious resemblances with Gatsby's parties. Both are set in times of wealth and decadence. . . . The guests in each case are a motley collection of adventurers and entertainers, while the two hosts are *nouveaux riches* with the uncertain taste common to that position. In both entertainments the life and virtue are comic, and both reach their dramatic climaxes in scenes of comic disorder. Gatsby's pose—aloof, dignified, ceremonial almost—is in ludicrous contrast with the turmoil of farcical

4. Matthew J. Bruccoli, *Apparatus for F. Scott Fitzgerald's 'The Great Gatsby'*, Columbia, S.C., 1974, p. 6 and fn

misunderstandings and caterwauling motor-horns in his drive. The *débâcle* of Trimalchio's banquet has the same relation to the whole, and contains similar comic incongruities. In order to parade his wealth and liberality, he has his will brought in and read aloud. As his slaves and guests weep drunkenly, he is inspired by the thought that they can pretend the occasion is his funeral wake. He lies down on a couch as if he were the corpse, libations are poured out, and a brass band is summoned to play suitable music. But the leading performer gives such a piercing blast on his instrument that the whole neighbourhood is awakened. The fire brigade is aroused, and the guests flee in terror as the firemen rush in with their axes and buckets of water.

While it is almost certain that Fitzgerald learned something from Petronius about the dramatic organization of such scenes—about the mounting rhythms that run through huge entertainments—his comic sense is entirely his own. . . . *The Great Gatsby* is the only work in which Fitzgerald realized the full potentialities of his comic genius, but in this one novel he equalled the masters of world literature.

Gatsby Is a Pathological Narcissist

Giles Mitchell

A clinical analysis of Jay Gatsby's personality shows
that he is a pathological narcissist, observes Giles
Mitchell, professor of English at the University of
North Texas. The themes of perfection and omnipotence in Gatsby's character are classic symptoms of
narcissism, in which the "ego-ideal" has become inflated and destructive. Gatsby's grandiose lies, poor
sense of reality, sense of entitlement, and exploitive
treatment of others—particularly women—offer further evidence for this theory and help explain why
he has lost the will to live by the end of the novel.

Many critics of *The Great Gatsby* believe, as John Chambers
(1989) does, that Jay Gatsby "has a vitality and potential for
intense happiness" (p. 115). A few critics, of whom Bettina
(1963) is typical, believe that the best that can be said of
Gatsby is that he is "a self-made phony" (p. 141). Obviously,
those who admire Gatsby find Nick Carraway to be a reliable
narrator, and those who deplore Gatsby's character believe
Nick to be so morally obtuse that his ideas about Gatsby cannot be trusted. Critics who admire Gatsby, as well as those
who do not, adduce a great deal of evidence to support their
views. There is probably not a single image, act, or statement
in this short novel that has not been subjected to extensive
analysis in support of both the admiring and the denigrating
view of Gatsby. There is at least one item lacking, however,
in criticism of the novel, and that is a clinical profile of
Gatsby's personality. My thesis is that the novel contains in-
superable evidence that Gatsby is a pathological narcissist
who by the end of the novel has lost the will to live. . . .

I realize that Gatsby is not merely a sick character who
can be dismissed after diagnosis. The complexity and rich-

Excerpted from Giles Mitchell, "The Great Narcissist: A Study of Fitzgerald's Gatsby,"
American Journal of Psychoanalysis, vol. 51, no. 4, pp. 387–96 (1991). Reprinted by per-
mission of the *American Journal of Psychoanalysis*; © 1991 by the Association for the
Advancement of Psychoanalysis.

ness of *The Great Gatsby* resists any one approach. The analysis presented here is intended to analyze Gatsby in clinical terms only. It does not attempt to describe his entire personhood. . . .

PERFECTION AND OMNIPOTENCE

In a person with normal narcissism, the ego-ideal provides "meaning [and] self-esteem" (Menaker, 1977, p. 249). In such a person the "ego-ideal supports the ego" (Menaker, 1977, p. 250) with a realistic sense of self and realistic hopes and aspirations. However, in the narcissist, the ego-ideal becomes inflated and destructive because it is filled with images of "perfection and omnipotence" (Jasovic-Gasic and Vesel, 1981, p. 371). Such images have a "most uncompromising influence on conduct" (Menaker, 1977, p. 250). Two major themes constitute the ego-ideal of Jay Gatsby. One is the theme of perfection, which is expressed in his capacity for idealizing himself and Daisy to an extreme degree. The idealized Gatsby's perfection is manifested in the belief that as a "son of God" he is entitled to be exploitive in any way and to any extent consonant with his idealizations. The other major theme in Gatsby's ego-ideal is omnipotency, which is expressed in his belief that as a son of God he can control time.

Upon meeting and falling in love with Daisy, Gatsby "committed himself to the following of a grail," the "green light" that symbolizes the idealized Daisy. . . .

Early in the summer, Nick observes Gatsby standing on his lawn looking across the bay at the green, grail light that symbolizes his spiritualized Daisy. He lifts his hands "in idolatrous supplication to the green light" (Dahl, 1984, p. 195). In worshipping the grail as if it were a light emanating from the idealized Daisy, Gatsby is really worshipping himself in the mirror of Daisy's symbolism. Gatsby's self-worship reveals what Sugerman (1964) aptly calls the "egotheism" of the typical narcissist (p. 82). At the end of the summer, when Daisy repudiates him and disappears behind the barricade of Buchanan wealth, the grail light also disappears, for it is Daisy's symbol. Nick says that on the night before his death, Gatsby was "clutching at some last hope" for Daisy's call. By the afternoon of the next day, Gatsby probably "didn't believe it would come, and perhaps he no longer cared." Although Nick says, on the last page of the novel, that Gatsby "believed in the green light," if in the last hours of his life he no longer believes that Daisy will call or cares about whether or not she will, then it follows that he no longer believes in the grail.

ENTITLEMENT, EXPLOITIVENESS, AND GRANDIOSITY

There is no evidence in the novel that Gatsby feels any moral conflict about urging Daisy to marry him—to marry into a life supported by criminal activities. In Rothstein's words, "People with narcissistic personality disorders feel entitled to have what they want just because they want it" (1985, p. 67). It is of crucial importance to note that Gatsby evinces no conscious sense of guilt for deceiving Daisy. Furthermore, there is no hint in the novel that he feels guilt unconsciously, because the feeling of narcissistic entitlement typically "serves as a substitute for normal repression" (Murray, 1964, p. 492).

Gatsby is a poseur in the most serious sense of the word. Therefore, he can have no genuine emotional contact with Daisy, and he compensates for this deficiency as, according to Stern, the narcissist typically does: by "making exploitive demands" (1977, p. 191) upon Daisy and upon the world in general. Exploitiveness with regard to women appears early in his life—in his mid-teens:

> He knew women early, and . . . he became contemptuous of them, of young virgins because they were ignorant, of the others because they were hysterical about things which in his overwhelming self-absorption he took for granted.

When he first met Daisy, "He took what he could get, ravenously and unscrupulously. . . . He had deliberately given Daisy a sense of security; he let her believe that he was a person from much the same stratum as herself." Gatsby's exploitiveness derives in part from what Kernberg refers to as the narcissist's "extreme self-centeredness" (1975, p. 228), or in Fitzgerald's phrase, "overwhelming self-absorption."

Gatsby's sense of entitlement is a major force in his character. . . . Gatsby's entitlement justifies his grandiosity as well as his exploitiveness. The most extreme expression of his grandiosity has to do with his parentage, which "his imagination had never really accepted." Instead, he "sprang from his Platonic conception of himself. He was a son of God—a phrase which, if it means anything, means just that." The blasphemous, deific quality in Gatsby has a specific grandiose focus: "his Father's business, the service of a vast, vulgar, and meretricious beauty." This narcissistically inflated religious theme is elaborated in the statement that "to this conception he was faithful to the end." . . .

When Gatsby tells Nick it is "God's truth" that he had been "educated at Oxford," like all his ancestors, he is not telling an ordinary lie, for the grandiose, deific theme is implicit in his use of the word "God's." Whether or not Gatsby is telling the truth about his ancestry and his heroic war record does not matter. The point is that when he tells Nick about it, he is planning to use Nick as an intermediary in order to see Daisy again; and he doesn't want Nick to think he is "just some nobody." He wants Daisy to see his house, which, he tells her, he keeps full of "celebrated people," special objects in his "universe of ineffable gaudiness." Given his poor sense of reality and his pitiable grandiosity, it is neatly appropriate that Gatsby's mansion be an "imitation," and a "colossal" one at that. The note inviting Nick to a party there is signed by Gatsby "in a majestic hand." Grandiosity is a major motive force in his idealizations of Daisy. He projects onto her a kind of royal status. To him, she is "high in a white palace the king's daughter, the golden girl."

A TAWDRY ROMANTICISM

Gatsby is extremely adept at embuing his exploitiveness with a tawdry romanticism that Nick finds attractive. Like the typical narcissist studied by Kernberg (1975), Gatsby presents "a surface which very often is charming and engaging," and a subsurface of "coldness and ruthlessness" (p. 228). Nick says that when he first met him, Gatsby produced a smile "with a quality of eternal reassurance in it"; it "concentrated on *you* with an irresistible prejudice in your favor." But beneath his engaging surface, Gatsby is profoundly dishonest and manipulative with Daisy both when he first meets her and later when they are reunited. He tells her lies of a most serious nature in defending himself against Tom's revelations about how Gatsby has made his money. In short, in asking Daisy to leave Tom, he is being morally devious. Gatsby lies to Daisy without the slightest compunction because she is the idealized object of his projections and therefore not real. Therefore, he unthinkingly assumes that he need not tell Daisy the factual truth of who he actually was when they met five years earlier and who he is now: a criminal.

If he loved her, he would want intimacy with her; but intimacy means knowing and being known, and Gatsby does not want Daisy to know him, for he is a criminal with a poor education and a background of impoverished, "shiftless and unsuccessful farm people." Furthermore, he does not want to know Daisy—the real Daisy—who is five years older than she was when he first met her and who has a husband whom she once loved and by whom she has had a child. The real Daisy runs far away from the scene of her crime and does not even bother to call Gatsby to say good-bye. Although she can weep over Gatsby's magniloquent display of shirts, the real Daisy has "impersonal eyes in the absence of all desire." It is likely that Gatsby is unknowingly attracted by Daisy's incapacity for intimacy and by the impersonality in her eyes: He discredits her love for Tom by describing it as being "just personal."

OMNIPOTENCE AND TIME

When Nick says to Gatsby, "You can't repeat the past," Gatsby is astounded at what he apparently regards as Nick's naivete: "'Can't repeat the past?' he cried incredulously. 'Why of course you can!'" Narcissists typically believe that they can control time, for time presents "threats to omnipotence" (Stern, 1977, p. 194). Therefore, it is often the case that narcissists illogically attempt to "repeat the same experience" (p. 194). What Gatsby wants in this regard is for himself and Daisy to be in Louisville again, in love, and then to "be married from her house—just as if it were five years ago." Controlling time by repeating an experience would be an attempt on Gatsby's part to stop and reverse time. Therefore, Gatsby "talked a lot about the past. . . . [He wanted to] return to a certain starting place and go over it all slowly." Gatsby's belief that he can delete the present and restore the idealized past reveals the perfection motif of his ego-ideal. And as Rothstein (1985) notes, "The pursuit of perfection is in itself self-destructive" (p. 99) because it radically diminishes one's humanness. But Gatsby rejects his mere humanness, and idealizes the wish to destroy the present—in which he must live if he *does* live. At the end of the novel, therefore, Gatsby may be choosing not to live. . . .

NOTHING BUT A MIRROR

Nick is probably right in surmising that, on the last day of his life, Gatsby "no longer cared" whether Daisy would call or not. (If so, Gatsby has ceased to care only a few hours after last seeing her.) The tone of the text suggests that Gatsby is grieving during the last hours of his life, but he is probably not grieving over Daisy: "When the object is lost, the narcissist mourns not the loss of the object in itself but rather the loss of the mirror" (Jasovic-Gasic and Vesel, 1981, p. 371). In other words, the narcissist does not experience loss of the person but of the person-as-mirror. . . .

Perhaps the most revealing thing about Gatsby's behavior during the last hours of his life is that he tells Nick the truth about his past, about his identity. Why does he do so? He has been lying steadily to Nick all summer. Do his revelations amount to a confession and a wish to atone, at least to himself, for a life of lies? I think not. Nothing he says suggests remorse. His revelations are, on the most simple and important level, an acknowledgment that he has "paid too high a price for living with a single dream." . . .

In telling the hopelessly unromantic truth about his identity, Gatsby is looking at the "universe of ineffable gaudiness" created for Daisy, and he is realizing that *it has been nothing but a mirror.* The parties for Daisy are over, and Gatsby has lost all interest in time, past or present. He has wanted too much for too long, and now he apparently is unable to want anything, including Daisy. She is, after all, irremediably imperfect. The price he pays for his narcissistic dream is a form of emotional suicide: He is now unable to care, at all, about his life. . . .

Nick is correct—in a way that he is unaware of—in believing that on the last day of his life Gatsby remains "faithful." But if he no longer cares about Daisy, then he is faithful only to the anomic image of *himself* that he "invented" at the age of seventeen. And this is the self that lives for images of perfection, which he sees reflected in Nick's words, "You're worth the whole damn bunch put together." At this moment, Gatsby's "face broke into that radiant and understanding smile, as if we'd been in ecstatic cahoots on that fact all the time." But Nick is only a minor, satellite mirror. Gatsby apparently regards Nick as being important enough to be told his true story, but he completely disregards Nick's advice that he go into hiding for a while. Gatsby enjoys Nick's praise, for losing Daisy as his mirror of perfection does not mean that he renounces his ego-ideal's images of perfection. On the contrary, to them he is so faithful that he may very well be the typical narcissistic suicide, of whom Menaker (1977) observes, "One dies for one's ego-ideal rather than let it die" (p. 259). For Gatsby to deliberately choose to shore up his ruins and live in the natural, real world—of unmanipulated time—would be to break faith with his ego-ideal.

REFERENCES

Bettina, Sister M. (1963). The artifact in imagery: Fitzgerald's *The Great Gatsby. Twentieth-Century Literature: A Scholarly and Critical Journal* 9: 140–142.

Chambers, John B. (1989). *The Novels of F. Scott Fitzgerald.* New York: St. Martin's Press.

Dahl, Curtis (1984). Fitzgerald's use of architectural styles in *The Great Gatsby. American Studies* 25: 91–102.

Jasovic-Gasic, Miroslava, and Vesel, Josif (1981). Fear of death and narcissism. *Psychology Today* 4: 369–372 (published in Prague).

Kernberg, Otto F. (1975). *Borderline Conditions and Pathological Narcissism.* New York: Jason Aronson, Inc.

Kernberg, Otto F. (1984). *Severe Personality Disorders: Psychotherapeutic Strategies.* New Haven: Yale University Press.

Menaker, Ruth (1977). The ego-ideal: An aspect of narcissism. In *The Narcissistic Condition: A Fact of Our Lives and Times,* M. L. Nelson (ed.). New York: Human Sciences Press.

Murray, John M. (1984). Narcissism and the ego ideal. *Journal of the American Psychoanalytic Association* 12: 477–511.

Rothstein, Arnold (1985). *The Narcissistic Pursuit of Perfection.* New York: International Universities Press.

Stern, Mark E. (1977). Narcissism and the defiance of time. In *The Narcissistic Condition: A Fact of Our Lives and Times,* M. L. Nelson (ed.). New York: Human Sciences Press.

Sugerman, Shirley (1964). *Sin and Madness: Studies in Narcissism.* Philadelphia: Westminster Press.

Gatsby Is a Fairy-Tale Hero for the Middle Class

Robert Emmet Long

The darkness of Fitzgerald's vision in *The Great Gatsby* comes from the exact center of postwar American society, writes essayist and book reviewer Robert Emmet Long. Gatsby's middle-class dream is a fairy tale, the product of a middle-class imagination. Fitzgerald drew from the resources and energies of the fairy tale to evoke the enchanted horror of a world in which the good prince is put to death and evil survives.

In Fitzgerald's early fiction, like that of his contemporaries, a young man figures prominently. Amory Blaine [in *This Side of Paradise*] and Anthony Patch [in *The Beautiful and Damned*] both serve in the army during World War I, and Amory, supposedly, is in combat overseas; but the war itself seems remote in Fitzgerald's work. It is the postwar world that he knows, and its upper-middle-class life that he records. The novels in which Amory and Anthony appear are "apprenticeship" works in the deepest sense, since in them Fitzgerald searches for a major theme without being able to give it full expression. It is in *The Great Gatsby* that everything comes together for him, that he finds his vision. It is a vision that, like that of Ernest Hemingway, John Dos Passos, and William Faulkner, repudiates the old assumptions of order firmly, makes the emptiness and estrangement of the present convincing and dramatic.

THE DREAM AT THE CENTER

In one specific respect, Fitzgerald's vision in *The Great Gatsby* is the most central to the twenties, since its darkness erupts from the exact middle of American society. Dos Passos's

Excerpted from Robert Emmet Long, *The Achieving of* The Great Gatsby: *F. Scott Fitzgerald, 1920–1925.* Copyright © 1979 by Associated University Presses, Inc. Reprinted by permission of Associated University Presses, Inc.

Manhattan Transfer has a leftist or Marxist orientation, and Faulkner's *Sartoris* is a study in regional or rural Southern realism. Hemingway's characters are characteristically somewhat at the edge of society, are suspicious of society, or are not fully committed to it, or are depicted at critical moments when they recognize their isolation, or must, like his bullfighters, prove their courage alone and under stress. But the darkness of the postwar world for Fitzgerald is felt at the exact social middle—and within a context of "manners." Unlike Hemingway's isolates, Fitzgerald's characters always belong to a social unit, function in a context of social differences, are socially defined. The difference of class in *The Great Gatsby* is essential to Fitzgerald's vision, a curiously dual vision, which delights in social discrimination and yet makes social order seem light-years in the past, is both classical and darkly apocalyptic.

It is the middle-class dream, the dream at the center, with which Fitzgerald deals in *The Great Gatsby*. Nick Carraway's voice is a "normal" one, suggesting a norm; it is solidly middle-class, sensitive within limits, a little complacent, even somewhat priggish. Gatsby himself comes out of the middle-class imagination. One of the great facts about him is his lack of familiarity with real wealth; when he acquires money he cannot quite believe in its reality, does not know what to do with it, converts it immediately into the material of romance, which had furnished his imagination earlier. He is nowhere with his dream, because he understands wealth only mythically; there is no fate he can embrace except estrangement and death. Gatsby's loneliness is emphasized even in the flaw of the novel's ending, the way in which Fitzgerald becomes entangled in the East versus West distinction, which he derived, apparently, from Willa Cather. At the end, Carraway returns to the West, where he can keep his moral distinctions straight. Or so he says. But there is a contradiction in terms in his return, since he has already envisioned a darkness spreading across the entire continent, including the West he returns to as sanctuary. Moreover, it is in the West, in the environs of Chicago, that the Buchanan money was made, that Gatsby was closed out of Daisy's life originally, that Daisy chose Tom. Further still, the frontier vision served first by Dan Cody and then by Gatsby, and exploded as a cruel illusion, was a dream of the West. Carraway returns to the West not, it seems, as fact so much as

SYLVIA PLATH FINDS A FAIRY-TALE METAPHOR IN GATSBY

The University of South Carolina's Matthew J. and Arlyn Bruccoli Collection of F. Scott Fitzgerald includes a heavily marked and annotated copy of The Great Gatsby *that once belonged to poet Sylvia Plath. Since the annotations show multiple close readings of the novel, Park Bucker surmises that associations could be made between Fitzgerald's lyrical prose and Plath's poetry. Here Bucker describes one of Plath's annotations.*

In one comment Plath expresses herself through metaphor. At the end of Chapter VII, after the murder of Tom's mistress, Nick sees the Buchanans through their kitchen window speaking intimately, almost "conspiring together." Nick leaves, passing Gatsby in the driveway. Plath underlined the final sentence in the chapter, "So I walked away and left him standing there in the moonlight—watching over nothing." In the margin underneath Plath wrote "knight waiting outside— dragon goes to bed with princess." With this note Plath's annotation rises from mundane commentary to incisive interpretation. Many of Plath's later poems employ fairy-tale allusions, usually with the inverted imagery she employs here.

Park Bucker, "Princess Daisy: A Description of Sylvia Plath's Copy of *The Great Gatsby,*" *Yemassee,* Fall/Winter 1995.

admitted illusion of adolescence, which means that he, like Gatsby, has no place to go, can envision no alternatives to the nightmare he has lived through. . . .

ENCHANTED HORROR

In its vision of modern emptiness, *The Great Gatsby* is a key document of the twenties, so much so that had it not been written the twenties would actually seem diminished. It is as vivid today (and as "surprising") as when it was written, and has an intense life. Gatsby's vividness has been reinforced on so many different levels of myth and folklore that it is difficult to say which most controls his conception. The woodchopper's son, the young man from the provinces come to the great city, Dick Whittington, Horatio Alger—all stand in the background of his conception. But perhaps as importantly as from any other source, Gatsby comes from the fairy tale; for if the novel has, in Henry James's phrase "the imagination of disaster," it also has the imagination of enchantment. There is a sentence in the manuscript, but not included in the book, that reveals Gatsby. It occurs when he is among Daisy's circle at Louisville. "He was a nobody with an irrevealable past," Fitzgerald comments, "and under the invisible cloak of a uniform he had wandered into a palace." With its palaces and invisible cloaks, Gatsby's imagination has a fairy-tale quality. Almost instinctively, he regards Daisy Fay as a princess, a girl in a white palace, and the spell of the fairy tale, too, marks his ascendancy from his midwestern farm to his own palace of a kind at West Egg. Gatsby becomes a kind of fairy-tale prince in disguise, is deprived of his princehood while retaining his princehood in essence, the consciousness of a noble inheritance, of an inner sovereignty belonging to a prince, even though he wears a shepherd's garments.

Fitzgerald refers to Long Island by name very rarely in the novel; it seems disembodied as well as real and is a region of wonder. Carraway's recall of his adolescence at the end is, too, part of the child's perception of life as wonder, as in the fairy tale. And there is a strong demarcation in the novel between good and evil; the Buchanans' world, and the Wilsons', seem somehow bewitched by evil forces, which are beyond containment or control. The evocative energies of the fairy tale help to account, I think, for the helplessness one feels before the enchanted horror of the world Fitzgerald creates in the novel, a world in which the good prince is put to death, and the dark prince reigns. Other American novelists before Fitzgerald drew from the fairy tale; Henry James did so in *The Portrait of a Lady* and other novels. But Fitzgerald is alone in the twenties in drawing from the resources of the fairy tale to create his age, to touch the depths of its irrationality, and at the same time to create one of the most memorable characters in the American fiction of the 1920s.

Since World War II there have been novels published in America that have some claims to seriousness, and yet after one has read them one can hardly remember their characters. Compare with these the power of dramatic projection in *The Great Gatsby*, the way in which Jay Gatsby lives in one's imagination, refusing to be dislodged. Such enduring life is the mark of exceptional achievement, can only be the result of a creative conception of astonishing depth and power, which *The Great Gatsby* continues to give the impression of being.

CHAPTER 2

Reflections of America in *The Great Gatsby*

The Cynical Views of an American Literary Generation

William Goldhurst

Although Fitzgerald and his contemporaries shared certain literary values, such as the importance of personal experience as a basis for art, their themes and treatments varied widely. But many authors of the 1920s agreed on one concept, writes William Goldhurst, Professor of Humanities Emeritus at the University of Florida: They reacted against the popular aspirations and values of post–World War I Americans. In Fitzgerald's case, that reaction leads to a suggestion that religious belief has degenerated into just another business, while business has attained the status of a new religion.

The literary community or artistic "cluster" is a commonplace of history.[1] But the feeling persists that the literary community of the nineteen-twenties was unique, that it was distinguished from earlier fellowships by its closeness and by the intensity of its activity. "They had more experiences in common than any other generation in American history," Malcolm Cowley accurately observes. *Exile's Return*, which is based on Cowley's own experience, traces some of the typical patterns of the time: childhood in a small town in the Midwest; a university education interrupted by the compelling patriotic impulse of 1917; service with the Armed Forces in Europe; return, restlessness, expatriation—and above all the fascination with literature, the joint projects and manifestoes, the plethora of *avant-garde* magazines, the

---

1. See A.L. Kroeber, *Configurations of Culture Growth* (Berkeley, Calif., 1944). This voluminous study documents what Kroeber calls "the tendency in human culture for successes or highest values to occur close together in relatively brief periods within nations."

Excerpted from William Goldhurst, *F. Scott Fitzgerald and His Contemporaries* (Cleveland: World, 1963). Copyright © 1963 by William Goldhurst. Reprinted by permission of the author.

common dedication among men who shared a profound interest in their craft.

On the other hand, the writers of the twenties formed no school or specific movement; they had no "program," nor did they limit themselves to doctrinaire principles. The American authors of the postwar decade, in fact, consisted of a number of small separate groups and a great many unaffiliated individuals—all of whom participated freely in public feuds and differences of opinion. . . .

Cliquishness and uniformity, undeviating mutual praise and agreement were held in low esteem by the more serious artists of the time, some of whom opposed such things on principle. Perhaps the best perspective on writers of the time reveals a community of literary spirits who were argumentative, self-defensive, and mutually critical, but who nonetheless shared similar ideals and underlying convictions.

This basic unity of attitude found its way into many essay collections and symposiums. By far the most famous of these, *Civilization in the United States* (New York, 1922), suggests the close harmony of opinion among intellectuals and artists on the subject of American culture. Harold Stearns (who also crops up in Ernest Hemingway's *The Sun Also Rises*) edited the collection and contributed a grim essay on "The Intellectual Life." Conrad Aiken lamented the plight of the American poet. J.E. Spingarn decried the fear of personality and intellect in the universities. H.L. Mencken, in a brief survey of American politics, blasted away at the ignorance and dishonesty of our officeholders. Lewis Mumford depicted the horrors of modern industrialization in our cities. Ring Lardner called attention to the "asininity" of American sports spectators. Van Wyck Brooks commented unhappily on "The Literary Life": "The chronic state of our literature," he observed, "is that of a youthful promise which is never redeemed." In his Preface, Stearns summed up one of the basic attitudes which pervaded the entire collection: "the most moving and pathetic fact in the social life of America today is emotional and aesthetic starvation. . . ." Stearns also declared that the volume attempted an "uncompromising analysis" of numerous aspects of American life; only religion had been omitted from the general indictment. "It has been next to impossible to get any one to write on the subject," Stearns confessed. Five years later Sinclair Lewis published *Elmer Gantry*, thereby contributing a powerful supplement to Stearns's symposium and correcting its most notable deficiency. . . .

FITZGERALD AND HIS CONTEMPORARIES

There is no "key" to an understanding of the literature of the nineteen-twenties. Anyone attempting to reduce it to a single essential "formula" courts the error of oversimplification. Yet there are large areas in the works of Fitzgerald and his contemporaries that reveal a fundamental agreement of interest and approach. These writers seem particularly in accord in their selection of themes and their attitudes toward literary technique. . . .

The writers of the period were united, moreover, in their approach to their sources of literary material: they stressed the importance of the immediate personal experience as a basis for art. Invention, of course, was still important; but the rendering of the actual, the concrete, the observed phenomena of life was given new emphasis. "It was, in fact, an age of indirect or direct 'transcription,'" writes Carlos Baker, "when the perfectly sound aesthetic theory was that the author must invent out of his own experience or run the risk of making hollow men out of his characters." The consistency with which the writers of the twenties and early thirties adopted this theory gives the literature they produced its intense documentary flavor and accounts for its many *romans à clef.* The serious authors of the time felt that they had first to see for themselves before starting to work; they spared no effort to achieve a verisimilitude based on experienced, rather than imagined, reality. . . . Scott Fitzgerald and his contemporaries reversed the doctrine of Shakespeare's Theseus and started, rather than ended, with "a local habitation and a name."

They drew their themes, in the same spirit, from the life around them. The writers of the twenties and early thirties were realists in this respect, too: each recorded with remarkable fidelity the issues and events—as well as the developing, ever-changing attitudes—of his time and place. There are, however, no simple patterns of agreement here. Fitzgerald, Lardner, and John Dos Passos, for example, all contributed treatments of the Younger Generation: but each one differs in its perspective. Fitzgerald was the chief historian of the emergent debutantes and playboys, and much of his early fiction is devoted to a romantic portrayal of their adventures. Lardner made the same group targets of his satire.

Dos Passos drew a picture of the flapper and her escort that emphasizes still another aspect of the subject: the girl is mildly insane and the boy is ignorant and self-interested. The reader discovers variety rather than uniformity in these treatments of a prominent theme of the twenties. Still, there is agreement in this instance—and in many others—in the writers' selection of subjects and materials to be treated in fiction.

Furthermore, many authors not only elected the same subjects, but shared similar attitudes toward them. They were particularly unified in their outspoken, sometimes vehement reaction against the popular aspirations and values of the American majority. "Never in history," remarked one of the most famous critics of the period, "did a literary generation so revile its country." Perhaps "revile" is too strong a word; but it is certain that many novelists and short-story writers turned out cynical interpretations of our habits and attitudes. We might consider, for example, fictional treatments of village life in the United States. President Harding had expressed an opinion on the subject that may be taken as representative of the popular sentiment: "What is the greatest thing in life, my countrymen? Happiness. And there is more happiness in the American village than in any other place on earth." Sherwood Anderson did not agree, as is demonstrated by *Winesburg, Ohio* (1919); neither did Sinclair Lewis in *Main Street* (1920), Ring Lardner in "Haircut" (1925), Herbert Asbury in "Hatrack" (1925), or the Lynds [Robert S. and Helen Merrill Lynd] in their documentary study, *Middletown* (1929).

A number of authors also turned their attention to the automobile, a commodity that had begun to assume significant proportions in the life of the average American citizen. Sinclair Lewis showed Babbitt's childish dependence on his motorcar for social status and self-esteem. William Faulkner, in *Sartoris*, made the automobile a symbol of the returned veteran's reckless and futile quest for speed and excitement; indeed, for the hero of this Faulkner novel the motorcar is a means of escape from life in a peace-torn world. Other writers extended Faulkner's implication: in Lardner's "There Are Smiles," in Fitzgerald's *The Great Gatsby*, and in Dos Passos' *The Big Money*, the automobile is an instrument of death. Such treatments reflect not only the tremendous increase in production and purchase of automobiles during the twenties, but also the tendency toward machine worship in the public imagination of the time.

In other areas Fitzgerald, Mencken, and Theodore Dreiser protested Puritanism and "Comstockery" [vigorous censorship; prudery]. These same writers, along with Dos Passos and Hemingway, rejected the high-sounding slogans of World War I propaganda. On occasion writers even adopted the same imagery: Faulkner (in *Soldier's Pay*), Fitzgerald (in *The Great Gatsby*), and Hemingway (in *The Sun Also Rises*) all owed a profound debt to the sterile landscape of T.S. Eliot's *Waste Land*, one of the most influential depictions of twentieth-century society. These examples, which could easily be multiplied, illustrate the close communion of attitude shared by many of the major writers of the time; but they also suggest, as does the consistent emphasis upon experimental technique, the rebellious tendency of their fiction.

No Time for Their Elders

The members of Fitzgerald's generation were not interested at the time in underlying social movements, any more than they were interested in local or international politics. What they felt in their hearts was that they had made an absolute break with the standards of the older generation. There was not the sharp distinction between highbrow and lowbrow (or liberal and conservative) that would later divide American society; in those days the real gulf was between the young and the old. The younger set paid few visits to their parents' homes and some of them hardly exchanged a social word with men or women over forty. The elders were discredited in their eyes by the war, by prohibition, by the Red scare of 1919–20 and by scandals like that of Teapot Dome. So much the better: the youngsters had a free field in which to test their own standards of the good life.

Malcolm Cowley, Introduction, *The Stories of F. Scott Fitzgerald*, 1951.

Rebellious they were, certainly, and critical of native mores, of which they were perceptive students. Many aspects of the "rebellion" have been recorded; yet the term is misleading if it creates an image of a spontaneous indictment of American institutions and customs. Taken as a whole, this body of fiction is emphatic in its iconoclasm and its vigorous assault on our weaknesses and illusions. But the same strain is evident in the works of earlier writers. In all periods of its relatively short history, in fact, American literature exhibits a rich vein of social satire and social criticism. Especially prominent since the Civil War, the theme of social criticism may be traced from the beginnings of our tradition to the present, from Hugh Brackenridge to Jack Kerouac. The fiction of the twenties differs, of course, in historical particulars; but it is still very much a traditional body of work in its preoccupations and its philosophy: it is part of the continuity of American letters rather than an isolated episode in its development.

We might accurately call their fundamental theme Democracy in America, after Alexis de Tocqueville's keen and detached study of our society. The subject is dramatic and multifarious, and it was given particular relevance in the nineteen-twenties by the social and economic forces operating during the postwar era. At no other time in our history have the potential misfortunes of equalitarianism seemed so conspicuous and so close to realization. Brackenridge had observed some of these unwholesome tendencies during the first twenty years of the republic. In his conclusion to *Modern Chivalry* he states that the great moral of his book is "the evil of men seeking office for which they are not qualified." This assertion has familiar echoes to readers of H.L. Mencken, whose era provided abundant material for a similar "great moral" ("I am not fit for this office and should never have been here," confessed Warren Gamaliel Harding). Nineteenth-century writers as diverse as Nathaniel Hawthorne, Mark Twain, and Henry James had focused disillusioned eyes on the subject of the American "aristocracy"; the same theme occupies a prominent position in the works of Lardner, Mencken, Lewis, and Scott Fitzgerald.

In the eighteen-thirties [in *Democracy in America*] Alexis de Tocqueville had mapped the contours of our culture that would engage native writers almost a century later. Tocqueville saw clearly the rationale of self-interest that dominated American business and the fluidity of movement that characterized our social structure:

> It is strange to see with what feverish ardor the Americans pursue their own welfare and to watch the vague dread that constantly torments them lest they should not have chosen the shortest path which may lead to it. . . . A native of the United States clings to this world's goods as if he were certain

never to die: and he is so hasty in grasping at all within reach
that one would suppose he was constantly afraid of not living
long enough to enjoy them. . . . If in addition to the taste for
physical well-being a social condition be added in which neither laws nor customs retain any person in his place, there is
a great additional stimulant to this restlessness of temper.
Men change their track for fear of missing the shortest cut to
happiness.

Tocqueville's comments on national pursuits and motives
might easily be applied to the post–World War I period. The
spirit of our commercial enterprise during those years of unprecedented prosperity was based in large measure upon
the practice and principle of "grasping at all within reach"
and a "clinging to this world's goods." The social aspirations
of the aggressive middle class (in Tocqueville's telling
phrase "the many men restless in the midst of abundance")
were recorded time after time by the writers of the nineteen-
twenties. These tendencies of democracy in America
claimed the attention of Fitzgerald and his contemporaries,
as they had attracted the notice of the astute European visi-
tor to our shores almost a century earlier.

The writers of the twenties saw numerous possibilities for
variation in these dominant motifs: they contained tragic
implications, as in Dreiser's *American Tragedy;* they provided material for comedy, invective, and satire—as in Lardner, Mencken, and Sinclair Lewis; they inspired the powerful sagas of social displacement by William Faulkner; they
gave authority and universality to the fictional autobiogra-
phies of Thomas Wolfe; and they were the backdrop for the
melancholy romances of Scott Fitzgerald.

REFLECTING AND SHAPING AN AGE

Whence the emphasis in the novels and stories of the
nineteen-twenties upon the social milieu, the pronounced
interest in the aspirations of the different classes, in their
motives and values? The fiction of the time only directs our
attention back to the time itself; and both yield fruitfully to
analysis when we understand the process, well known to
cultural historians, whereby a literature reflects an age and
simultaneously helps to shape it. If we add, further, the
forces that work upon the writer's imagination to shape his
art, our comprehension of the cycle approaches a state of
fullness, however imperfect or incomplete in an absolute
sense. In the twenties, few authors worked in isolation. The

majority were "involved" in two ways: with the issues and the events of the life around them, and with the ideas and attitudes of other contemporary writers. But a specific example at this point will help to clarify the process by which one fictionist of the era derived from his reading the materials of his art, and how those materials crystallize brilliantly an episode in actual national experience. An example appropriate to the purpose is the image of T.J. Eckleburg in Scott Fitzgerald's novel *The Great Gatsby*.

THE ECKLEBURG EYES

Eckleburg is introduced early in the novel, in the section describing the "valley of ashes" that serves as a Waste Land backdrop for some of the book's crucial action. This bleak area, actually a dumping ground just outside Manhattan, is dominated by a large billboard showing two enormous eyes wearing spectacles and captioned "Doctor T.J. Eckleburg." Presumably this is an optometrist's advertisement placed among the ash heaps to attract the notice of passing commuters. But Fitzgerald suggests that Eckleburg's brooding presence has a larger significance, that the gigantic eyes symbolize some implacable modern deity. Across the road from the desolate valley of ashes lives George Wilson, the spiritless garage owner whose wife, Myrtle, is having an adulterous affair with Tom Buchanan, the unscrupulous and well-to-do representative of Fitzgerald's American "aristocracy" in *The Great Gatsby*. Later, after Myrtle Wilson's death (which occurs in the neighborhood of the dumping ground), George Wilson entertains a curious delusion:

> Wilson's glazed eyes turned out to the ashheaps, where small gray clouds took on fantastic shapes and scurried here and there in the faint dawn wind.
> "I spoke to her," he muttered after a long silence. "I told her she might fool me but she couldn't fool God. I took her to the window"—with an effort he got up and walked to the rear window and leaned with his face pressed against it—"and I said 'God knows what you've been doing, everything you've been doing. You may fool me, but you can't fool God!'"
> Standing behind him, Michaelis saw with a shock that he was looking at the eyes of Doctor T. J. Eckleburg, which has just emerged, pale and enormous, from the dissolving night.
> "God sees everything," repeated Wilson.
> "That's an advertisement," Michaelis assured him.

Eckleburg has symbolic reflections elsewhere in the novel; one of Gatsby's party guests reminds us of the optometrist's advertisement "A stout, middle-aged man, with enormous owl-eyed spectacles. . . ." When we meet this character, who is later referred to as "Owl-Eyes," he is seated in the library musing over Gatsby's books. The amazing thing, Owl-Eyes tells some of the other guests, is that the books are real—"they have pages and everything." Considering the context of Gatsby's world and his papier-mâché palace with its tinsel trappings, Owl-Eyes' surprised discovery is not without relevance. Fitzgerald has extended the implication of Eckleburg's divinity and applied it to Owl-Eyes, one of the few characters in the novel who can distinguish between the apparent and the real.

It should be noted, not incidentally, that Owl-Eyes is the only attendant, aside from Gatsby's father and Nick Carraway, at Gatsby's funeral. And it is he who utters a Jazz Age benediction of sympathy over Gatsby's grave:

He took off his glasses and wiped them again, outside and in.

"The poor son-of-a-bitch," he said.

The image of T.J. Eckleburg—as well as his counterpart, Owl-Eyes—has an important function in the overall rationale of Fitzgerald's novel, and is properly seen as one of its central symbols. The optometrist's advertisement suggests the degenerate state of religious belief in the modern society Fitzgerald is depicting. The image—"God is a billboard"—is appropriate to the morality of self-interest that animates most of the major characters in the novel. Eckleburg broods, not only over the valley of ashes with its quasi-human figures and fantastic shapes, but also over the actions of Tom and Daisy Buchanan, Jordan Baker, and George and Myrtle Wilson—each of whom, in his own way, demonstrates an indifference to ethical standards of conduct. In these respects, Eckleburg is pervasive, integral and significant—an organic part of the intricate metaphorical texture of *The Great Gatsby*.

But the eyes of Doctor Eckleburg constitute more than an effective poetic image; they are also a strikingly accurate distillation of history. In the symbolic representation of God as an advertisement, Fitzgerald documented the peculiarly American, peculiarly modern association of business and religion. . . .

Fitzgerald was not the only writer of the period to comment critically on the business-of-religion phenomenon; Chapter XVII of Sinclair Lewis's *Babbitt* describes George Babbitt's campaign to "revitalize" the Sunday school of his parish church—according to the best sales methods and modern public-relations procedure. The same theme is touched upon earlier in the novel by the appearance of Mike Munday, the Prophet with a Punch, "the world's greatest salesman of salvation." In a later novel, *Elmer Gantry*, Lewis has the Reverend Gantry cultivate the good will of Zenith newspapermen, who later provide free advertising for his program of salvation. Walter Lippmann, in *A Preface to Morals*, observed sadly that "the modern emancipated man" no longer believes the words of the Gospel: instead, he "believes the best advertised notion." In illustration, Lippmann cited the case of a New York church that sold investment bonds with an interest rate of five percent; this was to be "an investment in your fellow-man's Salvation," and the church proclaimed itself a combination of "Religion and Revenue."

The business-of-religion was paralleled by the development of the religion of business, which became a powerful factor in everyday commercial transactions during Coolidge's administration. "The man who builds a factory," Coolidge himself contended, "builds a temple. . . . The man who works there worships there." . . .

All these comments have some relationship to Fitzgerald's rendering of the religion-business theme in the Eckleburg symbol of *The Great Gatsby*. But there is a more specific connection between that image and the essay on advertising by J. Thorne Smith in *Civilization in the United States*. Smith protested against the pervasiveness of this new national industry and the "false and unhealthy" appeal it was exercising on the American public. "Do I understand you to say," asked Smith, "that you do not believe in advertising? Indeed! Soon you will be telling me that you do not believe in God!" To many observers of the mores of the Harding-Coolidge era, this was no irrelevant or merely playful association of ideas. Smith's question, rather, suggested the larger religious and economic patterns of the period. The informed reader will recognize in Fitzgerald's synecdoche a compelling poetic reference to those patterns and their relevance to our behavior.

The American Dream: All Gush and Twinkle

Louis Auchincloss

In creating a hero out of a monster, Fitzgerald creates an illusion of an illusion, writes author and lawyer Louis Auchincloss. Daisy—"dreadful Daisy"— who is both Gatsby's dream and the American dream, is able to transform Gatsby into a romantic hero through the spell of her superficial charm. By investing a shallow, dull, drab world with a romantic glow, Fitzgerald catches the folly as well as the magic of the dream, and illuminates the lonely business of living.

I have classified Nathaniel Hawthorne's *The Scarlet Letter*, Emily Brontë's *Wuthering Heights*, and F. Scott Fitzgerald's *The Great Gatsby* as "perfect" for a special reason. In each case the author has created something totally unreal, yet at the same time totally satisfying, a dazzling artifact, compact, cohesive, a fine hard jewel that can be turned round and round, and admired from every angle. In each case the author has stripped himself, or herself, of the aids on which a reader normally relies to relate the page before him to some familiar aspect of his own environment. The author has deliberately chosen to be exotic. We see the conjurer, the magician at work.

A woman punished for life for a single fault, a monster of inhumanity on the Yorkshire moors, a bootlegger who lives in a fantasy world—the creators of such protagonists cannot rely on their readers' recognition or identification. They are dealing almost with myths.

Now just what do I mean by that? I mean that they are dealing with human stories which, with the use of a little imagination, can be made to relate to any time or condition of man. We can be thrilled by these stories without ever

Reprinted with the permission of Scribner, a division of Simon & Schuster, from *The Style's the Man: Reflections on Proust, Fitzgerald, Wharton, Vidal, and Others* by Louis Auchincloss. Copyright © 1994 by Louis Auchincloss.

wholly understanding them. Are myths ever meant to be wholly understood? Like Delphic oracles, they invite each man's interpretation. They have something to say to everybody. . . .

THE GREAT GATSBY

In *The Great Gatsby* Scott Fitzgerald makes a hero out of a kind of monster. Jay Gatsby, born James Gatz, acquires a fortune, or at least what appears to be one, by the age of thirty, by means that are far from clear but that are certainly dishonest. He starts with bootlegging, but in the end he seems to be engaged in the theft or embezzlement of securities. As Henry James leaves to our imagination how his heroes made their money (because he did not really know), so Fitzgerald allows us to make up our own crimes for Gatsby. But there is no doubt that he is a crook and a tough one, too. He has no friends, only hangers-on, no intellectual interests, no real concern for people. His entire heart and imagination are utterly consumed with his romantic image of Daisy Buchanan, a selfish, silly, giddy creature, who turns in the end into a remorseless hit-and-run driver. What seems to attract him to Daisy is the sense of financial security that she emanates: she has always been, and somehow always will be, abundantly, aboundingly rich. She is the tinselly department store window at Christmastime to the urchin in the street. Her very voice, as Gatsby puts it, "is full of money."

Fitzgerald is a courageous author. For what is Daisy, dreadful Daisy, but his dream and the American dream at that? He seems to make no bones about it. Vapid, vain, heartless, self-absorbed, she is still able to dispel a charm the effect of which on Gatsby is simply to transform him into a romantic hero. The American dream, then, is an illusion? Certainly. It is all gush and twinkle. But nonetheless its effect on a sentient observer is about all life has to offer.

Is Fitzgerald then seriously telling us that to fall in love with a beautiful heiress with a monied laugh, even if she's superficial, selfish, and gutless, is a fitting goal for a man's life, and one to justify years of criminal activity? Perhaps not quite. What he may be telling us is that he, the author, by creating the illusion of that illusion, may be doing the only thing worth doing in this vale of constant disillusionment.

To create his illusion of illusion Fitzgerald must set down

the dismal atmosphere of Gatsby's life: the senseless, drunken parties, the dull, hard people, the inane conversations, the curious juxtaposition of the luxury of West Egg with the huge garbage dumps of Flushing—and yet make the whole gleam with a hard brittle beauty. It is difficult to see just how he does it, but he does. It is a book of beautiful sentences. Consider this passage in the epilogue:

> Most of the big shore places were closed now and there were hardly any lights except the shadowy, moving glow of a ferryboat across the Sound. And as the moon rose higher the inessential houses began to melt away until gradually I became aware of the old island here that flowered once for Dutch sailors' eyes—a fresh, green breast of the new world. Its vanished trees, the trees that had made way for Gatsby's house, had once pandered in whispers to the last and greatest of all human dreams; for a transitory enchanted moment man must have held his breath in the presence of this continent, compelled into an aesthetic contemplation he neither understood nor desired, face to face for the last time in history with something commensurate to his capacity for wonder.

THE BURDEN OF THE NOVEL

Because of the skillful construction of *The Great Gatsby* the eloquence and invention with which Fitzgerald gradually reveals [Gatsby's] heroism are given a concentration and therefore a power he was never able to achieve again. The art of the book is nearly perfect.

Its limitation is the limitation of Fitzgerald's own nearly complete commitment to Gatsby's romantic attitude. "That's the whole burden of this novel," he wrote to a friend, "—the loss of those illusions that give such color to the world so that you don't care whether things are true or false as long as they partake of the magical glory."

Arthur Mizener, *The Far Side of Paradise*, 1965.

To me there is much in common between Fitzgerald's prose and the paintings of Edward Hopper. Hopper selects dull houses, drab streets, plain people, and invests them with a glow that is actually romantic. No matter what we think of Jay Gatsby and the triviality of his dream, it is impossible not to see what he sees and even feel a bit what he feels. I find myself almost embarrassed, in the end of the book, at regretting his sorry death. As one character says,

"He had it coming to him." He certainly did. But Fitzgerald has caught the magic as well as the folly of Gatsby's dream.

A LONELY EXPERIENCE WITH LONELY CHARACTERS

There is a peculiar power in these three novels that may stem from the isolation of their protagonists. [*The Scarlet Letter*'s] Hester lives in a world that is consistently cruel to her. Even those who care about her treat her harshly: her husband tortures her; her lover allows her to be punished alone. [In *Wuthering Heights*,] Heathcliff lives in a world that hates him and that he despises. Gatsby lives in a world where nobody understands him, except, in the very end, the narrator. Yet Nick Carraway's ultimate understanding of his friend costs him his own romance with Jordan Baker. He perceives at last that with *her* he does not even have the short-lived hope that Gatsby had of sharing with Daisy a perfect life.

The reader's experience with these three lonely characters is itself a lonely one. It is difficult to say just why one's reaction is so intense. Sometimes I think it is only self-pity. One likes to identify with a person as unjustly treated as Hester; it makes one feel the single sensitive soul in a world of horrid gaolers, and hence something finer than the world. One likes to identify with a dreamer like Gatsby whose dreams are better than anyone else's. Or even with Heathcliff, who revenges himself on a world that has mistreated him and then throws that world away. But the term "self-pity" may be simply denigrating. The business of living is a lonely one for all of us, and these novels repeat, embellish, and illuminate our own inner feelings.

Delusions of American Idealism

Joyce A. Rowe

In *The Great Gatsby*, Fitzgerald illustrates the tension between idealism and reality in American history: the heroic spiritual quest to create oneself anew, as urged by Ralph Waldo Emerson, has been replaced by a materialistic quest for the grail of wealth and power. So says Joyce A. Rowe, author of *Equivocal Endings in Classic American Novels*, who finds that many critics have overlooked Gatsby's delusion in thinking of himself as heroic. Rowe argues that Gatsby's self-delusion matches that of America, which similarly refuses to own up to its exploitive nature and, she asserts, maintains a "historical innocence about the sources of its own wealth."

Fitzgerald's novel might be conceived as a latter-day meditation on that persistent American faith in the power of the individual to transcend his history, to create himself anew, for which Ralph Waldo Emerson's early essays serve as master text. For despite standard interpretations, *The Great Gatsby* seems to me no simple dramatization of either the moral futility of the American dream of success, nor the destruction of innocent aspiration in a fallen world; but, in fact, . . . [a] historically self-conscious consideration of the contradictory nature of American idealism and the social cost of its attempt to subdue the facts of history to the faith of myth. . . .

Jay Gatsby, born of his Platonic conception of himself but nourished on the meretricious commodities of popular fantasy, rises in his quest for a transcendent identity from one level of experience to another. From the idolization of a dime-novel cowboy hero, he progresses to the filiopietism [excessive reverence for forebears], and patronage, of a debauched pioneer—a millionaire speculator in precious metals. Initiated into the world and its betrayals through Dan Cody and his paramour Ella Kaye, Gatsby climbs higher, aspiring to the thing that lies behind or beyond earthly show. But Gatsby is no Ahab [central character in Herman Melville's *Moby-Dick*] bursting through the world's pasteboard mask in search of the moral essence of the universe. His vision represents a kind of aestheticized materialism—the pursuit of a grail which conjoins wealth and power with all the beauty, vitality, and wonder of the world, which he incarnates in the fragile loveliness of the rich, well-born American girl.

Gatsby's biography can thus be read as an ironic recapitulation of the blueprint for spiritual ascent that Emerson lays out in "Nature." And just as Emerson's assimilationist ethos works to deny problems of conflict, or dualism, by obliterating all tension between individual will and the world's resistance (the latter is termed the "NOT-ME" and includes everything but the individual soul, i.e., "nature and art, all other men and my own body"), so it does for Gatsby, the gangster-idealist, who claims for himself the power to dominate space and time, to repeat the past at will and bring the natural world (microcosmically expressed in East and West Egg) under his imaginative dominion.

It is this Emersonian myth of the individual as sovereign state, inviolable to the conditions and categories of other lives, that Fitzgerald presents as the persistent dream-wish of our national life. It is a vision of freedom that is not only cast as a backward longing but is also, paradoxically, reaffirmed precisely by that historical consciousness which must attest to its failure. . . .

THE TENSION BETWEEN MYTH AND HISTORY

Alan Trachtenberg has observed that the tension between myth and history is central to all Fitzgerald's work; that myth and history project two opposing modes of consciousness, two ways of knowing the world which provide perspectives on each other.[1] Although I do not believe Fitzgerald to have been as disinterested an observer of American life as this definition implies, it seems an especially suggestive insight for understanding how the interplay of the novel, de-

1. Alan Trachtenberg, "The Journey Back: Myth and History in *Tender Is the Night*" in *Experience in the Novel*, ed. Roy Harvey Pearce (New York, Columbia Univ. Press, 1968), pp. 134–5

spite our contrary expectations, prepares us for an ending in which history comes to validate myth, and myth to ennoble history. For though the major distinction between myth and history would seem to be dramatized in the neighborly opposition of Gatsby, the man of mythic action—whose home, with Gothic library, Norman towers, Marie Antoinette music room "is a world complete in itself"[2]—and Nick Carraway, the ironic historian of reserved judgments and limited hopes—whose utilitarian bungalow houses the secrets of Midas and Morgan in the form of brokerage reports—their characters interpenetrate one another like the cut and uncut grass of their adjacent lawns.

If Gatsby is god-like, with his sun chariot car, his pink and gold accoutrements, his Olympian feasts,[3] he is also a gilded Jimmy Gatz, self-created through getting. The corrupt materialism that dogs his aspirations creates morally antithetical meanings for all the symbols that surround him—gold, most obviously, representing both the impersonal energy and glory of the sun and a base metal dug out of the earth which has the most ancient associations with carnal power and avarice. Gatsby is, finally, . . . trapped by circumstances that mock the gorgeous possibilities of his dreams, and are themselves conceptualized by Nick, the historian, as nightmare myth—a spreading hell of dust and ashes which devours the spirit as it does the body and turns living men into impoverished specters, indistinguishable from the industrial wasteland they inhabit. Indeed, the very form that Gatsby's mythic impulse takes, his aspiration to evade the present by repeating the past, reflects the popular taste on which he has been nourished. For, as Richard Hofstadter has noted, this longing was historically conditioned, bred out of post–Civil War disillusion with the corruption of the Gilded Age and had been part of American sentimental and popular rhetoric at least since William Jennings Bryan.[4]

But what seems generally to have been overlooked among critics' observations provides, to my mind, the most significant historical perspective on Gatsby's character. This is not

2. R.W. Stallman, "Gatsby and The Hole in Time," *The Houses that James Built and Other Literary Studies* (East Lansing, Mich. State Univ. Press, 1964), p. 132 3. For two views, among many, of Gatsby mythography see Bruce Michelson, "The Myth of Gatsby," *Modern Fiction Studies*, 26 (Winter, 1980–81), pp. 563–78; and Peter L. Hays, "Gatsby, Myth, Fairy Tale, and Legend," *Southern Folklore Quarterly*, no. 40 (1977), pp. 213–33. 4. Richard Hofstadter, *The American Political Tradition* (New York, Vintage, 1974), p. xxxv

the obvious fact of his crypto-gangster dealings, but the implications to be drawn from the social form which his enterprise takes. The constant irruption of the telephone into Gatsby's public life reminds us that despite his apparent isolation, Gatsby does not act alone. The calls that link him to agents in the West hint at a labyrinth of "gonnections" which replicates in negative the interlocking corporate structures of the legitimate world in which Nick labors at his more conventional version of the bond business. It is these "gonnections" that provide the pedestal of wealth on which Gatsby seems to stand in lonely splendor. From this perspective his heroic individualism is a self-deluding sham, fittingly expressed in the meretricious guise of "castle," car, and clothing. It represents a popular dream-wish which serves as a defense against the dislocations and complexities of a changing society.

ROMANTIC DELUSION ON A MYTHIC SCALE

As the common, middle-class ideal of the self-made man rising through his own efforts to a position of social and economic power . . . was becoming an obsolete reality, so his fictional counterpart was more intensely romanticized in the image of the lone cowboy or outlaw, loyal to his own moral code and enduring a solitary existence in the wilderness. In *The Incorporation of America*, Alan Trachtenberg has shown how this popular myth persisted to deny the reality of corporate control which arrived with post–Civil War industrial expansion.[5]

Gatsby, through his two surrogate fathers, the buccaneer Dan Cody and the gangster Meyer Wolfsheim, unites the imagery of free-wheeling plunder in the Gilded Age [late nineteenth century] to that of the Jazz Age [end of World War I through the 1920s], but by traditional codes of loyalty, both these fathers ultimately betray him. Dan Cody promises him a legacy, but the debauched old frontiersman no longer has the mind or will to ensure its disposition. Wolfsheim, who

5. Alan Trachtenberg, *The Incorporation of America* (New York, Hill & Wang, 1982), p. 82. Even as English social philosopher Herbert Spencer's Social Darwinism was being used to justify business success as a law of nature, new forms of monopoly capitalism that depended upon doing away with competition were taking shape. "Increasingly, the instrument of success proved to be more effective organization, the restructuring of enterprises into corporations in which financing and sales along with production fell under control of a single entity." Though proclaimed as an age of individualism, actually there was a "decisive decline of proprietors, family businesses, simple partnerships: the familiar forms of capital."

claims to have "made" Gatsby, to look on him as a son, will not risk appearing at his funeral. Far from personifying those qualities of rugged individualism associated with the frontier myth, both Cody and Wolfsheim are victims of 'forces" and "circumstances" which they seem unwilling or unable to control. When Gatsby met Cody the latter was already a vacuous, played-out figure, captive to a scheming woman, Ella Kaye—whose name, it has often been noted, rhymes with Daisy Fay. Meyer Wolfsheim's name, like his molar cufflinks, may allude to the ferocity of the forest, but he is more akin to the ambiguous "grandma" of the "Little Red Riding Hood" fairy tale than to a feral beast. In his office, he hides from Nick behind a woman and then excuses himself from attending Gatsby's funeral with a string of sentimental platitudes worthy of Uriah Heep [fawning, hypocritical clerk in Charles Dickens's *David Copperfield*].

Ultimately, Gatsby's relation to these fathers seems more contractual than personal. Their betrayals are largely failures of obligation; on either side, there is little energy of personal feeling. As Nick learns when he confronts Wolfsheim, questions of affection and emotional concern only mask the real interest—which is business. ("I raised him up out of nothing, right out of the gutter," says Wolfsheim proudly. "I saw right away he was a fine-appearing, gentlemanly young man, and when he told me he was an Oggsford I knew I could use him good.") Gatsby's relations with these men, as with his agents, turn out to be a paradigm of the larger social order depicted in the book—a collection of isolated beings whose interconnections are coded in terms of the use each can make of the other.

Yet, if the Great Gatsby, viewed from an historical perspective, is only a self-deluded con-man, the energy of his delusion matches the mythic scale of America's own. Guilt-free but deeply secretive, guileless but amorally corrupt, Gatsby embodies the essential contradictions of our national history and our national faith. . . .

His unblinking indifference to the ugly and criminal aspects of his own nature serves as the psychic counterpart to America's historical innocence about the sources of its own wealth, its tie to the exploitative realities of a fallen world, which Daisy (the driver of the "death car") comes to embody. Like his country's, Gatsby's illusions about the self and its powers are matched by his illusions about history, by his faith that "of course you can" repeat the past. He may be better than the other characters ("worth the whole damn bunch put together"), but Nick's obsessive ambivalence toward him ("I disapproved of him from beginning to end") would seem to suggest that ultimately he is not good enough.

THE LOST PROMISE

That Gatsby is not just the mythic embodiment of an American type but personifies the outline of our national consciousness is demonstrated by his structural relation to the other characters and, in particular, to the narrator, Nick Carraway.

Despite differences of class and taste, despite their apparent mutually antagonistic purposes, all the characters in this book are defined by their nostalgia for and sense of betrayal by some lost, if only dimly apprehended, promise in their past—a sense of life's possibilities toward which only Gatsby has retained the ingenuous faith and energy of the true seeker. It is in the difference between vision and sight, between the longing for self-transcendence and the lust for immediate gain—for sexual, financial, or social domination— that Nick, his chronicler and witness, finds the moral distinction which separates Gatsby from the "foul dust" of the others who float in his wake. And this moral dichotomy runs through the structure of the entire work. For the rapacious nature of each of the others, whether crude, desperate, arrogant or false, is finally shown to be a function of their common loss of vision, their blurred or displaced sense of possibilities—punningly symbolized in the enormous empty retinas of the oculist-wag, Dr. T.J. Eckleburg. Thus Gatsby and those who eddy around him are, reciprocally, positive and negative images of one another; but whether faithless or true all are doomed by the wasteful, self-deluding nature of the longing which controls their lives and which when it fails leaves its adherents utterly naked and alone, "contiguous to nothing."

THE SIREN SONG OF THE AMERICAN CONTINENT

However, Nick's insight into the distinction between Gatsby and others does not free him from his own involvement in the world he observes. His acute awareness of his own self-division (toward Gatsby as toward all the others) turns out to be the mirror inversion of his subject's unconscious one; it accounts for the sympathetic bond between them. . . .

Moreover, it is Nick's own confused responsiveness to his cousin's sexual power and charm that allows him subsequently to understand Gatsby's equation of Daisy with all that is most desirable under the heavens—ultimately with the siren song of the America continent. Nick cannot help but be compelled by the buoyant vitality which surrounds her and the glowing sound of her "low, thrilling voice," which sings with "a promise that she had done gay, exciting things just a while since and that there were gay exciting things hovering in the next hour." But, as the shadow of his double, Nick's response to Daisy is qualified by his discomforting awareness of the illusory and deceptive in her beauty. Her smirking insincerity, her banal chatter, the alluring whiteness of her expensive clothes—most of all, the languid boredom which enfolds her life—suggest a willing captivity, a lazy self-submission to a greater power than her own magical charms: the extraordinary wealth and physical arrogance that enable Tom Buchanan to dominate her. And Nick's visceral dislike for the man Daisy has given herself to, fanned by his intellectual and moral scorn for Tom's crude attempt to master "ideas" as he does horses and women, allies him with, as it prefigures, Gatsby's bland disregard of Tom as a factor in Daisy's existence.

Nick's experience of Daisy is, in fact, commensurate with his experience of the East. For like Daisy and her husband, transplanted Westerners who have drifted to the new center of energy and power, the East turns out to be the America of the moment—America experienced as a wilderness of opportunity, with all the ambiguity this implies.

West Egg, with its raw wealth and promiscuous mix of classes and types, is a metaphoric reminder of frontier society; while East Egg has all the decorum and snobbery of those who have "arrived" at least one generation earlier. (The Buchanans live in a house built by "Demaine, the oil man.") Together, the Eggs, with their smashed bottoms, serve as a metaphor for American actuality—the social barnyard of the present in which money and power breed ever-more-corrupt versions of a once-bright historical ideal . . . But from a distance their shore lines are enticing.

Nick comes East for the same reason that his forebears went West—he is restless, seeking adventure, excitement, freedom from the monotonous regularity and control of an established pattern of life and established social expectations. In the East he feels like a path-finder. There is a sense of things growing faster, of time and motion speeded up (as in a movie), of unexpected if illusory joy. The towers of New York rise "up across the river in white heaps and sugar lumps. . . . The city seen from the Queensboro Bridge is always the city seen for the first time, in its first wild promise of all the mystery and beauty in the world." Like the aura that emanates from Daisy, it is a magical place where anything can happen. "Even Gatsby could happen." And yet the ugliness, greed, and human sterility he discovers in this raucous wilderness are far worse than anything in the grey world of worn-out traditions that he has left behind. . . .

Although some critics claim to find in Nick's return to the Midwest a saving alternative to the futility of Gatsby's example, this reading seems to me to be itself a wishful dream out of a more sober historical moment. For the Midwest of Nick's allusions is hardly the moral alternative to the East that it has often been taken to be.[6] Rather, the moral distinction at issue . . . turns out to be a choice between the world [and] one's vision of it—not between what life might offer in one or another geographical context.

THE DECLINE AND FALL OF AMERICAN HOPES

The actual West, we are told at the beginning of the book, is a place of chronic anxiety, the "ragged edge of the universe," where an evening is hurried "toward its close, in a continually disappointed anticipation or else in sheer nervous dread of the moment itself." Daisy and Jordan, with their cool, impersonal "absence of desire," buoyed by privilege and wealth, serve as the vanguard of a process symbolized in the drift from West to East that includes all characters in the book. More than malaise, it is a creeping spiritual paralysis that shows itself in chronic anxiety and dread before it

---

6. Henry Dan Piper, in *F. Scott Fitzgerald: A Critical Portrait* (New York, Holt, Rinehart & Winston, 1965), sees Nick's traditional, inherited values as saving him from "Gatsby's terrible mistake"; sending him back home to take up "his responsibilities as a member of the Carraway clan" and grow up (p. 111). Arthur Mizener, in "The Poet of Borrowed Time," *F. Scott Fitzgerald: The Man and His Work*, ed. Alfred Kazin (New York, Collier Books, 1967), pp. 23–45, sees the East as representing corruption and sophistication and culture; the West as representing the simple moral virtue of Nick and Gatsby. James Tuttleton, in *The Novel of Manners in America* (Chapel Hill, Univ. of North Carolina Press, 1972), p. 179, says: "Nick's return to the Midwest is a return to the origins of his existence, to the wisdom of his father, to the middle-class 'fundamental decencies' marked by the inner check, by the family noted through generations in the same place, by social stability." These critics apparently read the prologue without noticing the ironies and contradictions in Nick's portrait of himself. Nor do they consider it in relation to Nick's subsequent remarks about the Midwest and his assertion to Gatsby that you can't repeat the past, can't go home again.

reaches the acute stage of anomie that Nick finds at the pin-
nacle of American social power. Ironically, it is the restless
rich, with their greater freedom to experience life's possibilities, to seek fulfillment in action and experimentation, who
most clearly reveal the aridity at the heart of the American
faith that the way to wealth is the way to a new status, a new
essence, that through wealth one may rise "to a loftier place
in the mysterious hierarchy of human worth."[7] They have
moved farther and faster from the old America that Nick recognizes in the dreams of Gatsby and the still unquenched
longings of the Wilsons—the coarse vitality of Myrtle's body,
the "damp gleam of hope" in George's eyes. It is, therefore,
metaphorically fitting that it should be Daisy and Tom who
together cause the "holocaust" in which these three give up
their lives.

Nick reminds us at the end of the book that all the characters are Westerners, "that this has been a story of the West,
after all." I take this to mean a story of the decline and fall of
American hopes—the West in its largest sense standing for
the westward course of empire, for the dream of America as
mankind's last best hope for social and moral redemption.[8]

---

7. Malcolm Cowley, "F. Scott Fitzgerald: The Romance of Money," *The Western Review*
(Summer, 1953), p. 245. Cowley notes the relation between money and vitality or potency. 8. Bercovitch, *Puritan Origins*, pp. 145–6, emphasizes the distinction between the
classical theory of *translatio studii*—civilization moving in a "westward course"—
based on a cyclical view of history, and the American transmutation of it. Here, the rise
and fall of empire is recast as redemptive history, with America as mankind's "last act
in the drama of salvation." Though this initially was the work of Puritan theorists,
Bercovitch finds its effect consistent throughout nineteenth-century American
thought. Fitzgerald, who was well-read in American history, would seem to have in-
tuited the same attitude toward his country's moral promise and moral failure as he
found in those works whose conventions form the body of his own consciously allusive text.

The True Heir of the American Dream

Marius Bewley

Some critics believe Fitzgerald approved of the
American dream, writes Marius Bewley, literary
critic and author of *The Eccentric Design: Form in
the Classic American Novel.* On the contrary, he asserts, *The Great Gatsby* offers close and severe criticism of the deficiencies of American values in the
1920s. Gatsby, according to Bewley, is a mythical
incarnation of "the aspiration and the ordeal of his
race." As such, he is pitted against Tom Buchanan,
who not only virtually murders Gatsby but tries to
destroy his vision. Since, in the end, Buchanan fails,
Gatsby is an affirmation of the American spirit in a
world that denies the soul.

Critics of Scott Fitzgerald tend to agree that *The Great Gatsby*
is somehow a commentary on that elusive phrase, the American dream. The assumption seems to be that Fitzgerald approved. On the contrary, it can be shown that *The Great
Gatsby* offers some of the severest and closest criticism of the
American dream that our literature affords. Read in this
way, Fitzgerald's masterpiece ceases to be a pastoral documentary of the Jazz Age and takes its distinguished place
among those great national novels whose profound correc-
tive insights into the nature of American experience are not
separable from the artistic form of the novel itself. That is to
say, Fitzgerald—at least in this one book—is in a line with
the greatest masters of American prose. *The Great Gatsby*
embodies a criticism of American experience—not of manners, but of a basic historic attitude to life—more radical
than anything in Henry James's own assessment of the deficiencies of his country. The theme of *Gatsby* is the withering
of the American dream.

Excerpted from Marius Bewley, "Fitzgerald's Criticism of America," first published in
the *Sewanee Review*, vol. 62, no. 2, Spring 1954. Copyright 1954, 1982 by the University
of the South. Reprinted with the permission of the editor.

Essentially, this phrase represents the romantic enlarge-
ment of the possibilities of life on a level at which the material and the spiritual have become inextricably confused. As
such, it led inevitably toward the problem that has always
confronted American artists dealing with American experience—the problem of determining the hidden boundary in
the American vision of life at which the reality ends and the
illusion begins. Historically, the American dream is
anti-Calvinistic, and believes in the goodness of nature and
man. It is accordingly a product of the frontier and the West
rather than of the Puritan Tradition. The simultaneous oper-
ation of two such attitudes in American life created a tension
out of which much of our greatest art has sprung. Youth of
the spirit—perhaps of the body as well—is a requirement of
its existence; limit and deprivation are its blackest devils.
But it shows an astonishing incapacity to believe in them:

> I join you . . . in branding as cowardly the idea that the human
> mind is incapable of further advances. This is precisely the
> doctrine which the present despots of the earth are inculcat-
> ing, and their friends here re-echoing; and applying espe-
> cially to religion and politics; "that it is not probable that any-
> thing better will be discovered than what was known to our
> fathers." . . . But thank heaven the American mind is already
> too much opened to listen to these impostures, and while the
> art of printing is left to us, science can never be retrograde.
> . . . To preserve the freedom of the human mind . . . every
> spirit should be ready to devote itself to martyrdom. . . . But
> that the enthusiasm which characterizes youth should lift its
> parricide hands against freedom and science would be such
> a monstrous phenomenon as I could not place among the
> possible things in this age and country.

That is the hard kernel, the seed from which the American dream would grow into unpruned luxuriance. Thomas
Jefferson's voice is not remote from many European voices
of his time, but it stands in unique relation to the country to
whom he spoke. That attitude was bred into the bone of
America, and in various, often distorted, ways, it has lasted.
Perhaps that is where the trouble begins, for if these virtues
of the American imagination have the elements of greatness
in them, they call immediately for discriminating and prac-
tical correctives. The reality in such an attitude lies in its
faith in life; the illusion lies in the undiscriminating multi-
plication of its material possibilities.

The Great Gatsby is an exploration of the American dream
as it exists in a corrupt period, and it is an attempt to deter-

mine that concealed boundary that divides the reality from the illusions. The illusions seem more real than the reality itself. Embodied in the subordinate characters in the novel, they threaten to invade the whole of the picture. On the other hand, the reality is embodied in Gatsby; and as opposed to the hard, tangible illusions, the reality is a thing of the spirit, a promise rather than the possession of a vision, a faith in the half-glimpsed, but hardly understood, possibilities of life. . . .

Gatsby never succeeds in seeing through the sham of his world or his acquaintances very clearly. It is of the essence of his romantic American vision that it should lack the seasoned powers of discrimination. But it invests those illusions with its own faith, and thus it discovers its projected goodness in the frauds of its crippled world. *The Great Gatsby* becomes the acting out of the tragedy of the American vision. . . .

A MYTHIC CHARACTER

In an essay called "Myths for Materialists" Mr. Jacques Barzun once wrote that figures, whether of fact or fiction, insofar as they express destinies, aspirations, attitudes typical of man or particular groups, are invested with a mythical character. In this sense Gatsby is a "mythic" character, and no other word will define him. Not only is he an embodiment (as Fitzgerald makes clear at the outset) of that conflict between illusion and reality at the heart of American life; he is an heroic personification of the American romantic hero, the true heir of the American dream. . . .

Gatsby is not merely a likable, romantic hero; he is a creature of myth in whom is incarnated the aspiration and the ordeal of his race.

"Mythic" characters are impersonal. There is no distinction between their public and their private lives. Because they share their meaning with everyone, they have no secrets and no hidden corners into which they can retire for a moment, unobserved. An intimacy so universal stands revealed in a ritual pattern for the inspection and instruction of the race. The "mythic" character can never withdraw from that air which is his existence—that is to say, from that area of consciousness (and hence of publicity) which every individual shares with the members, both living and dead, of his group or race. Gatsby is a "mythic" character in this sense—he has no private life, no meaning or significance that depends on the fulfillment of his merely private destiny, his happiness as an individual in a society of individuals. In a transcendent sense he touches our imaginations, but in this smaller sense—which is the world of the realistic novel—he even fails to arouse our curiosity. At this level, his love affair with Daisy is too easily "placed," a tawdry epic "crush" of no depth or interest in itself. But Gatsby not only remains undiminished by what is essentially the meanness of the affair: his stature grows, as we watch, to the proportions of a hero. We must inquire how Fitzgerald managed this extraordinary achievement.

Daisy Buchanan exists at two well-defined levels in the novel. She is what she is—but she exists also at the level of Gatsby's vision of her. The intelligence of no other important novelist has been as consistently undervalued as Fitzgerald's, and it is hardly surprising that no critic has ever given Fitzgerald credit for his superb understanding of Daisy's vicious emptiness. Even Fitzgerald's admirers regard Daisy as rather a good, if somewhat silly, little thing; but Fitzgerald knew that at its most depraved levels the American dream merges with the American debutante's dream—a thing of deathly hollowness. . . .

Fitzgerald's illustration of the emptiness of Daisy's character—an emptiness that we see curdling into the viciousness of a monstrous moral indifference as the story unfolds—is drawn with a fineness and depth of critical understanding, and communicated with a force of imagery so rare in modern American writing, that it is almost astonishing that he is often credited with giving in to those very qualities which *The Great Gatsby* so effectively excoriates.

A VULGAR LOVE AFFAIR

But what is the basis for the mutual attraction between Daisy and Gatsby? In Daisy's case the answer is simple. We remember that Nick Carraway has described Gatsby's personality as an "unbroken series of successful gestures." Superficially, Daisy finds in Gatsby, or thinks she finds, that safety from human reality which the empty gesture implies. What she fails to realize is that Gatsby's gorgeous gesturings are the reflex of an aspiration toward the possibilities of life, and this is something entirely different from those vacant images of romance and sophistication that fade so easily into the nothingness from which they came. But in a sense, Daisy is safe enough from the reality she dreads. The true question is not what Gatsby sees in Daisy, but the direction he takes from her, what he sees *beyond* her; and that has, despite the immaturity intrinsic in Gatsby's vision, an element of grandeur in it. For Gatsby, Daisy does not exist in herself. She is the green light that signals him into the heart of his ultimate vision. *Why* she should have this evocative power over Gatsby is a question Fitzgerald faces beautifully and successfully as he re-creates that milieu of uncritical snobbishness and frustrated idealism—monstrous fusion—which is the world in which Gatsby is compelled to live.

Fitzgerald, then, has a sure control when he defines the quality of this love affair. He shows it in itself as vulgar and specious. It has no possible interest in its own right, and if it did have the pattern of the novel would be ruined. Our imaginations would be fettered in those details and interests which would detain us on the narrative level where the affair works itself out as human history, and Gatsby would lose his "mythic" quality. But the economy with which Gatsby is presented, the formal and boldly drawn structural lines of his imagination, lead us at once to a level where it is obvious that Daisy's significance in the story lies in her failure to represent the objective correlative of Gatsby's vision. And at the same time, Daisy's wonderfully representative quality as a creature of the Jazz Age relates her personal failure to the larger failure of Gatsby's society to satisfy his need. In fact, Fitzgerald never allows Daisy's failure to become a human or personal one. He maintains it with sureness on a symbolic level where it is identified with and reflects the failure of Gatsby's decadent American world. There is a famous passage in which Gatsby sees Daisy as an embodiment of the glamor of wealth. Nick Carraway is speaking first to Gatsby:

> "She's got an indiscreet voice," I remarked. "It's full of—" I hesitated.
>
> "Her voice is full of money," he said suddenly.
>
> That was it. I'd never understood before. It was full of money—that was the inexhaustible charm that rose and fell in it, the jingle of it, the cymbals' song of it. . . . High in a white palace the king's daughter, the golden girl . . .

Gatsby tries to build up the inadequacy of each value by the support of the other; but united they fall as wretchedly short of what he is seeking as each does singly. Gatsby's gold and Gatsby's girl belong to the fairy story in which the Princess spins whole rooms of money from skeins of wool. In the fairy story, the value never lies in the gold but in something beyond. And so it is in this story. For Gatsby, Daisy is only the promise of fulfillment that lies beyond the green light that burns all night on her dock. . . .

ANTAGONISTIC ASPECTS OF AMERICA

Tom Buchanan and Gatsby represent antagonistic but historically related aspects of America. They are related as the body and the soul when a mortal barrier has risen up between them.

Tom Buchanan is virtually Gatsby's murderer in the end, but the crime that he commits by proxy is only a symbol of his deeper spiritual crime against Gatsby's inner vision. Gatsby's guilt, insofar as it exists, is radical failure—a failure of the critical faculty that seems to be an inherent part of the American dream—to understand that Daisy is as fully immersed in the destructive element of the American world as Tom himself. After Daisy, while driving Gatsby's white automobile, has killed Mrs. Wilson and, implicitly at least, left Gatsby to shoulder the blame, Nick Carraway gives us a crucial insight into the spiritual affinity of the Buchanan couple, drawing together in their callous selfishness in a moment of guilt and crisis:

> Daisy and Tom were sitting opposite each other at the kitchen table, with a plate of cold fried chicken between them, and two bottles of ale. He was talking intently across the table at her, and in his earnestness his hand had fallen upon and covered her own. Once in a while she looked up at him and nodded in agreement.

> They weren't happy, and neither of them had touched the chicken or the ale—and yet they weren't unhappy either. There was an unmistakable air of natural intimacy about the picture, and anybody would have said that they were conspiring together.

They instinctively seek out each other because each recognizes the other's strength in the corrupt spiritual element they inhabit.

There is little point in tracing out in detail the implications of the action any further, although it could be done with an exactness approaching allegory. That it is not allegory is owing to the fact that the pattern emerges from the fullness of Fitzgerald's living experience of his own society and time. In the end the most that can be said is that *The Great Gatsby* is a dramatic affirmation in fictional terms of the American spirit in the midst of an American world that denies the soul. Gatsby exists in, and for, that affirmation alone.

When, at the end, not even Gatsby can hide his recognition of the speciousness of his dream any longer, the discovery is made in universalizing terms that dissolve Daisy into the larger world she has stood for in Gatsby's imagination:

> He must have looked up at an unfamiliar sky through frightening leaves and shivered as he found what a grotesque thing a rose is and how raw the sunlight was upon the scarcely created grass. A new world, material without being real, where poor ghosts, breathing dreams like air, drifted fortuitously about.

"A new world, material without being real." Paradoxically, it was Gatsby's dream that conferred reality upon the world. The reality was in his faith in the goodness of creation, and in the possibilities of life. That these possibilities were intrinsically related to such romantic components limited and distorted his dream, and finally left it helpless in the face of the Buchanans, but it did not corrupt it. When the dream melted, it knocked the prop of reality from under the universe, and face to face with the physical substance at last, Gatsby realized that the illusion was *there*—there where Tom and Daisy, and generations of small-minded, ruthless Americans had found it—in the dreamless, visionless complacency of mere matter, substance without form. After this recognition, Gatsby's death is only a symbolic formality, for the world into which his mere body had been born rejected the gift he had been created to embody—the traditional dream from which alone it could awaken into life.

As the novel closes, the experience of Gatsby and his broken dream explicitly becomes the focus of that historic dream for which he stands. Nick Carraway is speaking:

> Most of the big shore places were closed now and there were hardly any lights except the shadowy, moving glow of a ferryboat across the Sound. And as the moon rose higher the inessential houses began to melt away until gradually I became aware of the old island here that flowered once for Dutch sailors' eyes—a fresh, green breast of the new world. Its vanished trees, the trees that had once made way for Gatsby's house, had once pandered in whispers to the last and greatest of all human dreams; for a transitory enchanted moment man must have held his breath in the presence of

this continent, compelled into an aesthetic contemplation he neither understood nor desired, face to face for the last time in history with something commensurate to his capacity for wonder.

It is fitting that this, like so many of the others in *Gatsby*, should be a moonlight scene, for the history and the romance are one. Gatsby fades into the past forever to take his place with the Dutch sailors who had chosen their moment in time so much more happily than he.

INDICTMENT OF—AND TRIBUTE TO—THE AMERICAN DREAM

We recognize that the great achievement of this novel is that it manages, while poetically evoking a sense of the goodness of that early dream, to offer the most damaging criticism of it in American literature. The astonishing thing is that the criticism—if indictment wouldn't be the better word— manages to be part of the tribute. Gatsby, the "mythic" embodiment of the American dream, is shown to us in all his immature romanticism. His insecure grasp of social and human values, his lack of critical intelligence and self-knowledge, his blindness to the pitfalls that surround him in American society, his compulsive optimism, are realized in the text with rare assurance and understanding. And yet the very grounding of these deficiencies is Gatsby's goodness and faith in life, his compelling desire to realize all the possibilities of existence, his belief that we can have an Earthly Paradise populated by Buchanans. A great part of Fitzgerald's achievement is that he suggests effectively that these terrifying deficiencies are not so much the private deficiencies of Gatsby, but are deficiencies inherent in contemporary manifestations of the American vision itself—a vision no doubt admirable, but stupidly defenseless before the equally American world of Tom and Daisy. Gatsby's deficiencies of intelligence and judgment bring him to his tragic death—a death that is spiritual as well as physical. But the more important question that faces us through our sense of the immediate tragedy is where they have brought America.

The Grotesque End Product of the American Dream

Richard Lehan

Jay Gatsby marks the logical end of the Horatio Alger rags-to-riches tradition, maintains Richard Lehan, professor of English at the University of California, Los Angeles. Although the former poor farm boy has acquired considerable wealth, Gatsby's idealism crashes against the brute strength and power of Tom Buchanan and his materialistic world. Gatsby never learns that his dream is dead, but that realization is Nick's nightmare: the loss of the new green land of the past to the modern ash heaps parallels the loss of the hopes of Gatsby, the young army officer who pinned his idealistic dreams to a wealthy young woman named Daisy Fay.

The American writer, torn between mutually exclusive cultural imperatives, has long suffered from a kind of schizophrenia. Over and over, he has tried to reconcile a materialism which he could not accept with an idealism that he could not realize. Henry James is a case in point. His Christopher Newman in *The American* turns his back on a greedy America and goes to Europe in search of vague cultural ideals. What he finds in Europe is that such ideals do not exist—that if America has money without tradition, Europe has tradition without the means to finance it. Honor has become meaningless. . . .

James himself discussed America as a kind of cultural limbo in *The American Scene*, written in 1904, after his long absence from America. The horror he expressed in the face of a growing American materialism is the same kind of horror that Henry Adams voiced in *The Education of Henry Adams*, where he symbolized the new materialism in terms of the dynamo, which for Adams represented a principle of uncontained, even destructive energy, an apocalyptic threat.

While Mark Twain was perhaps more ambiguous, he treated the same duality in *A Connecticut Yankee in King Arthur's Court*, and once more showed modern man tearing down an old world of hierarchy and principle for a new world of western "know-how." An American sense of pragmatism competed once again with a world of fixed values.

F. Scott Fitzgerald was as much concerned about these cultural dualities as were James, Adams, Twain, and the host of other American writers who have treated this theme. In many ways, the problem for Fitzgerald focused upon his father, a Southerner who embodied "the old courtesies" in a new industrial world where success demanded the kind of ruthless energy that his father lacked. Fitzgerald was both embarrassed by and proud of his father's failures—embarrassed because it revealed that the times were too much for his father; proud because conversely his father was better than the times.

THREE EQUATIONS

Nick Carraway has these same ambivalent feelings about Gatsby. Gatsby is obviously not with it. He is no match for Tom Buchanan, who represents the kind of energy and force—the spirit of Adams' dynamo—which is necessary for success in a materialistic America. Gatsby, who is really a phony broker, has become a grotesque distortion of the successful man, a pathetic extension of what Tom Buchanan embodies. Yet Gatsby's fidelity to an ideal, to a dream, is an admirable, albeit a romantic quality of mind. Fitzgerald equated the dream with the spirit of the past, with the spirit of the Dutch sailors for whom America was a dream, a matter of possibility, a new world waiting to be formed. He also equated it with the spirit of Benjamin Franklin, who best embodies the kind of western pragmatism which finally won out as well as the rags-to-riches ideal which Gatsby accepted so completely. And lastly, he equated the ideal with a woman, with Daisy Fay, who had abandoned Gatsby for Tom Buchanan, the man who best embodied the final heritage of Benjamin Franklin.

These three "equations" are the source of Gatsby's dream and Nick Carraway's nightmare, for Gatsby never learns that the dream is dead, and Nick's discovery of this fact leaves him . . . hopeless . . . [and] culturally displaced. . . . Indeed, such is the fate of the new man in the land discovered by Christopher; and if we look closely at these three "equations," we can clearly see what Fitzgerald was trying to tell us about America and how, as a novelist, he was saying it.

The references to America as a new world are "laid on" the novel—that is, this idea is never systematically developed but is instead implied. Nick thinks of himself as a Westerner, and here we have the suggestion of the frontier, long since gone, of course, when Fitzgerald was writing the novel. Nick also thinks of himself as a frontiersman when he gives directions to a man lost on West Egg. And lastly, Nick wonders what the Dutch sailors thought when they first saw Manhattan. All these references link Nick and Gatsby with a world that no longer exists, a world that has been lost in the back rush of time, a world that offered more in promise than has been realized in fact. While this theme is not the key one in the novel, it is important, because it sets the context within which Gatsby's story is told; it establishes the fact that, like Gatsby, all Americans live in a world of betrayed promise, a world that could never be—and "So we beat on, boats against the current, borne back ceaselessly into the past."

Here we have the theme that links Fitzgerald so closely with writers like James, Adams, and Twain, who contrast the values of modern America with those of the past. Fitzgerald's view is really as apocalyptic as Henry Adams' because it leaves no real basis for hope. We can only look nostalgically back at what could have been; we have no way to exercise the will to realize an ideal. Nick's return to the West is . . . [a] meaningless . . . gesture. . . . It is an act in and for itself, not heroic as the critics insist, but antiheroic, a subliminal recognition of cultural defeat—of a world that offers no basis for an act beyond itself, no basis for meaningful commitment.

THE DECLINE OF THE WEST

If Adams, James, and Fitzgerald share this theme among themselves, they also share it with Oswald Spengler. In a letter to Maxwell Perkins, Fitzgerald said that he read Spengler the summer he was writing *The Great Gatsby*, "and I don't think that I ever quite recovered from him." The importance of this remark has been somewhat belied by the fact that

Spengler's *The Decline of the West* was not translated into English until after Fitzgerald's novel was published, and Fitzgerald did not read German. To believe, however, that he did not know Spengler because he had not read him directly is to be a victim of literal-mindedness—and does not take into consideration the use that Fitzgerald often made of secondary sources and of what friends told him. Spengler was in the air during the early part of the twenties; there were countless summaries of his ideas (which is probably what Fitzgerald had in mind when he spoke of reading Spengler); and Fitzgerald could not long have talked with friends like Edmund Wilson without being exposed to these ideas. Moreover, many of Spengler's ideas had been approximated by Brooks Adams (Henry's brother) in *The Law of Civilization and Decay*, published in 1896.

Spengler discussed at great length two kinds of cultural periods—the Faustian and the Apollonian. The Apollonian, or classical period, was one of order and harmony with man generally self-satisfied. The Faustian or modern period is one of flux and disruption with man generally dissatisfied and longing for the unattainable. Spengler felt that there was nowhere to go after the Faustian period (that it marked the kind of cultural limbo within which Nick Carraway . . . [finds himself]) and that after the rise of the big cities controlled by the monied thugs ("the new Caesars," he called them) the last Faustian man would be destroyed, to be replaced by the "colored" races—the Negroes and the Chinese—who would use Western man's technological know-how against him.

Whether or not Spengler directly influenced *The Great Gatsby* can perhaps be argued. What cannot be argued, however, is the remarkable similarity between Spengler's ideas and the design of the novel. Gatsby is the last of the Faustian men, the modern man living in the flux of the big city, longing for the unattainable, doomed in his combat with the Tom Buchanans, the new Caesars, in a world that contrasts remarkably with an older order, a world that has been covered by the ashes of time—just as the green breast of the new world has given way to the Valley of Ashes in the novel itself. That Tom's world will in time give way to another, more primitive, culture is suggested in a number of ways. Tom, for example, discusses with some fear the rise of the colored races, and Nick and Gatsby see a white chauffeur driving two Negroes (an inversion of their [usual] roles) across the Queensboro Bridge.

When Tom is discussing these matters, he refers to Goddard's *The Rise of the Colored Empires,* a nonexistent book. Fitzgerald was obliquely referring to Lothrop Stoddard's *The Rising Tide of Color,* published by Charles Scribner's Sons in 1920. Like Spengler, Stoddard believed that the colored races would eventually control the world. He argued that the white man controlled four-fifths of the world but lived primarily in Europe and North America, which composed only one-fifth of the land. As a result, one-fifth of the white race, around 110 million persons, were expected to preserve the status quo in the face of a disgruntled colored population eleven times that number. The night of the big party, the owl-eyed man picks Volume 1 of Stoddard's lectures from a shelf in Gatsby's library.

Because so much of what Fitzgerald was saying about America was said obliquely, through the use of descriptive detail and allusion, the import of these matters has been lost on many of the critics. Fitzgerald placed his two principal characters, Gatsby and Nick Carraway, in a cultural limbo, where the past has been corrupted and where the idealists crash upon the hard rocks of ruthless materialism; he placed them in a world of Tom Buchanans, where the Faustian man is an intruder.

EMBODIMENT OF AN INVERTED DREAM

For if Gatsby cannot seal the hole in time, cannot buy back the past, he also cannot commit himself to the future. Fitzgerald inverted the rags-to-riches story and made Gatsby the victim of his Benjamin Franklin–Dan Cody (James J. Hill) dreams. One way that Fitzgerald did this was to make Gatsby an ersatz profiteer. Like a character in an inverted Horatio Alger novel, he struggles up from his bleak beginnings to make a great deal of money and to buy a mansion overlooking Long Island Sound. Only the mansion is on West Egg, which houses the new rich, and not East Egg, which houses the established rich; and the money comes from bucket shops [overly aggressive brokerage houses that push highly speculative stocks], bootlegging, and gambling.

Gatsby in many ways marks the logical end of the Alger tradition. He is, to put this differently, the end product of the

American Dream, the grotesque embodiment of what America can offer its ambitious young. At one point in the novel, Tom Buchanan buys a dog for Myrtle Wilson from "a gray old man who bore an absurd resemblance to John D. Rockefeller." Gatsby himself also has an absurd resemblance to the robber barons. To be sure, he lacks their ultimate refinement of taste and their final established status; but he shares their motives, wants what they want, and is just as unscrupulous in the way he operates. Rockefeller's dealings with Standard Oil share a quality of mind that Gatsby brought to Meyer Wolfsheim's operations. Enough money can buy respectability in America—just as today we know that the Mafia has moved into many "legitimate" businesses—and when Daisy leaves Gatsby because he lacks the proper social credentials, she is being more faithful to the letter than the spirit of the law.

As I pointed out in my *F. Scott Fitzgerald and the Craft of Fiction*, Gatsby grotesquely resembles Tom Buchanan. Both Gatsby and Tom are brokers—only Gatsby is a phony broker; but where the legitimate ends and the phony begins is a debatable point in Fitzgerald's world, where Gatsby's motives are in many ways at one with Tom's. Only Gatsby's lack of taste marks the substantial difference, and this is also a matter of degree—Gatsby with his silver suits, golden ties, and pin-striped shirts; Gatsby in his phony feudal castle built by a wealthy brewer (be it noted) who wanted to thatch the roofs of the surrounding houses; and Gatsby in his oversized yellow car embellished with chrome. Yet the grotesque qualities of Gatsby seem, at times, to extend to America itself, or at least to New York, which Nick at one point describes as a "city rising up across the river in white heaps and sugar lumps all built with a wish."

Gatsby becomes the absurd incarnation of Benjamin Franklin and the Gilded Age tycoon. Mr. Gatz makes the connection when he shows Nick the copy of *Hopalong Cassidy* in which Gatsby set down Franklin's formula to success and when he remarks that if Gatsby had lived he would have become another James J. Hill. Gatsby did not just become another Franklin or Hill; he went beyond them and became their grotesque extension in time. He came to embody the values that Henry James turned from in terror in *The American Scene*. He came to represent the decline of cultural ideals which Henry Adams warned us about in apocalyptic terms in his autobiography. . . .

WHAT MIGHT HAVE BEEN

When the dream fails them, Fitzgerald's characters look first nostalgically to the past and see it in terms of what might have been. Soon this nostalgia turns to horror as they realize how they have betrayed the promises of youth, how they have wasted their talents. Thus we move from one circle of experience to another in *The Great Gatsby*, the personal experience duplicating and reinforcing the cultural experience, Gatsby's sense of lost promise duplicating the lost promises of America itself. In *The Great Gatsby*, we move with Nick Carraway from dream to horror—from the dream of the early explorers who first saw the green breast of the new world, to the commuters who pass daily through the Valley of Ashes, which parallels our move from a young army officer named Gatsby to his grim and pathetic funeral.

When Nick leaves Gatsby the night of Myrtle Wilson's fatal accident, he says, "So I walked away and left him standing there in the moonlight—watching over nothing." At the very end of the novel, as Nick looks out into the dark of Long Island Sound, he realizes that both Gatsby's dream and that of the republic lie behind us, and his last sentence catches the rhythm of his previous words, "So we beat on, boats against the current, borne back ceaselessly into the past." Gatsby watches over nothing, and we beat on into the past. The two ideas merge on the level of style as well as on the level of narrative theme. We move from hope to despair, from the present to the past where the promises of a young country and a young man have given way to—"nothing. "

The meaning of Gatsby's story was not unknown to Henry James, Henry Adams, and Mark Twain. Gatsby was not the first of the nowhere heroes, and he is obviously not the last; but he is perhaps the most vital, and his story reveals a quality of mind that is our legacy from the Gilded Age.

Ethics in *Gatsby:* An Examination of American Values

Tony McAdams

Since *The Great Gatsby* expresses Fitzgerald's doubts about America's moral direction, it offers an excellent ground for an examination of American ethics, proposes Tony McAdams, professor of business law at the University of Northern Iowa. McAdams suggests several subjects for study: the individual characters (liars all); Nick's moral growth; and why Gatsby—a boorish fraud who uses others—is likable. On a broader scale, McAdams notes, *Gatsby* can provoke and inform an analysis of the values of wealth, class, and the American Dream of gleaming possibilities.

For some time a small but growing number of professors have employed fiction in studying ethics. Perhaps the most prominent exponent of that approach is the child psychiatrist Robert Coles of Harvard who argues that stories engage readers and stir "the moral imagination" in a manner that cannot be matched by other materials. Coles has employed *The Great Gatsby* at Harvard to examine ethics. A letter he received from a former Harvard Business School student suggests the power of literature to capture our moral attention:

> All of my friends are talking about Ivan Boesky. They want to know what made him tick. I want to know, too. But yesterday, as we talked, I realized that I did know—as much, probably, as anyone will ever know. I'd read *The Great Gatsby*, and suddenly, as I sat there, in a Wall Street restaurant, Jay Gatsby came to my mind, and our long discussions of what Gatsby is meant to tell us about ourselves. I told my buddies: go get *The Great Gatsby*, read it, think about it, and then we can talk some more about Boesky (Coles, 1987, p. 14).

For the past two semesters I have experimented with *The Great Gatsby* in our required, upper division Legal and Social

Excerpted from Tony McAdams, "*The Great Gatsby* as a Business Ethics Inquiry," *Journal of Business Ethics*, vol. 12, pp. 653–60 (1993). Copyright © 1993 by Kluwer Academic Publishers. Reprinted with kind permission from Kluwer Academic Publishers and the author. (Numbering of notes has been changed from the original.)

Environment of Business course. The preliminary response has been encouraging, and on that basis I am detailing here an approach to *Gatsby* as, in part, an expression of Fitzgerald's doubts about America's moral direction. . . .

CHARACTERS

Our first ethics inquiry is an exploration of the book's central characters as moral commentaries. In so doing, we introduce the key figures while beginning to treat *Gatsby* as an examination of American values. . . .

1. *Liars.* We simply proceed through the principal characters and examine their moral "images." For example, I argue that each character is a "liar" in some fundamental sense. We then talk about Tom Buchanan and his mistress, Daisy's failure to reveal her role in Myrtle Wilson's death, Gatsby's life as a lie and an illusion, and so on. Broadly, we note the characters' cavalier attitudes toward the truth. Nick sets that tone early in the book in commenting on Jordan's dishonesty:

> It made no difference to me. Dishonesty in a woman is a thing you never blame deeply—I was casually sorry, and then I forgot.

At that point, I acquaint the students with some studies attempting to measure the current incidence of lying in America including one poll reporting the remarkable finding that 91 percent of those surveyed admit to "lying regularly" although only 36 percent admit to telling "serious lies" (Patterson, 1991).

2. *Nick's moral growth.* Professor David Parker, in commenting on *The Great Gatsby*, raises the issue of Nick's moral growth from an inexperienced, complacent midwesterner to a much wiser, more mature man who, after his time in the East, had acquired an understanding of the complexity of humanity (1986, pp. 35–39).

Early on, we learn of Nick's traditional prescriptions for life. He recalls his father's advice chat "a sense of the fundamental decencies is parcelled out unequally at birth." Even after returning home from the East, Nick admits to wanting the world "at a sort of moral attention forever." During his first visit to Tom and Daisy Buchanan, his priggish, rule-bound view of life comes to the fore when he learns that Tom is taking a call from his mistress:

> To a certain temperament the situation might have seemed intriguing—my own instinct was to telephone immediately for the police.

Later, Nick admits to being "slow-thinking and full of interior rules." As we proceed through the story, however, Nick begins to sense the complexity in others and in life generally. He comes to admire a man, Gatsby, who breaks all of the rules. He comes to look at life from a variety of viewpoints in keeping with the remarkable array of personalities he had encountered on his sojourn East. Toward the end of the story, as he leaves Jordan behind, Nick acknowledges a new sense of perspective in his moral life.

Jordan: I thought you were rather an honest, straightforward person. I thought it was your secret pride.

Nick: I'm thirty, I said. I'm five years too old to lie to myself and call it honor.

Clearly, Nick is confused after his Gatsby experience. He wants to cling to the rules of his midwestern youth, but he senses that life provides more complexity than his rules suggested.[1] Nick's moral floundering thus provides an apt point of entry for examining contemporary theories of moral development. I rely on the work of noted developmental psychologist Lawrence Kohlberg (1981) as well as his critics and admirers, but others could be used. Kohlberg built an empirically based theory in which he identified six universal and progressively higher stages of moral development that depended in good part on age (at least up to the early twenties) and education:

Stage 1:   Obey rules to avoid punishment. Accept the dictates of those in authority.

Stage 2:   Follow rules only if doing so is in one's self-interest. Cooperate with others in order to secure rewards for oneself.

Stage 3:   Peer pressure. Conform to the expectations of others.

Stage 4:   Rule orientation. Obey the law. Uphold the social order.

Stage 5:   Social contract. Laws and duty are obeyed on the grounds of rational calculations to serve the greatest number.

Stage 6:   Moral autonomy. Follow self-chosen universal principles. In the event of conflict, principles override rules and laws.

---

1. At least one scholar argues that Nick's behavior over the course of the story suggests not moral growth but a retreat from his firm moral code. See Susan Resneck Parr (1982).

Nick's unambiguous rule orientation as he heads East stands in clear contrast with the confusion he feels as he prepares his return to the Midwest. Nick seems to be virtually the embodiment of Kohlberg's conception of moral growth as he gains increased moral maturity via the intellectual dissonance that leads to moral adjustments. . . .

3. *Gatsby and a life of illusion.* Jay Gatsby is a boorish fraud. He is adolescent in love. He makes use of others for his selfish purposes. His entire adult life is a lie. Nonetheless, we like and even admire Gatsby. As Nick says to Gatsby, "They're a rotten crowd. . . . You're worth the whole damn bunch put together." Still Nick goes on to note his disapproval of Gatsby "from beginning to end." Why . . . do we admire Gatsby? Of course, Gatsby exhibits great charm. In an important sense, he is the embodiment of the American Dream. He has faith in life. However, the theme that we dwell upon is Gatsby's zealous commitment to his cause: Daisy. However foolish that choice of causes may be, we admire Gatsby. That is so, I believe, because Gatsby has been true to himself or at least to his invented self. We admire him for taking a path that, in his case, seems to rise to the level of a moral conviction; that is, an absolute commitment to his personally conceived vision of life.

To illustrate that theme, I remind students of the famous passage in *Hamlet* (Act I, Scene 3) where Polonius advises his departing son, Laertes:

Be thou familiar, but by no means vulgar.
. — . — .
Give every man thy ear, but few thy voice;
Take each man's censure, but reserve thy judgment.
. — . — .
Neither a borrower nor a lender be;
. — . — .
This above all: to thine own self be true. (emphasis added)

We then spend some time talking about the utility and limitations of that single line, "To thine own self be true," as an ethical standard by which to guide one's professional and personal lives.

4. *Tom and Daisy.* We do not dwell upon these two rather transparent figures. We note that they are careless, shallow people living in eternal moral adolescence. Tom and Daisy serve as personifications of the doubts that Fitzgerald seemed to be feeling about the wealthy world that he yearned for and yet criticized.

Of course, Daisy does display some redeeming features. She is intelligent and charming. She shares Gatsby's romantic sensibilities. And at times, she seems to be aware of the shallow quality of her own life. Consider her account to Nick of her daughter's birth:

> Well, she was less than an hour old and Tom was God knows where. I woke up out of the ether with an utterly abandoned feeling, and asked the nurse right away if it was a boy or a girl. She told me it was a girl, and so I turned my head away and wept. "All right," I said, "I'm glad it's a girl. And I hope she'll be a fool—that is the best thing a girl can be in this world, a beautiful little fool."

Scholar Mary McCay argues that Daisy represents something of the emptiness of life for the many women of that era who really had no role of their own (1983, p. 311). Indeed, Fitzgerald regularly rebuked Zelda for what he took to be her empty values and underachievement.[2]

AMERICAN VALUES

1. *Wealth and class.* Clearly, in considerable part, *The Great Gatsby* is a commentary on the themes of wealth and class in America of the Roaring '20s. For example, Gatsby thinks of Daisy as a sort of icon of wealth:

> Gatsby was overwhelmingly aware of the youth and mystery that wealth imprisons and preserves, of the freshness of many clothes, and of Daisy, gleaming like silver, safe and proud above the hot struggles of the poor.

In one of the more famous and clever lines in American literature, Gatsby says of Daisy, "Her voice is full of money." And as Professor Milton Stern reminds us, Daisy "belongs to the highest bidder" (1970, p. 165).

Fitzgerald himself, while drawn to the pleasures of high society, apparently was troubled by what he took to be the unfairness of a culture marked by great divisions of wealth. Like Gatsby, Fitzgerald had sought a "golden girl," a young Chicago socialite named Ginevra King. King, however,

---

2. Some scholars, perhaps most notably Judith Fetterley (1978), see *The Great Gatsby* as, in part, a story of the willful oppression of women. Fetterley sees *Gatsby* as "another American 'love' story centered in hostility to women . . . " (p. 72). Clearly, Fitzgerald was often critical of his female characters and often depicted them in a peripheral and subordinate manner. Whether that treatment can persuasively be read to reflect a double standard, based in gender, and inherently hostile to women seems doubtful (Aldrich, 1989, p. 131).

Perhaps Daisy and Fitzgerald's other female characters should be seen, not as the products of gender-based animus, but as reflections of Fitzgerald's evolving views in a time of great societal confusion over expectations for women (Fryer, 1988). After all, women had only recently earned the right to vote, and they were manifesting an increased sexual/social liberation. At the same time, they remained economically dependent upon men.

married a wealthy suitor. Fitzgerald later sought to marry Zelda, but she put him off on the grounds that his prospects were uncertain. Fitzgerald then published his first novel, *This Side of Paradise*, Fitzgerald and Zelda married, and eventually Ginevra and Zelda served as "models" for Daisy. Class divisions in America became a central theme in Fitzgerald's thinking and writing:

> "That was always my experience," he wrote near the end of his life, "a poor boy in a rich town; a poor boy in a rich boy's school; a poor boy in a rich man's club at Princeton. . . . I have never been able to forgive the rich for being rich, and it has colored my entire life and works." He told a friend that "the whole idea of Gatsby is the unfairness of a poor young man not being able to marry a girl with money. This theme comes up again and again because I lived it" (Stern, 1970, p. 164).

We then look briefly at the United States of the 1920s, the Jazz Age, and the conspicuous affluence of the upper class of the time. In that context, we investigate the issue of wealth in contemporary America. . . . Thus *Gatsby* becomes a helpful vehicle for examining whether dramatic inequalities in wealth constitute a moral issue.

2. *The American Dream.* The gleaming *possibilities*, both spiritual and material, in a youthful, potent, exuberant America are central to *Gatsby*. However, as scholar Marius Bewley (1954) argues, *Gatsby* is also the story of the withering of that American Dream in a dissolute era.

The roots of the American Dream seem particularly to lie in the movement westward with its accompanying optimism and faith in humanity's inherent goodness. At the same time, the American Dream is also a product of our historical pursuit of spiritual progress and liberty. The Dream has taken on new dimensions for changing times, but its core, as we passed through the remarkable entrepreneurial/industrial successes of the nineteenth century, resided increasingly in material abundance. Professor Charles Sanford argues that doubts about the emergent materialist Dream have become a staple of American letters:

> The main theme in American literature during the twentieth century has been . . . America's abandonment of the security and innocence of an earlier day through some essentially sinful act, an act most frequently associated with industrialism and the commercial ethic (1961, p. 255).

What is Gatsby's dream? We remember that Gatsby "invented" himself. Hence, he and his vision are the expression of his dream. We catch glimpses of that dream via his heroic, ultimately foolish, quest for Daisy, and we find it embellished in Fitzgerald's picture of Gatsby: his youth, his beauty, his faith in life, his capacity for wonder, his romantic commitment, his idealism; indeed, his very capacity to dream. Fitzgerald seems to be suggesting that the American Dream lies in the limitless possibilities in being human while warning of the risks in losing sight of those possibilities in the glare of wealth and its accoutrements.

THE ETHICS OF EDITING

Fitzgerald's reputation for ignorance or carelessness has resulted in at least two pernicious editorial-critical positions. The first—which has lost most of its adherents—is that since he was incapable of correctness, the correctness of his texts does not matter. The second position—which compounds error—is that editors have the freedom to emend anything in Fitzgerald that is problematical. Thus when [Edmund] Wilson edited *The Great Gatsby* in 1941 he emended the celebrated line "Gatsby believed in the green light, the orgastic future, that year by year recedes before us." On 26 February 1965 Wilson wrote George M. Schieffelin of Scribners:

> I ought to report to you an error I made in editing *The Great Gatsby* for the volume that contained *The Last Tycoon*. The word *orgastic* on the last page I took to be Scott's mistake for *orgiastic*—he was very unreliable about words. But it appears from a letter to Max Perkins that he actually meant *orgastic.* Max has evidently remonstrated with him. I find that my false correction has been carried through all the reprints I have seen as well as my well-advised one of changing *Wolfshiem* (I think that's the name) to *Wolfsheim.*

Fitzgerald's intention is certain; when Perkins queried *orgastic* in the proofs, Fitzgerald replied on 24 January 1925 that "it expresses exactly the intended ecstasy."

Matthew J. Bruccoli, Introduction to the Cambridge Edition of *The Great Gatsby,* 1991.

Hence, *The Great Gatsby* simultaneously depicts both the allure of wealth and moral disapproval of the sometimes empty, corrupt, unsatisfying lives of those who achieve wealth (Hearn, 1977). Fitzgerald evidences this tension in his characterizations of Tom and Daisy, on the one hand, and Gatsby on the other. The Buchanans' materialist American Dream is at least as authentic as Gatsby's romantic version, but Tom and Daisy's spiritual corruption denies the American soul, while Gatsby's idealism affirms it (Bewley, pp. 243–6).

Gatsby should not be read as a yearning for some imagined, Edenic, pre-commercial past that needs only to be recaptured. Rather Fitzgerald mourns the loss of possibilities. Bewley explains:

> *The Great Gatsby* is an exploration of the American Dream as it exists in a corrupt period, and it is an attempt to determine that concealed boundary that divides the reality from the illusions. The illusions seem more real than the reality itself. Embodied in the subordinate characters in the novel, they threaten to invade the whole of the picture. On the other hand, the reality is embodied in Gatsby, and as opposed to the hard, tangible illusions, the reality is a thing of the spirit, a promise rather than the possession of a vision, a faith in the half-glimpsed, but hardly understood, possibilities of life (pp. 224–5).

Scholar Letha Audhuy (1980) provides further support for this "Dream corrupted by materialism" analysis. She points to the picture of emptiness and sterility in life that was the theme of T.S. Eliot's great work "The Waste Land" (a poem Fitzgerald very much admired). . . .

A TRIO OF RESERVATIONS

In closing I am obliged to note a trio of important reservations regarding the narrative approach to moral education. First, this suggested use of stories risks a charge of indoctrination in that one is necessarily teaching a particular content and probably a particular point of view thus violating the neutrality that we normally seek in moral education. Presumably, some element of indoctrination is virtually unavoidable. My inclination has been to willfully and openly take a pointed position and endeavor to counterbalance it with an equally pointed rebuttal. Specifically, our discussion of *Gatsby* and Fitzgerald's questions about America's direction follow an aggressive defense of the free market vision of Milton Friedman, Ronald Reagan, *et al.*

Secondly, we must simply remind ourselves that we are dealing with fiction. The characters and themes are constructs reflecting the author's world view, the nature of the times, the state of knowledge in that era, and so on. In this case, Fitzgerald drew, as noted, upon his own experiences and acquaintances in building his story. His values, his sense of the direction of America, his interpretation of the economic climate of the Jazz Age—these forces and many more are at work in this book. Obviously, *The Great Gatsby* cannot be understood to be an effort at an objective depiction of the reality of America in the Twenties. *Gatsby* can, however, be understood to be a provocative instrument for raising a variety of enduring ethics/values themes so long as we recognize that we are doing so via the mediating influence of a particular author in a particular time and place.

Finally, while stories have always been a staple of moral development efforts we have never been sure that they really do much good. We still do not have definitive evidence although recent scholarly developments provide encouragement.[3] As noted, my students have responded quite affirmatively to *Gatsby* as a moral lesson, but whether that satisfaction translates to improved moral insight or moral decision making is simply unknown.

References

Aldrich, E.K.: 1989, '"The Most Poetical Topic in the World": Women in the Novels of F. Scott Fitzgerald', in Lee, A.R. (ed.), *Scott Fitzgerald: The Promises of Life* (Vision Press, London), pp. 131, 153.

Audhuy, L.: 1980, 'The Waste Land Myth and Symbols in *The Great Gatsby*,' in Bloom, H. (ed.), *F. Scott Fitzgerald's The Great Gatsby* (Chelsea House Publishers, New York, 1986), p. 109.

Bewley, M.: 1954, 'Scott Fitzgerald's Criticism of America', *The Sewanee Review* 62(2) (Spring), 223.

Coles, R.: 1987, 'Storytellers' Ethics', *Harvard Business Review* 65 (2) (March–April), 8.

Coles, R.: 1989, *The Call of Stories* (Houghton Mifflin Company, Boston), p. 159.

Fetterley, J.: 1978, *The Resisting Reader* (Indiana University Press, Bloomington).

Fryer, S.B.: 1988, *Fitzgerald's New Women* (UMI Research Press, Ann Arbor, MI), pp. 1–17.

Hearn, C.: 1977, *The American Dream in the Great Depression* (Greenwood Press, Westport, CT).

3. See, e.g., Paul Vitz (1990).

Kohlberg, L.: 1981, *The Philosophy of Moral Development: Moral Stages and the Idea of Justice* (Harper and Row, San Francisco).

McKay, M.A.: 1983, 'Fitzgerald's Women: Beyond Winter Dreams', in Fleischman, F. (ed.), *American Novelists Revisited: Essays in Feminist Criticism* (G.K. Hall & Co., Boston).

Parker, D.: 1986, 'Two Versions of the Hero', in Bloom, H. (ed.), *F. Scott Fitzgerald's The Great Gatsby* (Chelsea House Publishers, New York).

Parr, S.R.: 1981, 'Individual Responsibility in *The Great Gatsby*,' *The Virginia Quarterly Review* 57(4) (Autumn), 662.

Parr, S.R.: 1982, *The Moral of the Story* (Teachers College Press, New York), p. 117.

Patterson, J.: 1991, *The Day America Told the Truth* (Prentice Hall, New York), pp. 45–6.

Sanford, C.: 1961, *The Quest for Paradise* (University of Illinois Press, Urbana).

Stern, M.: 1970, *The Golden Moment—The Novels of F. Scott Fitzgerald* (University of Illinois Press, Urbana).

Vitz, P.: 1990, 'The Use of Stories in Moral Development', *American Psychologist* 45(6) (June), 709.

Corruption and Anti-Immigrant Sentiments Skew a Traditional American Tale

Jeffrey Louis Decker

The Great Gatsby mirrors American uneasiness about the loss of white supremacy in the United States, declares Jeffrey Louis Decker, who teaches American literature at the University of California, Los Angeles. Fitzgerald took a traditional self-made-man tale as told by Horatio Alger and guided by Ben Franklin's precepts, but distorted the standard elements to reflect the fears, negative perceptions, and loss of faith of the early 1920s. Although the resulting story has been called "*the* novel of the American dream," Decker points out that the term "American dream" was created in the 1930s to offer a way to deal with the problems of the Great Depression; it is inappropriately used, he says, when applied to *The Great Gatsby*.

The Great Gatsby (1925) represents the diminishing moral authority of uplift stories in an age of declining faith in the nation's ability to assimilate new immigrants. Through the eyes of Fitzgerald's narrator, Nick Carraway, Gatsby appears in the guise of the archetypal, if somewhat misguided, self-made man in America. Gatsby's upward struggle is inspired by traditional purveyors of middle-class success, such as Ben Franklin and Horatio Alger Jr. However, another less virtuous narrative of Gatsby's self-making unfolds, which connects our hero's business schemes to the tainted hand of immigrant gangsters. A story of entrepreneurial corruption, accented by the language of nativism, competes with and ultimately foils the traditional narrative

Excerpted from Jeffrey Louis Decker, "Gatsby's Pristine Dream: The Diminishment of the Self-Made Man in the Tribal Twenties," *Novel: A Forum on Fiction*, vol. 28, no. 1, Fall 1994. Copyright © Novel Corp. 1994. Reprinted with permission. (Numbering of notes has been changed from the original.)

of virtuous American uplift. In this way, *Gatsby* stages a national anxiety about the loss of white Anglo-Saxon supremacy in the Twenties. . . .

RACIALIST AND NATIVIST DOCTRINE

Fitzgerald's familiarity with the grammar of nativism was likely informed by his professional affiliation with *The Saturday Evening Post* in the Twenties. During this period Fitzgerald placed many of his short stories with the *Post* and, as such, it became his most lucrative source of income while composing *Gatsby.* As the nation's most popular magazine, the *Post* began publishing nativist opinions in its pages as early as the spring of 1920. At this time *Post* editorials advocated the racialist doctrines of Madison Grant. During the same year the *Post*'s editor, George Horace Lorimer, sent Kenneth Roberts abroad to report on European immigration to the United States. According to historian John Higham, Roberts's articles, which appeared in the *Post* and which were published in a 1922 collection under the title *Why Europe Leaves Home,* became the most widely read effusions on Nordic theory of its day (265, 273). Roberts began from the twin premises of Nordicism: "The American nation was founded and developed by the Nordic race" and "Races can not be cross-bred without mongrelization." Writing overseas, Roberts speculated that "if a few more million members of the Alpine, Mediterranean and Semitic races are poured among us, the result must inevitably be a hybrid race of people as worthless and futile as the good-for-nothing mongrels of Central America and Southeastern Europe" (22).

Nordicism, a form of racial nativism that became popular in America following World War I, provides a context for understanding the production of classic American literature at mid-decade. For example, William Carlos Williams's relocation of the discovery of America in the voyages of "Red Eric" (father of Leif Ericson) in the opening page of *In the American Grain* (1925) might signal something more than the anti-Puritan impulse also common to writers of this era. Fitzgerald's Dutchmen [on the final page of *Gatsby*], like Williams's Norsemen, bear the inadvertent mark of nativism specific to the Twenties. Nick's invocation of the Dutch sailors' vision of the New World adheres to the nativist logic of President Coolidge's April 1924 Message to Congress on the passage of the Immigration Bill: "America must be kept American" (quoted in Grant 347). . . .

THE LIMITS OF AMERICAN DREAM SCHOLARSHIP

Lionel Trilling's statement that Gatsby "comes inevitably to stand for America itself" (251) best exemplifies the consensus among Fitzgerald critics who have turned *The Great Gatsby* into *the* novel of the American dream.[1] This sentiment, I believe, carries with it residual traces of 1920s nativism that are embedded in the book's ending. One of the earliest critics to identify the theme of the American dream in *The Great Gatsby* was Edwin Fussell. In "Fitzgerald's Brave New World" (1952), he suggests that Gatsby is corrupted "by values and attitudes that he holds in common with the society that destroys him." Within a "mechanized" world, Fussell points out, "a dream like Gatsby's cannot remain pristine, given the materials upon which the original impulse toward wonder must expend itself" (295).[2]

Nevertheless, we are left with the persistent question. Despite mounting evidence supporting Tom's accusations regarding his rival's entrepreneurial corruption through shady associations with immigrant gangsters, how does Gatsby maintain "his incorruptible dream" in the eyes of the narrator and readers alike? The standard procedure among critics is to interpret Gatsby's dream according to Nick's narrative demands: like Nick, critics usually separate modern corruption from a pristine dream located in the nation's distant past. This type of commentary reads *Gatsby* according to an opposition between present and past, between Gatsby's unethical business connections and the pastoral promise he inspires.[3] Marius Bewley, in his "Scott Fitzgerald's Criticism of America" (1954), was one of the first commentators to use this now widespread formulation. "The theme of *Gatsby*,"

1. Troy, in his 1945 essay "Scott Fitzgerald—the Authority of Failure," was the first critic to use the term "American dream" in an interpretation of *The Great Gatsby*. 2. Kenner similarly places not only the American dream in the distant past but Gatsby's sensibility as well: "It has been dreamed since the Renaissance, and Gatsby is the last Renaissance Man. . . . [I]n 1925 it was still possible to recapture the Dream, or at least how it had felt to be one of the Renaissance voyagers who had dreamed it" (27–28). More recently, Steinbrink has suggested that in Fitzgerald's novel "any attempt to realize the dream is destined not only to fail but to sully the dream itself. The actual settlement of this country, by the Dutch and others, gave rise not to edenic bliss but to mercantile avarice, divisiveness, and war" (167). 3. Nowhere, institutionally or pedagogically speaking, is the use of these analytical binaries more evident than in the criticism contained under the section headings "Crime and Corruption" and "The American Dream" in the well-worn Scribner's Research Anthology entitled *Fitzgerald's* The Great Gatsby: *The Novel, The Critics, The Background* [, edited by Henry Dan Piper].

A NOTE ON THE SWASTIKA

One of Meyer Wolfsheim's enterprises is called the Swastika Holding Company. . . . To those like Fitzgerald who were intimate with the night life of New York City the swastika had a significance altogether remote from Nazism. It was associated with the prohibition underworld and with two of its most flamboyant personalities, Larry Fay and Texas Guinan. . . . Fay, a bootlegger who also operated a fleet of taxi cabs and other legitimate enterprises, decorated his cabs with the swastika, his good luck emblem. He had seen it on the blanket of a horse on which he had bet and won at odds of one hundred to one, thereby financing his career.

Dalton Gross and Mary-Jean Gross, "F. Scott Fitzgerald's American Swastika: The Prohibition Underworld and *The Great Gatsby*," *Notes and Queries,* September 1994.

Bewley flatly states, "is the withering of the American dream" in industrial society (223).[4] "We recognize that the great achievement of this novel," he concludes, "is that it manages, while poetically evoking a sense of the goodness of that early dream, to offer the most damaging criticism of . . . deficiencies inherent in contemporary manifestations of the American vision itself" (245–46). Regardless, Fussell's and Bewley's interpretive models share the assumption that Gatsby's dream is principally a product of the past. These critics assume that the emergence of the American dream is conterminous with either European discoveries of the New World or the birth of the United States as a nation.

Alternatively, I want to argue two points. First, the "American dream" is not a trans-historical concept but, as I discuss at the end of this paper, a term invented *after* the Twenties in an effort to address the crisis of the Great Depression. Second, the social climate of the early 1920s, specifically as it is

---

4. Bewley's model for interpreting *The Great Gatsby* has found numerous restatements. In the early 1970s, for example, Callahan stated: "In its totality *The Great Gatsby* sketches the evolution of America from . . . continent with a spirit . . . to place of nightmare, exhaustion, and death. Founded on the myth of a new Eden, the history of the United States has displaced that vision into an industrial, excremental reality" (12). Callahan concludes that while the industrial nightmare we call modern society is our ugly reality, the nation's spiritual dream is an idealized "aesthetic impulse . . . in opposition to the rest of life" (215). Likewise, Bicknell parallels Fitzgerald's worldview to T.S. Eliot's by asserting that the author of *The Great Gatsby* perceives "modern corruption in contrast to a lost rather than to an emergent ideal" (72). More recently, Rohrkemper argues that the power of *The Great Gatsby* issues from "juxtaposing that corrupted present with the luminous possibilities in a rapidly receding past" (153). He too concludes that "Fitzgerald seems to suggest that America has become Thomas Jefferson's Disgusting City, and that the presiding spirit of Jefferson, no less than Franklin, has been corrupted in modern America" (160).

expressed in increasingly racialized forms of nativism, creates the conditions under which Fitzgerald's narrator imagines Gatsby as a figure for America. Gatsby's dream is a pure product of the Tribal Twenties. This latter point builds upon the provocative work of Walter Benn Michaels, who situates American national literature of the period, including *Gatsby*, within a discourse of nativism. . . .

THE RISING TIDE OF IMMIGRANT ENTERPRISE

Higham reports that around 1920 Nordicists began attacking new immigrants—particularly Catholics and Jews, but Japanese on the Pacific Coast as well—under a nativist banner which now tied racial to more traditional religious xenophobia (266).[5] During the latter half of 1920, the gathering tide of anti-immigration sentiment was fueled by both an economic downturn and a sharp increase in the importation of cheap labor from abroad. These twin factors, the state of the economy and the scale of immigration, regularly play a role in establishing the level of nativism in the United States. However, Higham puts forward a third determinant in nativist politics that exploded on the scene in 1920 and assumed greater importance than ever before: namely, the connection between foreigners and crime (267).

The conflation of new arrivals and unethical business practices provides obvious motivation for reading *The Great Gatsby* according to the rise of nativism and the fall of the self-made man. Gatsby's association with immigrant crime, particularly in the form of bootlegging, jeopardizes both the purity of his white identity and the ethics of his entrepreneurial uplift. The association of immigrants with lawlessness was crystallized during Prohibition, which was no less than a moral crusade to preserve the American Way through social control and conformity. The Eighteenth Amendment propelled organized gangsterism to new heights and, in

5. This trend was best exemplified in the changing philosophy, membership, and activities of the Ku Klux Klan. The first official post-war Klan appearance did not occur until 1920, and, with the "Red Summer" of 1919 behind it (which witnessed numerous race riots and lynchings), the organization began focusing its attacks on white foreigners. The Klan was not less race conscious than before but it did introduce a number of changes into its fold. The Knights of the Invisible Empire made extensive use of eugenics to justify its new interest in nativism. Klan activity shifted from exclusive attacks on Negroes to a broad-based hatred of foreigners who seemed less-than-white, particularly Italians and Jews. For the first time, Klan membership was extended only to white Americans of Anglo-Saxon Protestant descent. As a result, membership expanded geographically from the rural South to the small Midwestern town and the urban North. The ranks of Klansmen also swelled to unprecedented heights, estimated at 4.5 million in 1924 (Higham 277, 286ff).

doing so, opened opportunities for new arrivals by creating a lucrative trade in illicit alcohol. It also activated the stereotype of the non-Anglo-Saxon immigrant as gangster. . . .

Gatsby, although apparently not the child of an immigrant, is a bootlegger who associates with unsavory new arrivals and vile members of the underworld. The association forces Gatsby to make up improbable stories about his past because, as he explains to Nick, "I didn't want you to think I was just some nobody." While Nick desperately wants to believe in Gatsby's grand self-descriptions, contemporary reviewers were not always so sympathetic. One insists that the "Great Gatsby wasn't great at all—just a sordid, cheap, little crook" (Kenny). Evidence marshaled by Tom Buchanan's investigation into Gatsby's past supports such a reading.

> "Who are you anyhow?" broke out Tom. "You're one of that bunch that hangs around with Meyer Wolfsheim—that much I happen to know. I've made a little investigation into your affairs. . . . I found out what your 'drug stores' were." He turned to us and spoke rapidly. "He and this Wolfsheim bought up a lot of side-street drug stores here and in Chicago and sold grain alcohol over the counter. That's one of his little stunts. I picked him for a bootlegger the first time I saw him and I wasn't far wrong."

Gatsby brazenly refuses to deny Tom's accusation of his rival's bootlegging activities, responding politely: "What about it? . . . I guess your friend Walter Chase wasn't too proud to come in on it." Tom's findings not only implicate his rival in various unnamed criminal schemes by providing almost irrefutable evidence of his involvement in the illegal sale of alcohol. Tom, hoping to play to the nativist fears of his audience, binds Gatsby's identity to the Jewish gangster Wolfsheim.

Nick's stereotypical description of Wolfsheim is colored by racial nativism to the extent that it carries with it traces of degeneracy associated with Semites. Upon being introduced by Gatsby to his friend, the narrator provides the following description of Wolfsheim: "A small flat-nosed Jew raised his large head and regarded me with two fine growths of hair which luxuriated in either nostril. After a moment I discovered his tiny eyes in the half darkness." Nick repeatedly characterizes the man he finds "looking for a business gonnection" according to his gross physical appearance, typified by references to "his tragic nose." The descriptions implicate Nick in a form of what Sander L. Gilman calls "pathological stereotyping" (18). Immutable stereotyping of this sort licenses the construction of a rigid difference between the vigorous Anglo-Saxon, Tom Buchanan, and degenerate Jew, Meyer Wolfsheim. Gatsby, whose original surname ("Gatz") carries a Jewish inflection, is caught in a no-man's-land between the two ethnic extremes.

Wolfsheim's business activities are not merely illegal. They threaten the integrity of the national sporting event, baseball's World's Series. Eventually we learn that Wolfsheim runs his illicit business out of "The Swastika Holding Company," a name that continues to befuddle readers. It is unlikely that Fitzgerald would have known that Hitler was using the swastika as the symbol of his fledgling Nazi party. Instead the swastika was widely recognized at the time as an ancient Aryan symbol of good luck. Wolfsheim's possession of the swastika as the name of his holding company manifests the widely perceived threat to an Aryan nation posed by enterprising immigrants, particularly Jews. Burr, in his book *America's Race Heritage* (1922), insists that the "most objectionable classes of the 'new' immigration are rapidly breaking down American institutions and honorable business methods." In the context of discussing recent Jewish arrivals, he describes "business trickery" as a "trait . . . so ingrained that one may doubt whether it could be eradicated for generations" (195).[6]

Gatsby's illicit business association (indeed, his friendship) with immigrant gangster Meyer Wolfsheim compromises the ethics of our hero's self-made success while undermining the stability of white ethnic difference. His enterprising efforts among shady foreigners stages the nation's growing suspicion of immigrants after World War I. This sentiment is confirmed, for instance, in a contemporary commentator's use of an anti-Catholic slur to describe Gatsby upon his first encounter with Daisy. Stated Thomas Chubb, in his review of the novel in the August 1925 issue of *Forum* magazine: "He is still poor as an Irishman on Sunday morning" (311). Even Nick, after meeting the mysterious

---

6. It is important to remember that, with a loss of faith in Progressive Era efforts to assimilate immigrants, Jews (as much if not more than any other new immigrant group) became a national menace in the eyes of post-war nativists. For example, in the early months of 1920, Henry Ford—the country's leading industrialist, folk-hero to millions, and one-time melting-pot model advocate—began using his company organ, the *Dearborn Independent*, to wage an anti-Semitic propaganda campaign against what he called "international Financiers" operating in America.

Gatsby for the first time at one of his gala parties, immediately thinks of his host as a stranger in his own home: "I would have accepted without question the information that Gatsby sprang from the swamps of Louisiana or from the lower East Side of New York."

TALES OF "LUCK AND PLUCK"

Nick's suspicions about the source of Gatsby's wealth are heightened just after he is introduced to Wolfsheim. Gatsby, having boasted that it took him only three years to earn his fortune, is caught off guard and becomes noticeably upset when Nick points out that he was under the impression that Gatsby "inherited" his money through a legacy of family wealth. In the chapter which follows this uneasy exchange, Nick casts young Jimmy Gatz in the role of Alger boy-hero who has a fortunate encounter with wealthy yachtsman Dan Cody.[7] Nick's telling of Gatsby's "luck and pluck" tale suggests the loss of faith in stories of the self-made man at this time. For example, Gatsby's benefactor, Cody, is not the genteel aristocrat of Alger's stories but "the pioneer debauchee." He is a product of "the savage violence of the frontier brothel and saloon," and thus a considerable cry from even the celebrated frontier individualist imagined by Progressive Era historian Frederick Jackson Turner. When he sets sail for the West Indies and the Barbary Coast (places associated with pirating, the African slave trade, and colonialism), Cody employs the impressionable teenager in some "vague personal capacity" and gives him a "singularly appropriate education" before he dies suddenly. Fitzgerald's appropriation of the Alger formula reflects the fact that the traditional ideal of virtuous uplift, recently associated with the melting-pot model of immigrant success, was undercut by a growing interest in get-rich-quick schemes and a declining commitment to assimilating new arrivals during the Roaring Twenties.[8] In this social climate, the moral efficacy of Alger's respectable "rags to riches" stories began to lose their appeal in America. . . .

7. Gatsby's struggle upward is structured, according to Nick's narrative, along the lines of Alger's popular formula. For a discussion of the relationship between *The Great Gatsby* and Alger's stories, see Scharnhorst's "Scribbling Upward." 8. Alger's juvenile fiction reached its height in popular readership around 1910, at the height of the Progressive movement and at the moment when Gatsby and Nick would have been in their youth. At this time, Progressive reformers advocated self-help and uplift as, in part, a way of managing the greatest wave of immigration in the nation's history. For an account of Alger's readership, see Scharnhorst and Bales (149–56).

Another illustration of Gatsby's original ambition, one apparently modeled on the prescriptions of middle-class morality, . . . takes a page out of Benjamin Franklin's autobiography. However, because it mocks the conventions of the self-made man, this illustration ultimately functions to undermine evidence for Gatsby's virtuous uplift. More specifically, the reader is presented with Jimmy Gatz's transcription, on the flyleaf of a dime novel, of a Franklin-style timetable and resolves.[9] Unlike young Ben Franklin, who builds the "perfect Character" by pondering questions of inner goodness before setting out for a day of hard work (72–73), sixteen-year-old Gatsby's morning itinerary is conspicuously devoid of moral questions. Instead, Fitzgerald's boy-hero focuses on the enhancement of self-image through "Dumbbell exercise and wall-scaling." Furthermore, his general resolves focus more on external presentation of self ("No more smoking or chewing") than on Franklin's interest in cultivating the virtuous inner person in the "Project of arriving at moral Perfection" (66).

Fitzgerald's mock-representation of young Gatsby's attempt at Franklinesque uplift demonstrates the extent to which, with the consolidation of consumer society in the twentieth century, the cult of "personality" (based on image-making and competitiveness) eclipses an earlier producer-oriented notion of "character" (founded on an inner sense of duty and piety). The displacement of character by the newer concept of personality did not alone undermine traditional narratives of virtuous success. However, when coupled with rising suspicions regarding the rectitude of new immigrants, the apparent excesses of the personality craze contributed to the diminishing authority of the myth of the self-made man in the Twenties. The resultant crisis in an American national identity is represented by Fitzgerald through the figure of Gatsby. . . .

THE AMERICAN DREAM

The decline of the national myth of the white Anglo-Saxon self-made man during the 1920s predates the birth of the term "American dream." The term was not put into print until 1931, when middle-brow historian James Truslow Adams used it in his popular history of the United States

---

9. Watkins was the first critic to give extensive treatment to the influence of Franklin's writing on *The Great Gatsby*.

entitled *The Epic of America.* Thus, despite a half-century of
literary criticism on the expression of the American dream
in Fitzgerald's *Great Gatsby,* the phrase is a misnomer when
used to characterize the book's nationalist vision.

Adams makes no mention of Fitzgerald or *Gatsby* in his
book, nor should he. The author articulates the fledgling idea
of the American dream through a vague concept of moral
economics meant to address and subdue the imminent threat
of class antagonism caused by the Great Depression. By explicitly appealing to a shared, rather than tribal, sense of the
nation's dream, Adams steers clear of group conflict.

> The point is that if we are to have a rich and full life in which
> all are to share and play their parts, if the American dream is
> to be a reality, our communal spiritual and intellectual life
> must be distinctly higher than elsewhere, where classes and
> groups have their separate interests, habits, markets, arts,
> and lives. (411)

Adams's American dream is inspired by pre-war Progressive
ideals of individual uplift and ethnic assimilation, values
intended to assist readers in managing the crises of the
Thirties.[10] It comes as little surprise when, at the very end
of *The Epic,* the historian offers a lengthy quotation from
Mary Antin's optimistic autobiography of Russian Jewish
melting-pot success, originally published in 1912.

Nothing could be further from the Nordic inflection given
to the national imaginary as it is expressed in Fitzgerald's
fiction. Gatsby's pristine vision of America past does not belong to the American dream of the Great Depression. Rather,
it is a product of the rising tide of anti-immigrant sentiment
in the 1920s, which activated narrowing definitions of
whiteness and, in doing so, weakened the moral authority of
the myth of the self-made man. If we want to interpret *The
Great Gatsby* historically, we should stop using the American dream as an analytical category altogether. Yet it is not
enough to say that Gatsby's dream is simply an aspect of
what Fitzgerald coined the Jazz Age. It is also swept along by
racial nativism peculiar to the Tribal Twenties.

---

10. My assessment of the meaning that Adams gives to the term "American dream" in
The Epic of America concurs with his biographer's description of the historian's politic
outlook at the outset of the Great Depression. Nevins writes that Adams "carried the
principles of T[heodore] R[oosevelt]'s New Nationalism and Wilson's New Freedom
into the years of Franklin D. Roosevelt's New Deal" (90).

WORKS CITED

Adams, James Truslow. *The Epic of America.* Boston: Little, 1931.

Alger, Jr., Horatio. *Ragged Dick; or Street Life in New York.* Boston: Loring, 1868.

Antin, Mary. *The Promised Land.* Boston: Houghton, 1912.

Bewley, Marius. "Scott Fitzgerald's Criticism of America." *Sewanee Review* 62 (1954): 223–46.

Bicknell, John. "The Waste Land of F. Scott Fitzgerald." In *F. Scott Fitzgerald: A Collection of Criticism.* Ed. Kenneth Eble. New York: McGraw-Hill, 1973. 67–80.

Burr, Clinton Stoddard. *America's Race Heritage.* New York: National Historical Society, 1922.

Callahan, John F. *The Illusions of a Nation: Myth and History in the Novels of F. Scott Fitzgerald.* Urbana: U of Illinois P, 1972.

Chubb, Thomas Caldecot. "Bagdad-on-Subway." *Forum* 74 (1925): 310–11.

Franklin, Benjamin. *Autobiography.* New York: Norton, 1986.

Fussell, Edwin S. "Fitzgerald's Brave New World." *ELH* 19 (1952): 291–306.

Gilman, Sander L. *Difference and Pathology: Stereotypes of Sexuality, Race, and Madness.* Ithaca: Cornell UP, 1985.

Grant, Madison. "America for the Americans." *Forum* 74 (1925): 346–55.

Higham, John. *Strangers in the Land: Patterns of American Nativism, 1860–1925.* New York: Atheneum, 1963.

Kenner, Hugh. *A Homemade World: The American Modernist Writers.* New York: Knopf, 1975.

Kenny, Jr., John M. "The Great Gatsby." *Commonweal* 3 (June 1925): 110.

Michaels, Walter Benn. "Anti-Imperial Americanism." *Cultures of United States Imperialism.* Eds. Amy Kaplan and Donald E. Pease. Durham: Duke UP, 1993. 365–91.

——. "The Souls of White Folk." *Literature and the Body: Essays on Populations and Persons.* Ed. Elaine Scarry. Baltimore: Johns Hopkins UP, 1988. 185–209.

————. "The Vanishing American." *American Literary History* 2 (1990): 220–41.

Nevins, Allan. *James Truslow Adams: Historian of the Am-er-ican Dream.* Urbana: U of Illinois P, 1968.

Piper, Henry Dan, ed. *Fitzgerald's* The Great Gatsby: *The Novel, The Critics, The Background.* New York: Scribner's, 1970.

Roberts, Kenneth L. *Why Europe Leaves Home.* Indianapolis: Bobbs-Merrill, 1922.

Rohrkemper, John. "The Allusive Past: Historical Perspective in *The Great Gatsby.*" *College Literature* 12 (1985): 153–62.

Scharnhorst, Gary. "Scribbling Upward: Fitzgerald's Debt of Honor to Horatio Alger, Jr." *Fitzgerald/Hemingway Annual 1978.* Eds. Matthew J. Bruccoli and Richard Layman. Detroit: Gale, 1979. 161–69.

Scharnhorst, Gary, and Jack Bales. *The Lost Life of Horatio Alger, Jr.* Bloomington: Indiana UP, 1985.

Steinbrink, Jeffrey. "'Boats Against the Current': Morality and the Myth of Renewal in *The Great Gatsby.*" *Twentieth Century Literature* 26 (1980): 157–70.

Trilling, Lionel. *The Liberal Imagination.* Garden City, NY: Doubleday, 1950.

Troy, William. "Scott Fitzgerald—the Authority of Failure." *Accent* 6 (1945): 56–60.

Watkins, Floyd C. "Fitzgerald's Jay Gatz and Young Ben Franklin." *New England Quarterly* 17 (1954): 249–52.

A Farewell to Flappers

Edwin Clark

Edwin Clark writes that a conflict between spirituality and commercial life animates *The Great Gatsby*.
Clark was the reviewer for the *New York Times* who
wrote the following review of *Gatsby* when the novel
was first published in 1925. Despite its "whimsical
magic," he says, the book portrays a tragic decay of
souls with insight and keen psychological observation. The characters, mean of spirit, careless, and
disloyal, are more to be pitied than despised because
they are unaware of their flaws. "The philosopher of
the flapper," declares Clark, "has turned grave."

Of the many new writers that sprang into notice with the advent of the post-war period, Scott Fitzgerald has remained
the steadiest performer and the most entertaining. Short stories, novels and a play have followed with consistent regularity since he became the philosopher of the flapper with
This Side of Paradise. With shrewd observation and humor
he reflected the Jazz Age. Now he has said farewell to his
flappers—perhaps because they have grown up—and is
writing of the other sisters that have married. But marriage
has not changed their world, only the locale of their parties.
To use a phrase of Burton Rascoe's—his hurt romantics are
still seeking that other side of paradise. And it might almost
be said that *The Great Gatsby* is the last stage of illusion in
this absurd chase. For middle age is certainly creeping up on
Mr. Fitzgerald's flappers.

In all great arid spots nature provides an oasis. So when
the Atlantic seaboard was hermetically sealed by law, nature
provided an outlet, or inlet rather, in Long Island. A place of
innate natural charm, it became lush and luxurious under
the stress of this excessive attention, a seat of festive activities. It expresses one phase of the great grotesque spectacle
of our American scene. It is humor, irony, ribaldry, pathos
and loveliness. Out of this grotesque fusion of incongrui-

From Edwin Clark, "A Farewell to Flappers," *New York Times Review of Books*, April
19, 1925; reprinted in the October 6, 1996, *New York Times Review of Books*. Copyright
© The New York Times Company. Reprinted by permission.

ties has slowly become conscious a new humor—a strictly American product. It is not sensibility, as witness the writings of Don Marquis, Robert Benchley and Ring Lardner. It is the spirit of *Processional* and Donald Douglas's *The Grand Inquisitor*; a conflict of spirituality caught fast in the web of our commercial life. Both boisterous and tragic, it animates this new novel by Mr. Fitzgerald with whimsical magic and simple pathos that is realized with economy and restraint.

A TRAGIC NOVEL

The most tragic novel about life as it may be lived in and near this city [New York] seems to me F. Scott Fitzgerald's *The Great Gatsby* (Scribner), and the first story in his new collection, *All the Sad Young Men* (Scribner), seems a preliminary study for it. I do not know if Mr. Fitzgerald wrote with a moral intention, but he certainly produces a moral effect. "Monstrous dinosaurs carried these people in their mouths," you meditate, "and now look at the darned things," and being launched upon meditation, come to the depressing truth that they are what they are not in spite of money and power, but because of these.

May Lamberton Becker, *Saturday Review of Literature*, June 12, 1926.

The story of Jay Gatsby of West Egg is told by Nick Carraway, who is one of the legion from the Middle West who have moved on to New York to win from its restless indifference—well, the aspiration that arises in the Middle West—and finds in Long Island a fascinating but dangerous playground. In the method of telling, *The Great Gatsby* is reminiscent of Henry James's *Turn of the Screw*. You will recall that the evil of that mysterious tale which so endangered the two children was never exactly stated beyond a suggested generalization. Gatsby's fortune, business, even his connection with underworld figures, remain vague generalizations. He is wealthy, powerful, a man who knows how to get things done. He has no friends, only business associates, and the throngs who come to his Saturday night parties. Of his uncompromising love—his love for Daisy Buchanan—his effort to recapture the past romance—we are explicitly informed. This patient romantic hopefulness against existing conditions, symbolizes Gatsby. And like the *Turn of the Screw*, *The Great Gatsby* is more a long short story than a novel.

Nick Carraway had known Tom Buchanan at New Haven. Daisy, his wife, was a distant cousin. When he came East Nick was asked to call at their place at East Egg. The post-war reactions were at their height—every one was restless—every one was looking for a substitute for the excitement of the war years. Buchanan had acquired another woman. Daisy was bored, broken in spirit and neglected. Gatsby, his parties and his mysterious wealth were the gossip of the hour. At the Buchanans Nick met Jordan Baker; through them both Daisy again meets Gatsby, to whom she had been engaged before she married Buchanan. The inevitable consequence that follows, in which violence takes its toll, is almost incidental, for in the overtones—and this is a book of potent overtones—the decay of souls is more tragic. With sensitive insight and keen psychological observation, Fitzgerald discloses in these people a meanness of spirit, carelessness and absence of loyalties. He cannot hate them, for they are dumb in their insensate selfishness, and only to be pitied. The philosopher of the flapper has escaped the mordant, but he has turned grave. A curious book, a mystical, glamourous story of today. It takes a deeper cut at life than hitherto has been essayed by Mr. Fitzgerald. He writes well—he always has—for he writes naturally, and his sense of form is becoming perfected.

CHAPTER 3

The Art of *The Great Gatsby*

READINGS ON
THE GREAT GATSBY

An Introduction to *Gatsby*

F. Scott Fitzgerald

In 1934 Random House asked Scott Fitzgerald to write an introduction to their Modern Library edition of *The Great Gatsby*. Fitzgerald took the opportunity to disparage the current crop of literary critics as being worse than useless and to defend his efforts at keeping his "artistic conscience" pure while he wrote the book. After reexamining his work, he decides that, while there might be some room for improvement in the novel, he has nothing to be embarrassed about.

To one who has spent his professional life in the world of fiction the request to "write an introduction" offers many facets of temptation. The present writer succumbs to one of them; with as much equanimity as he can muster, he will discuss the critics among us, trying to revolve as centripetally as possible about the novel which comes hereafter in this volume.

To begin with, I must say that I have no cause to grumble about the "press" of any book of mine. If Jack (who liked my last book) didn't like this one—well then John (who despised my last book) *did* like it; so it all mounts up to the same total. But I think the writers of my time were spoiled in that regard, living in generous days when there was plenty of space on the page for endless ratiocination about fiction—a space largely created by Mencken because of his disgust for what passed as criticism before he arrived and made his public. They were encouraged by his bravery and his tremendous and profound love of letters. In his case, the jackals are already tearing at what they imprudently regard as a moribund lion, but I don't think many men of my age can regard him without reverence, nor fail to regret that he got off the train. To any new effort by a new man he brought an attitude; he made many mistakes—such as his early undervaluation of Hemingway—but he came equipped; he never had to go back for his tools.

And now that he has abandoned American fiction to its own devices, there is no one to take his place. If the present writer had seriously to attend some of the efforts of political diehards to tell him the values of a métier he has practised since boyhood—well then, babies, you can take this number out and shoot him at dawn.

But all that is less discouraging, in the past few years, than the growing cowardice of the reviewers. Underpaid and overworked, they seem not to care for books, and it has been saddening recently to see young talents in fiction expire from sheer lack of a stage to act on: West, McHugh and many others.

I'm circling closer to my theme song, which is: that I'd like to communicate to such of them who read this novel a healthy cynicism toward contemporary reviews. Without undue vanity one can permit oneself a suit of chain mail in any profession. Your pride is all you have, and if you let it be tampered with by a man who has a dozen prides to tamper with before lunch, you are promising yourself a lot of disappointments that a hard-boiled professional has learned to spare himself.

This novel is a case in point. Because the pages weren't loaded with big names of big things and the subject not concerned with farmers (who were the heroes of the moment), there was easy judgment exercised that had nothing to do with criticism but was simply an attempt on the part of men who had few chances of self-expression to express themselves. How anyone could take up the responsibility of being a novelist without a sharp and concise attitude about life is a puzzle to me. How a critic could assume a point of view which included twelve variant aspects of the social scene in a few hours seems something too dinosaurean to loom over the awful loneliness of a young author.

To circle nearer to this book, one woman, who could hardly have written a coherent letter in English, described it as a book that one read only as one goes to the movies around the corner. That type of criticism is what a lot of young writers are being greeted with, instead of any appreciation of the world of imagination in which they (the writers) have been trying, with greater or lesser success, to live—the world that Mencken made stable in the days when he was watching over us.

Now that this book is being reissued, the author would like to say that never before did one try to keep his artistic conscience as pure as during the ten months put into doing it. Reading it over one can see how it could have been im-proved—yet without feeling guilty of any discrepancy from the truth, as far as I saw it; truth or rather the *equivalent* of the truth, the attempt at honesty of imagination. I had just re-read Conrad's preface to *The Nigger [of the "Narcissus"]*, and I had recently been kidded half haywire by critics who felt that my material was such as to preclude all dealing with mature persons in a mature world. But, my God! it was my material, and it was all I had to deal with.

"I WAS AN ORIGINAL"

Although only five thousand copies were printed of the 1934 Modern Library edition of Gatsby *containing Fitzgerald's Introduction, a copy in the University of South Carolina's Bruccoli Collection of Fitzgerald material is marked "Discontinued Title," indicating that even that relatively small printing did not sell well.*

When the Modern Library edition subsided after one printing of 5,000 copies, Fitzgerald once again importuned Max Perkins [his editor at Scribner's] for some sort of reissue. Upon going to Hollywood in 1937, he was especially worried that his name might "sink out of sight." Perkins had mentioned the possibility of an omnibus volume containing *Paradise, Gatsby,* and *Tender.* "How remote is that idea, and why must we forget it?" he asked his editor in April 1938. Two years later, he had yet another question. Cheap paperbacks were just coming on the market, and he wondered if *Gatsby* might not make a fresh start in this form. "Would the 25-cent press keep *Gatsby* in the public eye— or *is the book unpopular?* Has it *had* its chance? Would a popu-lar reissue in that series with a preface *not* by me but by one of its admirers—I can maybe pick one—make it a favorite with classrooms, profs, lovers of English prose—anybody? But to die, so completely and unjustly after having given so much! Even now there is little published in American fiction that doesn't slightly bear my stamp—in a *small* way I was an origi-nal." Read nearly half a century later, when the sales of *Gatsby* run to 300,000 copies a year for those "classrooms, profs, lovers of English prose" Fitzgerald rightly conceived of as his eventual market, his May 1940 letter seems sadly ironic.

Scott Donaldson, Introduction, *Critical Essays on F. Scott Fitzgerald's* The Great Gatsby, 1984.

What I cut out of it both physically and emotionally would make other novel!

I think it is an honest book, that is to say, that one used none of one's virtuosity to get an effect, and, to boast again, one soft-pedalled the emotional side to avoid the tears leaking from the socket of the left eye, or the large false face peering around the corner of a character's head.

If there is a clear conscience, a book can survive—at least in one's feelings about it. On the contrary, if one has a guilty conscience, one reads what one wants to hear out of reviews. In addition, if one is young and willing to learn, almost all reviews have a value, even the ones that seem unfair.

The present writer has always been a "natural" for his profession, in so much that he can think of nothing he could have done as efficiently as to have lived deeply in the world of imagination. There are plenty other people constituted as he is, for giving expression to intimate explorations, the:

—Look—this is here!

—I saw this under my eyes.

—*This* is the way it was!

—No, it was like this.

—"Look! Here is that drop of blood I told you about."

—"Stop everything! Here is the flash of that girl's eyes, here is the reflection that will always come back to me from the memory of her eyes.

—"If one chooses to find that face again in the non-refracting surface of a washbowl, if one chooses to make the image more obscure with a little sweat, it should be the business of the critic to recognize the intention.

—"No one felt like this before—says the young writer—but *I* felt like this; I have a pride akin to a soldier going into battle; without knowing whether there will be anybody there, to distribute medals or even to record it."

But remember, also, young man: you are not the first person who has ever been alone and alone.

F. Scott Fitzgerald

Baltimore, Md.
August, 1934.

The High Cost of Immersion

Malcolm Bradbury

Although some critics believe Fitzgerald was little
more than a chronicler of American life during the
1920s, novelist and literary essayist Malcolm Bradbury holds that Fitzgerald's gift was the discovery
of and immersion in the psychic forces that drove
that frenzied life. As in *Tender Is the Night* and *The
Last Tycoon*, Fitzgerald's exploration of the society
and psychology of the times in *The Great Gatsby*
required a deep personal involvement that was reflected in his life, from the euphoria of the beginning
of the decade to the deep depression that ended it.

The writer of the nineteen twenties who most obviously feels
the intensity of modern American experience in all its spec-
ified and evolving detail is Scott Fitzgerald. The result is that
to many of his critics he has seemed little more than a chronicler, a man whose immersion in the social life and com-
merce of his times, in the prevailing ambitions, the shifting
lifestyles, the fun and the frenzies, the amusements and
tunes, the fashionable displays and the current mores, the
unwinding detail of history, gave him no real distance with
which to stand back and shape or criticize. It is true that
Fitzgerald was, more than most novelists, a novelist of immersion; it was the heart of his literary tactic. It was a tactic
paid for at high cost; it involved a competition for public
fame and attention which ran through his personal as well
as his public life and cut deep into his marriage and his psy-
che. Indeed in his essay 'The Crack-Up' Fitzgerald draws a
very precise analogy between the historical sequence of
America through the nineteen twenties and early nineteen
thirties and his own psychological career: the early euphoria
of the decade turning toward a sense of trauma and distur-
bance and then to Slump is an exact match for the psychic

Excerpted from Malcolm Bradbury, "Style of Life, Style of Art, and the American Novelist of the Nineteen Twenties," in Malcolm Bradbury and David Palmer, eds., *The
American Novel and the Nineteen Twenties.* Copyright © 1971 by Edward Arnold (Publishers) Ltd., London. Reprinted by permission of the publisher.

process that takes Fitzgerald through his own early joyous success to his crack-up, his alcoholism and his wife's schizophrenia. The identification could be so precise because Fitzgerald lived it as such; he bound himself tightly to the glossy and wealthy cosmopolitan life which was a species of the decade's experimentalism, and much of his style, in life and in writing, he took from that link. This has often been identified as his weakness; and we can see why it might be thought so. With *This Side of Paradise* Fitzgerald had set himself the task of catching the mood of youth, in a book that while energetic can hardly be thought of as good; its success encouraged him to take on the stance of style-setter for the times, to identify tightly with its emergent moods and fashions; and that identification satisfied many of his crudest ambitions and his obsession with wealth. He caught himself up in the American cosmopolite class at a time when it dominated, by its money and its high consciousness of contemporary fashion, the pace of modern style, substituting for the more rooted social culture of the wealthy in the past a life of flamboyant display, a kind of dream-behaviour. There was obviously something of the parvenu in his involvement, and it was often expressed in the simplest form in his writings, converted into a popular, easy and money-making kind of fiction. It is often supposed that what he acquired, by painful experience and effort, was the power to stand back and criticize; and it is that which explains the quality of his serious fiction. The truth is, I think, that Fitzgerald's creative gift is better understood from a slightly different emphasis; it was not his separation from the frenzied life of the times, but his discovery of the psychic forces which compel it, that made his best work what it is.

A TOUCH OF DISASTER

Fitzgerald said that his stories all had a 'touch of disaster' in them—a sense of the high emotional cost of human involvement in the times, a sense of the general spirit of psychic overextension involved in the commitment to youth and glamour, wealth and amusement. Fitzgerald's main characters are deeply immersed in their times, like Dick Diver [in *Tender Is the Night*], who feels compelled to risk his sanity and ordinariness by plunging into the melée of advanced social experience, as if the claims of consciousness and the responsibilities of the human condition demand this. The belief that the writer must know his times and serve in the places where the times are acted out most fully is a familiar literary conviction; it was one Fitzgerald shared with Ernest Hemingway. But where for Hemingway the urgent need becomes that of a line of control, a making of style of self and style in writing into protective instruments, Fitzgerald practised the opposite tactic. His style is a mode of involvement, a thrust into the society and psychology of the times. His narrator in *The Great Gatsby*, Nick Carraway, stills the voice of judgment; and by virtue of so doing he explores the complexities of a hero, Gatsby, who at all levels seems morally unsatisfactory. Gatsby is a former bootlegger; he is a parvenu; he is at the service of a vulgar and meretricious beauty. Carraway's peculiar tolerance—partly a condition of his own involvement in a fantastic life in which he, too, is something of a parvenu—is the instrument for a very oblique assessment, which Fitzgerald establishes by an underlayering of subdued symbolism which emerges naturally from the surreal environment of the story, the surreal environment of modern dream-life. *The Great Gatsby* is a novel of the modern city, and it throws up its startling detail in instants and images—in the shifting fashions in clothes and music, the decor of hotel rooms, the movements of traffic, the ashheaps and hearses, that catch Carraway's eye in his mobile way through the varied and populous society of the novel. Through Carraway, too, Fitzgerald establishes a very oblique sense of causality, so that Gatsby, who might well be thought of as the derivative of this world, is gradually distinguished from it and set against it, so that finally he becomes a victim of its contingency. The theme of the novel is the suffusion of the material by the ideal, so that raw stuff becomes enchanted object; and this is not only the basis of Gatsby's peculiar power and quality, but the basis of the writing itself, which manages to invest Gatsby's actions, his parties, his clothes, with this distinctive glow. Fitzgerald's effects are, as I say, surreal, the making bright of evanescent things so that they have the quality of dream; but of course at the end of the novel the dream is withdrawn, and another surreality, the nightmare of the unmitigated mass of material objects, it replaces:

> I have an idea that Gatsby didn't himself believe that it [the phone call from Daisy] would come, and perhaps he no longer cared. If that was true he must have felt that he had lost the old warm world, paid a high price for living so long

with a single dream. He must have looked up at an unfamiliar sky through frightening leaves and shivered as he found what a grotesque thing a rose is and how raw the sunlight was upon scarcely created grass. A new world, material without being real, where poor ghosts, breathing dreams like air, drifted fortuitously about . . . like the ashen, fantastic figure gliding toward him through the amorphous trees.

HISTORIAN OF INTERLOCKING WORLDS

Fitzgerald is in fact the great historian of these two interlocking worlds, the world of modern history invested with meaning and the world of that history without it, the modern wasteland, the city of culture and the city of anarchy. The great fact of his work is that he was able, as a young man in his twenties in the twenties, to humanize and internalize his times, to follow out their running sequences, catching the right tunes for the year and the right fashions and tones of voice. As with Hemingway, though with a tighter social detail, he follows out the psychic history of the times, the history of the great gaudy spree, of a 'whole race going hedonistic, deciding on pleasure'. This is a meaningful revolution for Fitzgerald, and he sees the pleasure in it as well as the pain in it. But the flaw is of course inherently there; the Beautiful are also the Damned. And, like Hemingway, Fitzgerald made not only emancipation but neurosis part of his personal history. *The Great Gatsby* is a completed, and is indeed a contained, work; the aesthetic controls are precise, and the way the hero is both valued and distanced involves a complex artistic strategy. But Fitzgerald's great novel of the nineteen thirties, *Tender Is the Night*, a novel coming after his own crack-up ('There was not an "I" any more—not a basis on which I could organize my self-respect. . . .'), is incomplete, fully enough written, but open to variants of organization; it is an incompleteness curiously apt to its theme, as in fact is the incompleteness of Hemingway's shrillest and most anguished work, *Islands in the Stream*. The central figure, Dick Diver, is himself shocked out of completeness in the course of the book; choosing, as Fitzgerald chose, to dive into his time, he finds his purity of position, his impersonality, his sanity, compromised by the need to act on the front edges of modern society, and especially with regard to Nicole. His humanism becomes famished; a redemptive figure at the beginning of the book, he is unable by the end to perform the trick—once done with elegant ease—of lifting a man on his back while surfing; his pastoral concern for others becomes a breakup of self, and he fades away from significant history at the end of the book. Like Fitzgerald, he becomes an implicated man; the implication draws him into the heart of that disaster, that psychic overextension, which was to become increasingly Fitzgerald's theme.

ACTING OUT HIS DREAMS

The point has to be made that Fitzgerald was not "typical" of his own age or any other. He lived harder than most people have ever lived and acted out his dreams with an extraordinary intensity of emotion. The dreams themselves were not at all unusual; in the beginning they were dreams of becoming a football star and a big man in college, of being a hero on the battlefield, of winning through to financial success and of getting the top girl; they were the commonplace aspirations shared by almost all the young men of his time and social class. It was the emotion he put into them, and the honesty with which he expressed the emotion, that made them seem distinguished. By feeling intensely he made his readers believe in the unique value of the world in which they lived.

Malcolm Cowley, Introduction, *The Stories of F. Scott Fitzgerald,* 1951.

By the nineteen thirties, Fitzgerald had come to feel the risks of what he had done, and *Tender Is the Night* is an exploration of those risks; it also takes them again, using once more as its hidden theme the notion that this contemporary and accelerating history might be redeemed, might be made valid. The result is a novel of singular power and force—superior, I think, to that other great expatriate novel, Hemingway's *The Sun Also Rises,* by its comparatively deeper quality of immersion, its attentiveness to the sequence of historical fact, its closeness of registering. But its power lies also in the way in which Fitzgerald, within a method that puts the emphasis on this, traces back causes and reasons, so that, just as Diver's psychic dislocation comes from his concern with the fragility of these front-line modern sensibilities, so in turn those sensibilities, and Nicole's above all, are tracked backwards to their social, cultural and economic roots. The novel becomes an energetic metaphor for the nineteen twenties and their turn into the nineteen thirties; it catches the force of the passion for emancipation and new consciousness, the accelerating tempo, the cultural exploration through shifting sexual morality and sensation-hunting; it is a psychology of all its characters. But the psychology is within a history, and Fitzgerald explains that history. Its awareness is psychological, economic and social at once; man is, so to speak, propelled by history and society into expressive action, but the action itself can come to express the dislocation in society, the energy and the threat of the active modern consciousness. Against the economic history, which he came to recognize as being more or less Marxist, Fitzgerald sought always to establish the alternative—history made luminous by its participants, involvement given meaning and transcendence. Both histories are currents, processes; Fitzgerald would have liked to unite them, as they are united in the great American success stories where American social history serves the American dream.[1] But what he gives us is a world that is both material and dross, a naturalistic world; and a world in which limited meanings can live—the result being neither realism nor autonomous symbolism but a distinctive surrealism. This kind of achievement, because it is not finally an achievement of form organizing matter, is the hardest for us to explore and to value, especially because Fitzgerald uncomfortably possessed the means—he could be a very bad as well as a very good writer—to make them impure. Yet in these two books, as incipiently in *The Last Tycoon,* Fitzgerald shows the enormity of the effort. Indeed . . . his reconciliation of the formalism and the historical realism of the novel—those two countervailing attributes of the genre from its beginning—offers a great artistic achievement.

1. Fitzgerald represents the two currents at the end of *The Great Gatsby;* it is perhaps significant that the directions in which they are moving seem confused, as if Fitzgerald could not determine which is the genuinely progressive force.

Using a Dramatic Narrator to Present a Bifocal View

Douglas Taylor

Using Nick Carraway to present an image of Jay Gatsby, Fitzgerald created a work artistically worthy of the intense moral and social passions of its time, declares author Douglas Taylor. The view of the somewhat detached narrator allows Fitzgerald to explore the tale from both sentimental and self-critical angles, revealing the subtle ironies of the tension between inner feeling and outer form. While the tawdry images of the world are presented to the reader through Nick's eyes, at the same time Nick embraces and chooses to validate Gatsby's romantic vision, presenting with sympathy the sadness and magic of unfulfilled youthful dreams.

Few critics dispute the superbness of Scott Fitzgerald's achievement in *The Great Gatsby*. In precision of workmanship, elegance of prose style, and control of dramatic point of view, it represents to my mind Fitzgerald's genius at its sustained best. No other novel of the period, with the exception of Ernest Hemingway's *The Sun Also Rises*, can be said to have succeeded so perfectly in transforming the mind and manners of its time into something artistically worthy of the intense moral and social conditions which produced them. The features of the book which stand out most strongly in one's mind—the swirling, sideshow anonymity of Gatsby's Long Island parties, the huge, ominous eyes of the oculist's sign brooding perpetually over the hot, desolate "valley of ashes," the shrill, oppressive atmosphere of Myrtle Wilson's flat, the brutal, cowardly truculence of Tom Buchanan, the poignant dream and pathetic bad taste of Gatsby himself—concentrate a multiple image of an America that had lost its

Douglas Taylor, "*The Great Gatsby*: Style and Myth." This essay originally appeared in *The University of Kansas City Review*, vol. 20, no. 1 (Autumn 1953). It is reprinted here with the permission of *New Letters* and the Curators of the University of Missouri–Kansas City.

standards and its sense of the moral fitness of things, and had given itself over to a self-deceiving myth that would some day come apart like wet cardboard.

A BIFOCAL VIEW

The book is so very good that one is tempted occasionally to go along with the assumption that some influence, other than his own moral growth, operated to aid his imagination in organizing and disciplining his thought and feeling as maturely as it did. Nevertheless, the use of a dramatic narrator to unify a series of swift and intensive scenes was a technique ideally adapted to a talent of Fitzgerald's kind, for, aside from the advantages of compositional compactness, such a method allowed his imagination to project in the form and subject of the novel a conception which enabled him to externalize and to exploit simultaneously from within and without both sides of a nature that was split between sentiment and self-criticism. Gatsby and Nick Carraway unquestionably are coextensive with his own feelings about each side of this nature, and are developed within a context of insights which control their precise moral and creative meanings through a bifocal view that manipulates at once the attitudes of intimacy and detachment with a distinctness that is never blurred.

Fitzgerald's bifurcated relation to his experience, so eloquently underscored in *Gatsby*, has been commented upon frequently by his critics, but Malcolm Cowley has provided the perfect figure to concretize the opposition in Fitzgerald's temperament between the wish to belong and the fear of being unaccepted, between the impulse to participate and the tendency to observe, a man who desired to do and yet to become. "He cultivated a sort of double vision," wrote Mr. Cowley—

> It was as if all his novels described a big dance to which he had taken . . . the prettiest girl . . . and as if at the same time he stood outside the ballroom, a little Midwestern boy with his nose to the glass, wondering how much the tickets cost and who paid for the music.[1]

This sense of "double vision" informs both the general organization of *Gatsby* and the arrangement of its smallest thematic details, and, at one point very early in the narrative, Fitzgerald seems to have imbedded in a casual reflection of

1. "Third Act and Epilogue," *New Yorker*, XXI (June 30, 1945), 54

Nick Carraway's an image which not only emphasizes this double view and represents what may be Fitzgerald's own evaluation of one of the major defects of his earlier novels, but offers a possible esthetic justification for the novel's form as well. It is when Nick, having settled at West Egg and looking forward to the long, quiet days of summer, decides to revive a somewhat neglected habit of reading, doing so with the feeling that "I was going to bring back all such things into my life and become again that most limited of all specialists, the 'well-rounded man.' This isn't just an epigram—*life is much more successfully looked at from a single window, after all.*" (Italics mine.) Invariably, Nick's experience will demonstrate both an aspect of his nature and the bifocal continuity of the book itself, as when he pauses wistfully amidst the busy loneliness of the New York evening to watch a thick congestion of crowded taxicabs moving toward the theatre district, and notes how "Forms leaned together in the taxis as they waited, and voices sang, and there was laughter from unheard jokes, and lighted cigarettes made unintelligible circles inside. Imagining that I, too, was hurrying toward gayety and sharing their intimate excitement, I wished them well." The fine control of language in this passage, with its precise use of detail that mingles several qualities of sensation in a swift interplay of mood, feeling, and idea, the tonal proportions of the colloquial rhythms of the first sentence that evoke and lengthen, through its strong liquid properties, the extent of Nick's longing for the warmth and attachment the experience suggests, the sudden withdrawal and running-away of the emotion expressed in the half-nostalgic, half-ironic "I wished them well," indicates the degree to which Fitzgerald's imagination had matured along with the sense of poetic artistry which could compress and modulate variations of action, character, and atmosphere in words that could feel through to the essential quality of a situation and reproduce its most accurate overtones. This flexible and lyrically differentiated kind of prose is duplicated on every page of the novel, and represents a very real development over the confused mixture of tonal and stylistic peccancies that cluttered his earlier writing, where his uncertainty and insufficiency of understanding tended to force him into the use of illegitimate rhetorical and incantatory devices of language in an attempt to communicate intensities of feeling inaccessible to his imagination.

A MORAL AND COMPOSITIONAL CENTER

In Nick Carraway, Fitzgerald conceived a figure who was to function as a center of moral and compositional activity which fused both the dramatic action and the values it implied. His character, though literally credible, can be regarded as a kind of choric voice, a man who embodies the moral conscience of his race, "a guide, a pathfinder, an original settler," who "wanted the world to be . . . at a sort of moral attention forever," but never forgets that "a sense of the fundamental decencies is parcelled out unequally at birth." The very form and larger idea of the novel allows for this possibility, and throughout the narrative, such a relation to the action is suggested both by the nature of his detached moral involvement and by the pitch and timbre of a diction that compels one to have an instinctive faith in his point of view.

Furthermore, it is the position of Fitzgerald to bring out some of the most subtle and ironic proportions of his subject matter by juxtaposing Nick's feelings and the context from which they issue. In the scene, for example, where Daisy and Gatsby meet after five years, Fitzgerald has used the image of a defunct mantelpiece clock to symbolize the discontinuity of time their reunion implies. Gatsby, nervous and miserably uncomfortable, and leaning against the mantel, had almost knocked the clock to the floor—

> "I'm sorry about the clock," [Gatsby] said.
>
> My own face had now assumed a deep tropical burn. I couldn't muster up a single commonplace out of the thousand in my head.
>
> "It's an old clock," I told them idiotically.
>
> I think we all believed for a moment that it had smashed in pieces on the floor.
>
> "We haven't met for many years," said Daisy, her voice as matter-of-fact as it could ever be.
>
> "Five years next November."
>
> The automatic quality of Gatsby's answer set us all back at least another minute.

The tonal and compositional elements of this passage develop with faultless imaginative detail a tension between inner feeling and outer statement which generates the most evocative kind of emotional and atmospheric irony: the awkward banality of the conversational surface which runs counter to the seriousness of the subject combines with Nick's "It's an old clock" to carry the irony forward in the phrase "smashed in pieces," and, moving with appropriate figurativeness through the diminishing segments of the re-membered time-sequence expressed in "many years" and "five years" to the audacious telescoping of Nick's "set us all back at least another minute," it functions to obliterate artistically the immensity of the moral and psychological distance which separates Gatsby's dream and Daisy's presence, and connects itself dramatically with the image of the defunct clock to complete and reinforce the unsensed irony. This running concentration both of intellect and emotion in Nick's central intelligence thus allowed Fitzgerald to control and intensify the internal and external proportions of his subject in modes which held its values in distinct but inter-animated states of sympathy and evaluation, a method which resulted in a dramatic effectiveness he had never before achieved.

Magic and Passion

Inasmuch as Nick Carraway's point of view represents the significant moral force of *Gatsby*, one is led inevitably to recognize the nature of Jay Gatsby's "incorruptible dream" through the continuous series of moral and emotional insights which reflect Nick's understanding of the importance of the values involved. In spite of the pathetically naive assumptions which lie behind Gatsby's vision of life, Nick chooses ultimately to commit himself to the beliefs it fosters, because, seen against the callous, destructive charm of Daisy and Tom Buchanan's world, it becomes, to his mind, not the gaudy, unsplendid show-piece which attracts the vagrant and the vulgar, but a creative dream of intense magic and passion of purpose that flows from an innate fineness of heart and feeling. It is the worth and dignity of which the human will and imagination is capable traduced by a specious conviction, inarguably American in character, that the noblest intensities of existence are available if the objects with which they are ostensibly synonymous can be possessed. Such a conviction impels Gatsby to believe that his pink suits and period rooms will somehow secure his dream's right to reality, and to disregard tragically the qualitative points of difference between the self-conscious standards of a superimposed wealth and those ingrained in the certitudes of an aristocratic moneyed class. He assumes, with all the immaturity of his race, that living across the courtesy bay from Daisy entitles him to share the complicated dimensions of her world, but the distance which separates them is of a greater and less tangible kind than any narrow extension of water or the green dock-light toward which he yearns: there are all the years of Daisy's assurance and certainty and self-indulgent pride, a way of life that has made her ignorant of unsatisfied longings and of wishes that could not be had, a whole cynical hierarchy of things taken for granted, like her expensive home in Louisville that always hinted of "bedrooms upstairs more beautiful and cool than other bedrooms," and seemed "as casual a thing to her as [Gatsby's] tent out at camp was to him." But enchanted by the amenity and charm of Daisy and her world, by the romantic possibilities for subtlety and graciousness of purpose its mystery and mobility promise, he commits the force of his idealizing imagination to the intense, allusive variousness of its life. His personal tragedy is his failure to understand the complex quality of the mind and motives which go into her fine-seeming world of wealth, for he is captivated by the delightful, exquisitely ordered surface without discerning the behind-the-doors ruthlessness, the years of infinite duplicity and subterfuge that a shrewd, self-preoccupied class has practiced to preserve the power and well-being such a surface implies. Only after the accident, when his vision starts to come to pieces like one of those toy clocks won at carnivals, and he has "lost the old warm world, paid a high price for living too long with a single dream," does he probably sense how very different the very rich are. "They were careless people," Nick concludes of Tom and Daisy, ". . . they smashed up things and creatures and then retreated back into their money or their vast carelessness, or whatever it was that kept them together, and let other people clean up the mess they had made. . . ," and the most eloquent irony of the novel is generated by the subtle interplay between, on the one hand, the elegance and charm of Daisy's world as opposed to the cunningness of its inner corruption and, on the other, the gaudy elaborateness of Gatsby's efforts to emulate its surface as contrasted with the uncontaminated fineness of his heart.

YOUTH AND WEALTH

In the frantic tenacity of Gatsby's belief that the conditions of both youth and love could be repeated if a way of life commensurate with their particular circumstances could be evolved, the whole complex tissue of Fitzgerald's feeling about time, money, and emotional innocence are developed along with the mixture of sympathy and insight his own divided temperament adopted toward these features of experience. Like Gatsby, Fitzgerald felt very strongly about the sadness and magic of the past and the remembrance of the youth and hope and feeling that had gone into its rush of individual moments, as he felt an intense fascination for the life of inherited wealth; but, unlike him, Fitzgerald, though committed imaginatively to both the charm and necessity of such sentiments, understood their value critically and creatively in relation to their total effect on human life and conduct. And in the themes of youth and wealth, two of the most brooding, compulsive images of the American mind, the one with all its overtones of romance, virtue, and emotional intactness, the other with its corresponding associations of happiness and a kind of millennial fulfillment—with the possible irony of corruption—Fitzgerald took hold of the essential qualities by which the American experience could be interpreted and expressed, and the last pages of the novel make explicit the significance of Gatsby as an avatar of a national consciousness that has committed the manifold vastness of its resources to the acquisition of "the orgastic future that year by year recedes before us." His story takes on the proportions of a mythic or archetypal idea: his dream becomes the tawdry, painted dream of a continent that has forfeited its will to the infinite, deceptive optimisms of film and advertising gauds which have the finality of excommunicatory edicts, while his parties, set in a world that is "material without being real, where poor ghosts, breathing dreams like air, drifted fortuitously about," crystallize into the whirling incoherence that stands for the obtrusive, unfeeling largeness of the American social experience itself.

Creating a Creator

David H. Lynn

In *The Great Gatsby*, it is impossible to know a character's essential qualities because the reader's perceptions are mediated by other characters, observes David H. Lynn, director of publications for the Council for Basic Education. For example, the reader is given Nick's private attempt to add flesh to the skeleton of Gatsby's public gestures; the portrait that emerges is Nick's interpretation, and as such illuminates him even more than it does Gatsby. As Nick straddles the traditions of realism and romanticism—a responsibility he accepted when he became narrator of Gatsby's tale—he synthesizes these different views into his ironic but affectionate vision of Gatsby as an exotic, romantic dreamer.

The distinction between character and personality suggested from the earliest pages of *The Great Gatsby* reveals just how fully Gatsby as a romantic hero is Nick's creation. Character as defined by Nick is essentially private; personality appears in public performance. This is an important reversal of the realist tradition . . . in which character—the fullest realization of an individual—lies precisely in the public, historical interplay of private impulses and social conventions. But in *The Great Gatsby* an individual's essential qualities remain forever hidden. Fitzgerald makes it clear that to know another person in any substantial way lies somewhere between a leap of imaginative faith and the sheerly impossible. . . . Nevertheless, . . . Carraway's entire relationship with Gatsby depends on his efforts to translate the mysterious man's dramatic gestures into a revelation of their hidden significance:

> If personality is an unbroken series of successful gestures, then there was something gorgeous about him, some heightened sensitivity to the promises of life.

Excerpted from David H. Lynn, *The Hero's Tale: Narrators in the Early Modern Novel.* Copyright © 1989 David H. Lynn. Reprinted with permission of St. Martin's Press, Inc.

Nick's interpretive imagination is thus at work from the outset. The conditional 'if' emphasizes the process; onto a skeleton of public gestures Nick fleshes a Gatsby, someone whose essential romantic hopefulness is expressed in his behaviour. Were any other figure in the novel to tell his story, to interpret the same gestures, however, Gatsby might well appear as a bootlegger living under an alias on Long Island, rather than the romantic hero we in fact encounter.

Much the same creative, interpretive impulse operates between other characters in the novel; Gatsby himself transforms Daisy's calculated dance—her everlasting freshness and gaiety, the music and extravagance of her voice—into the object of his dream. As our relation to Gatsby is mediated by Nick, so our perspective on Daisy is divided, with Gatsby performing as a narrator of her splendour, while Nick provides a less enchanted estimation. Marius Bewley makes a similar point:

> Daisy Buchanan exists at two well-defined levels in the novel. She is what she is—but she exists at the level of Gatsby's vision of her.[1]

It is important to add that even what Daisy 'is' emerges only through Nick's own private interpretation.

The dilemma for characters to interpret each other's gestures—and, just as important, the concurrent dilemma of the uncertain relation between public gesture and inner 'truth'—occurs throughout Fitzgerald's fiction. Rosemary Hoyt, in *Tender Is the Night*, falls in love with the carefully fashioned persona of Dick Diver, a persona that is the most ironic manifestation of the self-betrayal that rules his life.

As Fitzgerald's characters struggle to fathom each other, nevertheless, they must trust in a faithful relation between personality and character. Yet early in *The Great Gatsby* Daisy demonstrates that no such harmony is necessary. Sitting with Nick on the front porch of her house, she makes a grand and fashionable speech of disillusion.

> 'You see I think everything's terrible anyhow,' she went on in a convinced way. 'Everybody thinks so—the most advanced people. And I *know*. I've been everywhere and seen everything and done everything.' Her eyes flashed around her in a defiant way, rather like Tom's, and she laughed with thrilling scorn. 'Sophisticated—God, I'm sophisticated!'

1. Marius Bewley, *The Eccentric Design: Form in the Classic American Novel* (New York: Columbia University Press, 1963) p. 277

> The instant her voice broke off, ceasing to compel my atten-
> tion, my belief, I felt the basic insincerity of what she had
> said. It made me uneasy, as though the whole evening had
> been a trick of some sort to exact a contributory emotion from
> me. I waited, and sure enough, in a moment she looked at me
> with an absolute smirk on her lovely face, as if she had as-
> serted her membership in a rather distinguished secret soci-
> ety to which she and Tom belonged.

Daisy lacks any meaningful integrity between self and gesture. And Gatsby, therefore, can never fully fathom her; he is
too naive. His gestures and persona are too honestly an expression of the romantic self-image he has modelled himself
on—despite the submerged identity of James Gatz—for him
to understand Daisy's selfishness and charming duplicity.

NICK TRANSLATES GATSBY'S PERSONALITY

Although Gatsby's personality may bear an honest relation to
his private intentions, we must remember that the Gatsby we
are discussing is largely Carraway's creation. If we sense
something of Gatsby's hidden nature, an intimate knowledge
Fitzgerald would deny is ever fully valid, it is because Carraway believes in the sympathetic understanding he has, at the
last, for Gatsby. The sensibilities of Nick's own private character translate the public spectacle of Gatsby's personality into
an apparent three-dimensionality. Nick responds to Gatsby's
ludicrous poses and sentimental cliches and immense egoism
with imaginative sympathy because he believes these traits
are born of a romantic hopefulness that he shares.

From their first meeting, Nick translates Gatsby's gestures
with authority, as if his response were singularly attuned to
Gatsby's intended effect.

> He smiled understandingly—much more than understand-
> ingly. It was one of those rare smiles with a quality of eter-
> nal reassurance in it, that you may come across four or five
> times in life. It faced—or seemed to face—the whole exter-
> nal world for an instant, and then concentrated on you with
> an irresistible prejudice in your favor. It understood you just
> as far as you wanted to be understood, believed in you as
> you would like to believe in yourself, and assured you that it
> had precisely the impression of you that, at your best, you
> hoped to convey. Precisely at that point it vanished—and I
> was looking at an elegant young roughneck, a year or two
> over thirty, whose elaborate formality of speech just missed
> being absurd.

Gatsby's exotic behaviour [is] always at the threshold between the grand and the absurd. . . . Dramatic flair, defiant public gesture often constitute the heart of that ideal self-image pursued by romantic heroes as they define themselves against the conventions of the community. . . . Further, in Gatsby's dramatic behaviour W.J. Harvey discovers not simply a typical egoistic self-proclamation, but an articulation, even a partial, symbolic fulfillment, of Gatsby's dream.

> What we remember about [Gatsby] is not the restlessness or the drifting but 'an unbroken series of successful gestures' . . . above all, Gatsby stretching out his arms towards the green light that is the vain promise of his future. We remember these formal poses as something theatrical or religious, but they *are* poses, moments of suspended time, something static and as such are the stylistic equivalents of Gatsby's attempt to impose his dream on reality, his effort to make the ever-rolling stream stand still.[2]

An essential element of Gatsby's dream, therefore, and indeed of the romantic impulse itself, is the pursuit of a transcendent significance outside of society and beyond the mutability of history. The fact that we remember Gatsby's gestures outside of the narrative flow of events is evidence of how Gatsby and Carraway are truly in league: Gatsby poses and Carraway paints the picture, capturing the instant. Initially, Nick shares his fascination with other 'moths' drawn to Gatsby's Trimalchean fetes. However, Gatsby's extravagance is given form and meaning only in Nick's imagination; he comes alive when Nick first glimpses the intensity of his dream. That intimation arises without Gatsby himself even present, as Jordon Baker reveals the history of his affair with Daisy.

> 'Gatsby bought that house so that Daisy would be just across the bay.'

> Then it had not been merely the stars to which he had aspired on that June night. He came alive to me, delivered suddenly from the womb of his purposeless splendor.

As Harvey points out, Carraway recalls Gatsby in a series of photographic poses, each representing an aspect of Gatsby's romantic, idealized self-image. But Jordon's story reveals the key to translating the static tableaux. Not until then does Nick understand the significance of his first view of his neighbour standing in the darkness, arms stretched across

2. W.J. Harvey, 'Theme and Texture in *The Great Gatsby*', *Twentieth Century Interpretations of The Great Gatsby*, p. 99

the bay. The gesture acquires meaning only through the interpretation of an observer, someone whose own character provides a touchstone for understanding.[3]

PARADOX AND INCONSISTENCY

Nick responds powerfully to the bare suggestion of Gatsby's dream. He is drawn to Gatsby and repelled because of the paradoxical impulses within himself as much as by the inconsistencies of the other's nature. Throughout the course of the tale Nick remains one foot in the settlement of conventional society, one foot in the wilderness with this extraordinary fellow. He is anchored to a world of chronological time and mutability, to values that are fundamentally social. Yet he is drawn imaginatively to a figure who repudiates both time and an identity defined by the community. Nick's dilemma is similar to that of narrators in such novels as *Wuthering Heights* and *The Scarlet Letter*, who straddle the traditions of realism and romanticism. They are poised between the values of the community and the creative defiance of a rebellious hero. Nick's own form of heroism, when he too becomes a narrator, will be to synthesize these apparently disparate impulses within his vision of general irony. He will avow the value of Gatsby's imagination and energy and his yearning for significance, while also affirming a code of fundamental decencies that makes human intercourse meaningful. . . .

IMPOSING FORM ON A DREAM

In creating a portrait of Gatsby and in trying to explain his own sympathy for the man, Nick Carraway must himself attempt to impose form on Gatsby's dream, to articulate its beauty and energy and value, without deadening it within the constraints of language. . . . Both Nick's ambivalence towards Gatsby and the inevitable disjunction between the ideal and the material world are further reflected in the ways he fashions a suggestion of the dream into language. Carraway reports Gatsby's intimate confessions using three separate strategies precisely to heighten the manifold paradoxes. The first is the straightforward quotation of Gatsby's own words.

3. In *The Great Gatsby* only 'in Carraway's interpretation is the fullness of Gatsby's dream recovered'. David L. Minter, *The Interpreted Design as a Structural Principle in American Prose* (New Haven: Yale University Press, 1969) p. 186. See also Walter L. Reed, *Meditations on the Hero* (New Haven, Conn.: Yale University Press, 1974).

Gatsby's failure of language is [a] manifestation of the dream's adolescent conception. He is clumsy with language; his diction and images also belong to boyhood adventure fiction. And too, the flow of simple communication doesn't easily conform to staged poses. When he perseveres in trying to match words to gestures, he repeatedly crosses the threshold between the mysterious and the absurd.[4]

> 'I lived like a young rajah in all the capitals of Europe—Paris, Venice, Rome—collecting jewels, chiefly rubies, hunting big game, painting a little, things for myself only, and trying to forget something very sad that had happened to me long ago.'

> With an effort I managed to restrain my incredulous laughter. The very phrases were worn so threadbare that they evoked no image except that of a turbaned 'character' leaking sawdust at every pore as he pursued a tiger through the Bois de Boulogne.

By thus reporting Gatsby's speeches verbatim and then criticizing their heavy-handed cliches, Nick stakes out one dimension in Gatsby—with these brief glimpses the full, exotic, impossibility of such a creature becomes apparent. Indeed, the extravagance of this passage distances the reader so that he is taken aback by Nick's abrupt conversion moments later on seeing Gatsby's medal from Montenegro: 'Then it was all true.'

Yet absurdity is, of course, only one element of Nick's portrait of Gatsby. A second method is simple paraphrasis; Nick translates the gist of Gatsby's speech without being bound by the artificial constrictions of the other's syntax and diction.

> He talked a lot about the past, and I gathered that he wanted to recover something, some idea of himself perhaps, that had gone into loving Daisy. His life had been confused and disordered since then, but if he could once return to a certain starting place and go over it all slowly, he could find out what that thing was. . . . (Fitzgerald's ellipsis)

Nick's paraphrasing here keeps absurdity at a distance. Gatsby is *not* entirely unaware of the tyranny of change. The intensity of his first great love has shorn him of something of himself, some essence of vitality that nurtured his belief in romantic possibility. This narrative strategy conveys both

---

4. 'Gatsby's taste in language is as flashy and overblown as his taste in cars or clothes: when he talks about his feelings to Nick Carraway, the words he uses retain echoes from many cheap and vulgar styles. . . . Gatsby's feelings for Daisy, the moment he tries to define them, become the banal stereotypes of romantic magazine fiction, and so it is fitting that the language he uses should be vitiated by worn-out images and sentimental cliches.' (Brian Way, *F. Scott Fitzgerald and the Art of Social Fiction* [London: Edward Arnold, 1980], p. 105.)

the strength and pathos of Gatsby's yearning, along with Nick's own ironic awareness that, as he has said to Gatsby moments before, 'You can't repeat the past'.

Immediately after this last passage, Carraway abandons Gatsby's words entirely. He transforms into lyric the story of Gatsby in Louisville five years earlier.

> Now it was a cool night with that mysterious excitement in it which comes at the two changes of the year. The quiet lights in the houses were humming out into the darkness and there was a stir and bustle among the stars. Out of the corner of his eye Gatsby saw that the blocks of the sidewalks really formed a ladder and mounted to a secret place above the tree—he could climb to it, if he climbed alone, and once there he could suck on the pap of life, gulp down the incomparable milk of wonder.

Clearly this is more than a matter of substituting new words for Gatsby's—the perspective, the conception, as well as the language, are Nick's. He has, in fact, stolen away dream from dreamer, and reshaped it according to the possibilities of his own imagination. Here, when Gatsby's dream seems most vivid, we discover to what extent both Gatsby and his dream are Nick's creations. He can speak as Gatsby cannot, achieving lyric intensity rather than empty cliche, for as narrator he possesses at once an ironic detachment from and a sympathetic bond to Gatsby's romantic impulse.

But finally what Nick cannot say—and does not attempt— is the most potent testament that the two men share a dream that transcends either of them. Nick, like Gatsby, cannot circumscribe its energy, the vitality of all youth and hope and desire, within the boundaries of language. Instead, with Conradian impressionism, he *suggests* the dream's deeper significance.

> Through all he said, even through his appalling sentimentality, I was reminded of something—an elusive rhythm, a fragment of lost words, that I had heard somewhere a long time ago. For a moment a phrase tried to take shape in my mouth and my lips parted like a dumb man's, as though there was more struggling upon them than a wisp of startled air. But they made no sound, and what I had almost remembered was uncommunicable forever.

Nick acknowledges the greatness of the dream by not constraining it, not fashioning it fully into articulateness. Yet by evoking the dream through language, he achieves what Gatsby cannot—he translates the ideal into a medium of this world, affirming its value, and sustaining it.

NICK ASSUMES RESPONSIBILITY FOR GATSBY AND HIS DREAM

Just as the ideal cannot be brought into the physical universe without being tainted, Gatsby cannot survive in a world indifferent to his dream and unable to comprehend him. With Daisy, the object that has sustained his dream and given his life direction, lost forever, Gatsby's personality collapses. It will be Nick as narrator and hero who revives the dream and sets it in juxtaposition to a modern society always its foe.

Certainly Gatsby generates and bears his own fate; he has no place in a world that grants him everything but what he desires most, the right it cannot grant—to change time and history. Like a great carnival with tents struck and costumes shed, he ceases entirely to exist as far as society is concerned. Only Nick, acting according to the moral gyroscope of his identity, that code of fundamental decencies, insists on Gatsby's significance, his meaning as a human being, if not the transcendent significance Jimmy Gatz had dreamed of.

> [A]s he lay in his house and didn't move or breathe or speak, hour upon hour, it grew upon me that I was responsible, because no one else was interested—interested, I mean, with that intense personal interest to which every one has some vague right at the end.

The refusal of all the crowd who had swirled through Gatsby's parties to recognize such human responsibilities is finally more damning in Nick's eyes than any collective guilt for Gatsby's fate. All that holds this society together—and not just Tom and Daisy as representative of the very rich—is a vast, careless, self-interested association. No code of solidarity to the social weal, or moral responsibility, or human dignity, retains any forceful imperative.

The indifference of society itself to standards of human behaviour destroys Nick's faith in what Marlow [narrator in Joseph Conrad's *Heart of Darkness* and *Lord Jim*]called 'a sovereign code of conduct'. Carraway must henceforth wrestle with the fact that any such code is arbitrary, artificial, and, to a certain degree, an illusion. Right action, which in the innocence of youth had seemed automatic and unquestionable, becomes a matter of deliberate choice. Carraway's choice to assume responsibility for Gatsby is a response to the indifferent, to Meyer Wolfsheim and to Daisy, to the East and to the universe—a clear, unabashed claim of his own moral identity.

Of course, Gatsby has been no more committed than other members of Eastern society to a common code of shared values. While eagerly pursuing his own glory he could hardly be distracted with moral imperatives. Gatsby's physical existence, his methods of surviving and conquering, all the tools he has used in his quest, are as corrupt as any of the creatures around him.

Carraway's rejection of the East for its irresponsibility, therefore, is a rejection as well of that side of Gatsby's nature which . . . asserts the appetite and significance of the ego in disregard of larger forms of human relations. His enduring ambivalence towards Gatsby is not due solely to the conflict between the dream and the corrupt environment in which it is expressed, but to this essential aspect of the romantic impulse as well—that it celebrates the self alone, not the values that make community meaningful. . . .

Even as he repudiates its anti-social nature, Nick, as narrator, affirms Gatsby's dream with his own effort to create a meaningful tale that will endure. Gatsby sought to set himself free of worldly, temporal constraints. Nick's heroism is to succeed, at least partly, where Gatsby fails. The victory of the narrative itself is analogous to and greater than Gatsby's characteristic gestures or poses. W.J. Harvey suggested that those static poses were a 'stylistic equivalent' to Gatsby's goal, an existence momentarily free of time. Nick's narrative is a more enduring stylistic equivalent of what the dream promised—an existence outside of time, immutable, brought to life in the eyes of an audience.

The narrative is also the culmination of what Nick has begun by accepting responsibility for Gatsby. By telling the tale Nick assumes a further responsibility: for the dream itself. His narrative circumscribes its romantic egoism, while celebrating its vitality and faith, its capacity for wonder, and its determination to create significance. And the narrative fulfills that determination. It insists on the form—and the meaning—of a tale that has apparently ended in disaster and chaos. Out of the confusion following Gatsby's death, and the hypocrisy and indifference of New York society, emerges Nick Carraway's moral character, manifested in the controlling irony that shapes the tale and answers the chaos.

Fitzgerald's Remarkable Narrative Art

R.W. Lid

By using Nick Carraway as narrator, observes
R.W. Lid of San Fernando Valley State College in
California, Fitzgerald was able to create ingenious
solutions to the problems of tying together a compressed, episodic narrative. Such imaginative rhetorical movements constitute much of the technical
brilliance of the novel. Married to these technical
turns of artistry is Fitzgerald's strong narrative sense,
which allowed him to rearrange time and orchestrate
two threads of the story so that the threads continually complement each other as they develop toward
a mutual, horrific climax.

Critics of *The Great Gatsby* frequently, and quite under-
standably, focus their attention on the magnificent overt
symbolism of the novel, particularly Dr. Eckleburg and the
ashheaps his brooding presence dominates. So powerful
are these symbols, and certain others in *Gatsby*, that it is
sometimes assumed that the meaning of the novel resides
in them. Readings of the novel through the eyes of Dr. Eckleburg overlook a simple truth about fiction, which is that
narrative pattern is the total mode of symbol. The major
meaning of a work of fiction is by and large carried by the
narrative—and this narrative is in turn symbolic of the
novel's larger meaning. In terms of the structure of *Gatsby*
it is questionable whether symbolically Eckleburg is as important to the novel's meaning as the less eye-catching
dog-leash which Myrtle Wilson buys for her mongrel pup
and which, in a complex way, mirrors her relationship
with Tom Buchanan. What our fascination and preoccupa-
tion with the oculist's sign, with "owl eyes," the ashheaps,

Excerpted from R.W. Lid, "The Passion of F. Scott Fitzgerald," in Matthew J. Bruccoli
and C.E. Frazer Clark Jr., eds., *Fitzgerald/Hemingway Annual 1970.* Copyright © 1970
by The National Cash Register Company. Reprinted by permission of the editors.

and other such symbols, reflect, I think, is the depth of our immediate response to the powerful moral quality which pervades the book. At the root of Fitzgerald's success in *Gatsby* lies something we can only attribute to the author's personal passion. Ultimately, as I hope to show, Fitzgerald used his narrative art to curb and express this passion. In effect he manipulated the processes of his own heart, and in so doing enlarged the dimensions of narrative in twentieth-century fiction. . . .

Fitzgerald's narrative sense was in an extraordinarily personal way the direct expression of his moral experience as a man. I use the phrase "narrative sense" for lack of a more precise term. Yet what I mean is not very difficult to see. It resides in the fragmented narrative line of *Gatsby* and the skill which Fitzgerald, through the agency of his first-person narrator, Nick Carraway, exercised in putting it together. I would like to stop over one isolated instance of Fitzgerald's use of Nick Carraway at the beginning of Chapter VI to illustrate the point I wish to make. This is that Fitzgerald's swift, breathless, and apparently rather random ordering of his material is actually so tightly controlled that the reader's mind is led through each involution of narrative. . . .

The chapter begins in the following manner:

> About this time an ambitious young reporter from New York arrived one morning at Gatsby's door and asked him if he had anything to say.
> "Anything to say about what?" inquired Gatsby politely.
> "Why—any statement to give out."

The reporter, we learn, has come out to West Egg on his day off. Some rumor, some half-understood remark in the office, has sent him energetically in search of a story about Gatsby. "It was a random shot," Nick remarks, "and yet the reporter's instinct was right. Gatsby's notoriety . . . had increased all summer until he fell just short of being news."

> Contemporary legends such as the "underground pipe-line to Canada" attached themselves to him, and there was one persistent story that he didn't live in a house at all, but in a boat that looked like a house and was moved secretly up and down the Long Island shore.

"Just why," Nick goes on, concluding the paragraph with a sudden, and upon first sight seemingly unexpected, revelation. "Just why these inventions were a source of satisfaction to James Gatz of North Dakota isn't easy to say." And the next paragraph abruptly begins: "James Gatz—that was really, or at least legally, his name." With as little overt preparation as this single page of the novel, the misty grandeurs of the Gatsby legend are suddenly blown away to reveal an unglamorous patronymic and an unromantic birthplace. And then, before we have time to cease wondering over our new insight, the next sentence plunges us backwards in time, to Dan Cody and the incident of the *Tuolumne,* to events which Nick learns only later, on the final night he spent with Gatsby.

It is true, of course, that we have been expecting some such revelation about Gatsby's background for some time. The rumors spread by the guests at his parties, "the bizarre accusations that flavored conversation in his halls," have been compounded as Fitzgerald's tale has progressed. Gatsby's own account of himself to Nick in Chapter IV ("I'll tell you God's truth") has left Nick half incredulous. The luncheon with Meyer Wolfsheim has added another dimension to the mysteries surrounding the man, and Jordan Baker's account of Gatsby's relationship with Daisy has also contributed to our growing expectation of some revelation. But we have not expected it to come as starkly or as boldly as it occurs at the beginning of Chapter VI, and certainly not at this moment, in this way. Yet a closer examination of the passage shows that the revelation has been subtly prepared for.

The success of Fitzgerald's narrative boldness derives from the particular relevance of the apparently random occurrence of the newspaper reporter at Gatsby's door and the pattern of suggestion it creates. The reporter's instinct, that a story concerning Gatsby is about to break, is, Nick tells us, the right instinct to have; the truth about Jay Gatsby, the incident suggests, is near at hand. There is an added suggestion of this in the emphasis on the season; before summer is over, the implication runs, Gatsby will be news. Time, we are made to feel, is about to run out on Gatsby's masquerade—and before the paragraph is over, he has become James Gatz.

Gatsby, of course, doesn't have "any statement to give out" to the young reporter; but he does have, we know, a detailed statement to give Nick, and it is ultimately our knowledge of this that gives the incident its relevance and the transition its effectiveness. For Nick is our reporter. We are waiting for his account of Gatsby's life, for the "news" about James Gatz. The reporter's arrival and reaction have been merely the occasion for revealing the real story behind Gatsby. What we might call Fitzgerald's calculated "rhetoric of narrative" in this instance serves a similar function at a number of crucial junctures where Fitzgerald is bridging difficult gaps in his fragmented narrative scheme. Without such imaginative rhetorical movements on the part of Nick Carraway, no re-arrangement of chronology, however clever, would be effective. A good deal of the technical brilliance of *Gatsby* stems from Fitzgerald's narrative sense at precisely such moments.

COMPRESSING A SHORT STORY INTO A NOVEL

It was Fitzgerald's narrative sense, I think, which partly enabled him to achieve the extraordinary effect of compression *Gatsby* gives. Writing to the author some months before the novel's publication, Scribner's editor Maxwell Perkins remarked: "It seems, on reading, a much shorter book than it is, but it carries the mind through a series of experiences that one would think would require a book of three times its length." And Fitzgerald, in his Introduction to the Modern Library reprint of the novel, remarked: "What I cut out of it both physically and emotionally would make another novel." The contours of Fitzgerald's story would more than prove the truth of such a statement. For one problem Fitzgerald faced, and solved, was the burden of narrative. He had too much story on his hands. Any one of his isolated narrative fragments—Gatsby's courtship of Daisy, Tom's and Daisy's wedding, Dan Cody and Ella Kaye—could have commanded a great deal more space.

In *The Fictional Technique of F. Scott Fitzgerald*, James E. Miller, Jr., demonstrates at considerable length that Fitzgerald had a "sure touch" for selection, for knowing which events to dramatize, which to present obliquely, to summarize, to omit, and so on. Some similar account also has to be given of Fitzgerald's "sure touch" in the selection of his major narrative elements. For one reason for the brevity of the novel and its extraordinary effect of compression is that basically the plot of *Gatsby* is that of a short story, not a novel. Fitzgerald fashioned the narrative framework for a major American novel from the thin story-line of two sexual affairs (Gatsby and Daisy, Myrtle Wilson and Tom Buchanan), one of which he does not even recount, and he resolved both lines of action by a single violent action on the road to West Egg. So the novel appears in outline.

The narrative scheme of *Gatsby* is built around two strands of story—the story of Gatsby and the story of Myrtle

Wilson, parallel characters who share parallel dreams and parallel fates. In terms of structure, the novel is as much Myrtle Wilson's story as James Gatz's, and the novel's most tragic moment is when her body is found on the road to West Egg, the left breast "swinging loose like a flap." "There was no need to listen for the heart beneath. The mouth was wide open and ripped at the corners, as though she had choked a little in giving up the tremendous vitality she had stored so long." I am not suggesting for a moment that Myrtle Wilson is the central figure of the novel, or even that Fitzgerald was as absorbed by her story as Gatsby's, but that she carries the burden of narrative which her more glamorous counterpart cannot sustain. She is the ballast which prevents Fitzgerald's balloon of romance from sailing off into the blue and out of sight.

Myrtle Wilson, of course, was not part of the nucleus of fact out of which Fitzgerald first conceived his novel, and it is impossible to reconstruct what led him to seize upon her story and develop it to such lengths—except to say that his extraordinary narrative sense guided him. Her story is a second, less glamorous, more soiled version of the American Dream. Its realities are crude, its plot openly one of adultery and exploitation. Its characters are distinctly unpleasant people. Myrtle is seen at her most vulgar, Tom Buchanan at his ugliest. Then there is Wilson, a tragically broken man who lives in a blighted world with his own dreams of success. And at the party in Myrtle's and Tom's apartment, the dark counterpart of all the glamorous parties on Gatsby's estate, there is Myrtle's sister Catherine and the McKees, characters which reinforce Fitzgerald's point. The Sunday afternoon party occurs before we see any of the exotic affairs at Gatsby's on Long Island. It stands at the front of the novel providing ironic commentary and judgment on events to follow. The accidental violence which is to occur on the road to West Egg is prefigured by the violent outburst of emotions with which the party breaks up near midnight. . . .

A Stroke of Narrator Genius

Assuredly it was a stroke of narrative genius on Fitzgerald's part which found the resolution of his two narrative strands in a single event on the road to West Egg—but it was Fitzgerald's narrative sense which enabled him to join together his two fragmented lines of story so that they not merely reflect

UNTAINTED BY HINDSIGHT

Gatsby unfolds over the course of a long summer and follows the logic of a dream. One of the marvels of the book is the way in which the narration changes. Though Nick has alerted us in the first few pages to the crashing outcome, we forget. We forget because Nick forgets. His narration becomes fresh and expectant, untainted by hindsight.

Sven Birkerts, "A Gatsby for Today," *The Atlantic*, March 1993.

each other but become a single unit of narrative. The effect he achieves is much like that of a composer orchestrating two themes which sometimes reinforce each other, sometimes clash, but which always provide continuous commentary on each other. From the pattern of consonances and dissonances emerges the larger meaning of *Gatsby*.

It is in creating the resonances between the two narrative strands that Fitzgerald's narrator plays such an important role. . . .

It is often said by critics of *Gatsby* that Fitzgerald's narrator not merely records the events of the novel but also embodies the meaning of the experiences he witnesses. Certainly Nick Carraway is one of the most engaging narrators in twentieth-century fiction. He is warm, human, fallible. From the first page of the novel, when he presents his credentials in a humorous, self-deprecatory yet quietly authoritative voice, much like Herman Melville's Ishmael [in *Moby-Dick*], we consciously identify with him. . . .

Nick's function is another matter. If we turn to the most complex instance of Fitzgerald's weaving together of his narrative strands, his role becomes clearer. After the breakfast with Gatsby, on the morning after the accident, Nick goes up to the city. He tries "for a while to list the quotations on an interminable amount of stock," then falls asleep in his swivel chair. At noon he is awakened by the phone. It is Jordan Baker. "Usually," Nick remarks, "her voice came over the wire as something fresh and cool, as if a divot from a green golf-links had come sailing in at the office window, but this morning it seemed harsh and dry." Jordan tells Nick that she has left Daisy's house. "Probably," Nick remarks, "it had been tactful to leave Daisy's house, but the act annoyed me, and her next remark made me rigid." Jordan complains that Nick wasn't "so nice" to her the night before. ("How could it have mattered then?" he replied.) Nevertheless Jordan wants to see Nick that afternoon. But Nick, responding to the suggestion of cowardliness in her leaving Daisy's, and to her essential selfishness and lack of concern over what has happened, doesn't want to see her. "I don't know which of us hung up with a sharp click, but I know I didn't care. I couldn't have talked to her across a tea-table that day if I never talked to her again in this world."

> I called Gatsby's house a few minutes later, but the line was busy. I tried four times; finally an exasperated central told me the wire was being kept open for long distance from Detroit. Taking out my time-table, I drew a small circle around the three-fifty train. Then I leaned back in my chair and tried to think. It was just noon.

Now there occurs a space break on the page, possibly to suggest that the thoughts which follow could occur to Nick as he reclines in his chair, and then a time-shift carries us back to the morning.

> When I passed the ashheaps on the train that morning I had crossed deliberately to the other side of the car. I supposed there'd be a curious crowd around there all day with little boys searching for dark spots in the dust, and some garrulous man telling over and over what had happened, until it became less and less real even to him and he could tell it no longer, and Myrtle Wilson's tragic achievement was forgotten.

A final, abrupt sentence closes the paragraph: "Now I want to go back and tell what happened at the garage after we left there the night before." With that sentence time shifts first backward, to the night before and events at the garage, then forward to the events of the day leading to Gatsby's death.

About the detailed events crowding around Wilson and Michaelis in the hours after the accident—which Fitzgerald describes immediately after the paragraph quoted above—Nick can know only what newspaper accounts or Michaelis's testimony at the inquest revealed. Nick's "Now I want to go back and tell what happened . . ." seemingly violates point of view. A less assured and less skilled writer than Fitzgerald, one can theorize, would have handled the matter less swiftly and less boldly. Conceivably he might have had Nick interview Michaelis. More likely, he would have taken pains to show Nick piecing things out from various sources, or he would have planted an eyewitness who directly tells Nick what happened. But such devices used in this fashion would have obtruded technique upon subject matter, and Fitzgerald is too good a writer to do this. Actually Fitzgerald does use these devices but much more subtly and imaginatively. In scattered references to Michaelis's testimony and to newspaper accounts in the pages which follow Nick implies that he has gathered the information which he dramatically retells, while the suggestion of an eyewitness—"some garrulous man telling over and over what had happened"—is represented in the ghostly person of Nick. . . .

AUTHOR AS CHARACTER

Fitzgerald's rearrangement of time juxtaposes the deaths of Myrtle and Gatsby. It also allows Wilson's story of his life with Myrtle, his growing suspicion of her other life, his discovery of the dog collar, and his quarrel with her to be part of the main narrative instead of mere flashback or isolated story. But such re-ordering of chronology also produces unexpected breaks in narrative, sudden stops and swift starts, awkward gaps that have to be filled. It is precisely at these moments that the presence of Fitzgerald's narrator, who is not bound by time or scene, maintains the unbroken rhythm of the plot. But Nick is not merely the author's stand-in. The relationship between authorial intent and personality and narrative technique remains complex.

In his biography of Fitzgerald, Arthur Mizener remarks: "His use of a narrator allowed Fitzgerald to keep clearly separated for the first time in his career the two sides of his nature, the middle-western Trimalchio and the spoiled priest who disapproved of but grudgingly admired him." Mr. Mizener's remark, in the sense in which I think he intended it, is obviously true. *Gatsby* exhibits a measure of control over subject matter which Fitzgerald failed to achieve in his other books and this control resides in Fitzgerald having found, through his use of first person narration, a way not only to sort out the attitudes he shared with his characters but also to provide legitimate commentary on these attitudes. . . .

It is a commonplace of Fitzgerald criticism that the characterization in *Gatsby* is not deep, is at times no more than adequate; and we ourselves have seen how minimally Nick Carraway and Jordan Baker exist as people. But what has never been posited is that perhaps Fitzgerald is using first-person narration here to avoid characterization. That is, in *Gatsby* the deliberate pressure of narration frees Fitzgerald from a blinding sense of identity with any one character in the working out of his fable; in effect, he is able to curb and express his personal passion.

Ultimately, of course, Fitzgerald does create a magnificent figure in *Gatsby*, one with depth and possessed of profound moral seriousness, but that figure is neither Jay Gatsby nor Myrtle Wilson. Nor is it Nick Carraway. It is, I would suggest, Scott Fitzgerald, both man and writer, or, rather, the man-as-writer. Brooding over his domain of ashheaps and the drama which unfolds upon it are not merely the eyes of Doctor T. J. Eckleburg but the intelligence and conscience of the author. "I am not a great man," he wrote his daughter in 1939, "but sometimes I think the impersonal and objective quality of my talent and the sacrifices of it, in pieces, to preserve its essential value has some sort of epic grandeur."

From the vast biographical material available about Fitzgerald, including that provided by his *Letters*, it is clear that he wrote out of himself, in effect put himself directly on paper, in a way that earlier writers cannot be said to. His goal was the modern novelist's goal of self-understanding. What separates Fitzgerald from his immediate predecessors, it seems to me, is the extent of awareness of self in his fiction. It is not that Fitzgerald was more honest than, say, Conrad, but that by the time Fitzgerald wrote, it had become possible to accept blame. For Fitzgerald's generation, self-knowledge had become a human discovery, and Fitzgerald shared in that discovery. Overshadowing both the man and his work is the deeply tragic understanding that he is the personal author of his own wreckage.

Transforming Old Values into New Art

Robert Sklar

Before he wrote *The Great Gatsby*, Fitzgerald had brought a new perspective to a variety of themes and ideas, observes Robert Sklar, assistant professor in the University of Michigan's program in American culture. For example, he wrote variations on the genteel romantic formula in which the flapper heroine, rather than the hero, wields the ultimate power. He struggled with issues of wealth and class, especially the acquisition of sudden wealth, often "punishing" his characters for both their faults and their good fortune. Sklar follows the maturation of Fitzgerald's ideas through his early novels and short stories to the turning point of his career, *The Great Gatsby*.

Sometime in his last two years of life F. Scott Fitzgerald wrote down, on the inside back cover of André Malraux's *Man's Hope*, the sources in his own experience for chapters of *The Great Gatsby*. Under Roman numerals I through IX he marked down names and places; and though he added no heading or identifying title, their meaning cannot be mistaken. Why Fitzgerald should have put down this list, however, at so late a date, unidentified, and particularly in so obscure a place, is much less clear. Perhaps, reading the novel which had grown so obviously out of Malraux's experience in the Spanish Civil War, he was moved suddenly to record how deeply the roots of *The Great Gatsby* were laid in his own experience. For the opening chapter's scene in Tom Buchanan's East Egg mansion, Fitzgerald recalled the "glamor of Rumsies and Hitchcocks"; Tommy Hitchcock was a wealthy polo player whom the Fitzgeralds met on Long Island. Gatsby's first party in Chapter III was drawn, he wrote, from "Goddards, Dwans, Swopes." Herbert Bayard Swope was a well-known journalist, Allen Dwan a movie

From *F. Scott Fitzgerald: The Last Laocoön* by Robert Sklar. Copyright © 1967 by Robert Sklar. Used by permission of Oxford University Press.

director, who lived at Great Neck in the early twenties. Jordan Baker's story of Daisy's wedding, in Chapter IV, came from Fitzgerald's "memory of Ginevra [King]'s wedding"; and the details of Gatsby's career, as their mystery unfolded in Chapter VI, were taken from a story told to Fitzgerald by a man named Bob Kerr. The desolate setting of Wilson's garage, and Myrtle Wilson's secret apartment, in Chapter II, were places recalled: "Ash heaps, memory of 125th, Great Neck." Fitzgerald remembered 125th Street from his four unhappy months in New York during the spring of 1919; and he lived to see the ash heaps bulldozed for the Flushing Meadows site of the New York World's Fair. Carraway's drive with Gatsby to New York, and their lunch with Meyer Wolfsheim in Chapter IV, came from broader recollections of Fitzgerald's "Vegetable Days in New York." The second party in Chapter VI, and the climactic events of Chapter VII, in New York and returning, Fitzgerald listed without comment, for he had already accounted for their setting and their mood.

Yet Fitzgerald took pains also to show that much of the novel had not been drawn from parallel moments in his own life. The meeting between Gatsby and Daisy in Chapter V, the murder of Gatsby by Wilson in Chapter VIII, and Gatsby's funeral in Chapter IX, he listed explicitly as his own "invention"; and thus he laid claim to the structure, the conclusion, and the ultimate meanings of *The Great Gatsby* as original creations of his own mind and art. *The Great Gatsby* has undergone exceptionally intensive and quite informative criticism in recent years, yet of the many valid ways the novel has been interpreted, none provides so solid a foundation for its meanings as Fitzgerald's own. For all his extraordinary success in creating *The Great Gatsby* as a unified emotional and artistic gesture, Fitzgerald conceived the novel, not as a solid artifact, but as an act; and its fullest meanings may be most completely uncovered by approaching the novel as a process—a process whereby Fitzgerald transformed old values and experience in the crucible of his developing art and ideas.

NEW INSIGHTS INTO OLD IDEAS

To list the parallels between *The Great Gatsby* and Fitzgerald's earlier fiction would be to catalogue extensively the themes and issues of two novels, more than three dozen short stories, and a play. It was Fitzgerald's new intellectual and artistic maturity, stimulated by his sense of connection and participation in the modern movement of the arts, that made possible his capacity to understand and recast old themes in *The Great Gatsby*'s unforgettable form. For Fitzgerald *The Great Gatsby* was not a novel of new ideas, but of new insights into old ideas. The act of re-creation is more important than the substance thus reshaped, the process more necessary to understand than the material it reworked. Yet it is not possible simply to say, here then is Fitzgerald's stock of themes and problems. As H.L. Mencken warned, Fitzgerald was supplied with so much versatility as to be a danger to himself; and though his supply of issues may have been small, he was capable of many different emphases and resolutions, depending on his form, his audience, or his moods. There is no clear formula of progression in Fitzgerald's fiction before *The Great Gatsby*, . . . and thus it is difficult to ascertain in what form the problems rested when *The Great Gatsby* was begun. The one certainty about the material Fitzgerald brought to *The Great Gatsby* was that Fitzgerald had his problems with it, problems to which he had not yet found any lasting satisfactory solution.

But if there was a single, most pervasive theme that connected *The Great Gatsby* to Fitzgerald's earlier fiction, it was the problem of sudden and unmerited wealth. Fitzgerald struggled with the issue first in *This Side of Paradise*, through the character of Dick Humbird. Amory Blaine had looked on Humbird as "a perfect type of aristocrat." But in fact Humbird turned out to be the son of a grocery clerk, who had struck it rich by speculation in land. So Humbird suffered a violent and ugly death, almost as a punishment for Amory's self-deception. It was as if Fitzgerald regarded the Humbirds' financial success, and their rise to social status and power, as a crime; yet Amory Blaine, whose need to expunge Humbird's appeal went so far as to see a vision of him burning in hell, was himself an admirer of successful criminals. "It seemed to him that life and history were rife with the strong criminal, keen, but often self-deluding; in politics and business one found him and among the old statesmen and kings and generals."

Wealth and class, formal categories and real distinctions—these were the issues which Fitzgerald in his early fiction sought to clarify. In stories like "The Four Fists" the answers seemed to lie in morality; in stories like "Two for a Cent," in fate. Sometimes he seemed to find solutions in realism, and sometimes in fantasy. But no resolution was more than temporary, for even the terms of the issue were not yet clear. If Humbird had looked and acted like an aristocrat, but had to be punished because he was not, what then was an aristocrat?

Mencken's aristocrats formed a class of birth, fortune, and intellect, along the lines of eighteenth-century Virginia. Philosopher Friedrich Nietzsche limited his aristocracy to artists and philosophers alone. Fitzgerald pondered their ideas and even borrowed the language of their concepts, but he resisted their meanings. When he used the term "aristocrat" he meant the man of wealth alone—the "plutocrat." In *The Beautiful and Damned* Fitzgerald also claimed Anthony Patch as an aristocrat; and Anthony was punished, not by death, but by degradation and insanity. But Fitzgerald's animus against aristocrats was in truth directed against plutocrats in masquerade.

Rich young men with unearned wealth could bring out in Fitzgerald this confused instinct for punishment; poor young men who desired wealth were something else. In one of the stories he wrote right after *This Side of Paradise*, "Dalrymple Goes Wrong," Fitzgerald endowed Bryan Dalrymple with the criminal strength and will Amory Blaine had admired. Dalrymple won his success in the material world by a secret life of crime. But whatever the implications of this character, Fitzgerald could not maintain them. Thereafter his ambitious poor boys who became criminals in their quest for wealth— the most important is Curtis Carlyle in "The Offshore Pirate"—were in fact upper-class genteel heroes, acting out a romantic role to win the hearts of their upper-class girls.

New Life for an Outmoded Formula

The hero in criminal disguise—"The Unspeakable Egg," written in 1924 just before *The Great Gatsby*, provides a cruder example—was Fitzgerald's most significant variation on the genteel romantic formula. . . . The conventional genteel romantic hero, whom Fitzgerald inherited from one aspect of nineteenth-century American fiction, . . . was a young man who demonstrated the power of his independent will to prove a moral point, and thereby win fortune and the girl. His task was to perform unconventionally, though without breaking any of the moral or social conventions; his best means were cleverness and imagination, the capacity to do accepted tasks in humorous and entertaining ways. Fitzgerald's truly original contribution to this genre of American fiction was to prolong its life by shifting the focus from the young man to the young woman. He created the genteel romantic heroine, and thus, partly by accident and partly by design, was made the chronicler of the age of the flapper. In all the conventional genteel romantic stories he wrote for the popular magazines before *The Great Gatsby*—the two criminal disguise stories are the only exceptions—the power of independent will rests in the hands not of the male, but of the female. No matter how daring and arduous the task performed by the hero, control over his destiny remains with the girl. As a result the young men in Fitzgerald's conventional genteel stories are vague, rather shadowy figures, even if they always win the girl's love; what interest and excitement there is in the stories is always generated by the flapper heroine.

But for all her independent willfulness the flapper heroine does not break the genteel conventions any more than the romantic hero does. As Gloria Gilbert in *The Beautiful and Damned* insisted, she was free to do anything she pleased, but sexual promiscuity did not please her. Gloria, it is true, drank far too much, but she was punished for it by her loss of beauty. Nancy Lamar in "The Jelly-Bean," who drank and gambled, was the wildest of Fitzgerald's flappers, and she too was punished, by marriage to a man she did not love. The punishment of both girls was lightened, to be sure, by the fact that both their husbands were multi-millionaires. Despite occasional innuendo and a bit of innocent necking in parked cars, Fitzgerald's willful heroines kept themselves remarkably pure.

Thus in his conventional fiction Fitzgerald gave new life to an outmoded formula by shifting the focus of attention within it. It was in his novels that he confronted the implications of the formula's true obsolescence; for he argued in *This Side of Paradise* that the economic and social foundations for genteel romantic heroism were shattered in the First World War. The heroes of his novels, Amory Blaine in *This Side of Paradise* and Anthony Patch in *The Beautiful and Damned*, shared with the old nineteenth-century genteel romantic heroes—Tom Sawyer is the best example—an interesting mixture of romantic ideology and sentimental emotion in one mind. In the conventions of the genteel American tradition, . . . romanticism gave power to the deed, and sentiment held the results within socially acceptable bounds. Fitzgerald's significant effort in *This Side of Paradise* to provide an alternative to the genteel hero, through Amory Blaine's constructive individualism, reversed the process. Only sentiment held Amory's loyalty to a social system which had deserted him; but romantic ideology was to shape a new meaning for his sentimentally inspired acts. By the time of *The Beautiful and Damned*, however, romantic ideology had seemed to have proven itself incapable of providing any new meanings. The pathetic Anthony Patch was thus, like Amory Blaine, sentimental in his emotions, but capable only of regarding himself through a veil of romantic despair. Romantic meaning had given way to romantic meaninglessness, optimism and constructive power had been converted to pessimism and helplessness.

A Turning Point

The genteel romantic hero, who formed the backbone of Fitzgerald's best fiction as well as his worst, of his most original work as well as his most conventional, was never to fall lower. The process of recovery and growth that began after *The Beautiful and Damned* retained this hero, with his mingled romantic dreams and sentimental feelings. But as the conventional resolution of romance and sentiment had been rendered impossible by the war, so too were Fitzgerald's postwar alternatives—romantic meaning or romantic meaninglessness—outmoded by his maturing insight. The possibility of a resolution within society no longer mattered, for he had discovered a different realm whereby social failure or social success could be judged. Henceforth the genteel romantic hero would be a flawed superman, a man who, merely by his belief that the impossible was still possible, that sentiment and romance could still be resolved, placed himself beyond the safety, and beyond the comprehension, of conventional society. Society would judge him, to be sure, but so long as Fitzgerald through his art could provide another mode of judgment, the genteel hero's fate might be raised to the stature of a national tragedy.

This structure emerges only imperfectly from "The Diamond as Big as the Ritz," for Fitzgerald was torn between punishing Braddock Washington and exalting him. Yet the novella marks the single most important turning point, before *The Great Gatsby*, in Fitzgerald's mind and art. While turning "The Romantic Egotist" into *This Side of Paradise* the author had discovered that the genteel romantic hero was a victim of the First World War, and ever since he had been faced with a dilemma. He could please his slick magazine readers by writing as if the wealthy and clever old hero was still as lively as ever; or he could try in his novels to create new values in place of the moribund old, or coherently to portray the decadence of youth without values. No alternative had satisfied him, for the values of the genteel romantic hero were his own values, and the problem was to combine genteel romantic values with his own true perceptions of society. Of all Fitzgerald's early fiction "The Offshore Pirate" was the most cogent statement of his dilemma. There he had fused the conventional genteel romantic hero to his own conception of the unconventional, self-created individual, in the person of the ambitious, class-conscious, criminal band-leader, Curtis Carlyle, only to destroy his creation by a sentimental ending. By "The Diamond as Big as the Ritz" Fitzgerald had discovered new means in his maturing intelligence and artistry to re-create the fusion, and to make it stick. With "The Diamond as Big as the Ritz" the major dilemma affecting Fitzgerald's themes and values had been solved, and the first block in the foundation of *The Great Gatsby* was laid. . . .

A CHARACTER ADEQUATE FOR GREATNESS AND TRAGEDY

Though *The Beautiful and Damned* represents the nadir of Fitzgerald's capacity to comprehend and control his material, he had already, before his slight effort to revise the novel, begun to write "The Diamond as Big as the Ritz." He had never before felt such artistic despair and intellectual confusion; and yet at that moment his dangerous versatility, combined with the exceptional resilience of his talent, came up with a combination of elements almost perfectly right.

By writing the novella "utterly for my own amusement" [as he noted in *Tales of the Jazz Age*], Fitzgerald excused himself from the responsibility of either criticizing conventional forms or adhering to them, and gave license to his fancy to play freely on ideas of wealth. The fusion of his fantasy, completely unfettered for the first time from genteel formulas, with a not unfamiliar craving for luxury, gave birth to the diamond mountain and the man of wealth raised to the status of a god. Braddock Washington, the Prometheus Enriched who destroyed himself and his fortune instead of destroying human hopes and values, retained greater dignity than Fitzgerald had meant for him to have; thereafter it remained only for Fitzgerald to create a character adequate to his conception of greatness and of tragic plight.

The conception, then, was originally Fitzgerald's; the process whereby it attained *The Great Gatsby*'s perfection of form . . . began with his reading and reflection on the fiction of Joseph Conrad and James Joyce. From his reading of Conrad's "Youth" and *Nostromo* Fitzgerald grasped what he had not learned from the Romantic poets, that, as his favorite John Keats had written, "the excellence of every Art is its intensity, capable of making all disagreeables evaporate, from their being in close relationship with Beauty & Truth." The loss of youth and beauty, even the loss of life, could be overcome by an art which was intense enough to preserve the quality of romance and power, even though their substance must disappear; time, though it still conquered, might nevertheless lose its terror. . . .

With *The Great Gatsby* F. Scott Fitzgerald created his own vision of national tragedy and of high art, created a novel which with every passing year more clearly assumes a place among the imperishable works of American fiction. He had come a long way since the early moment in his career when he denied Keats's poetic statement that beauty was truth, and truth beauty. In *This Side of Paradise* and *The Beautiful and Damned* the beauty he rejected and the beauty that proved false was the beauty of a woman; in *The Great Gatsby* he found truth in the beauty of art, and beauty in its truths. With *The Great Gatsby* he found self-fulfillment and self-creation as an artist.

CHRONOLOGY

1896

Francis Scott Key Fitzgerald is born in St. Paul, Minnesota, on September 24.

1898

Edward Fitzgerald's business fails; the family moves to Buffalo, New York, where he takes a job as a salesman.

1900

Zelda Sayre is born in Montgomery, Alabama, on July 24.

1901

Fitzgerald family moves to Syracuse, New York. Annabel Fitzgerald, Scott's only surviving sibling, is born in July in Syracuse.

1903

Fitzgerald family returns to Buffalo.

1908

Edward Fitzgerald loses his job; the family returns to St. Paul. Scott enters St. Paul Academy.

1909

Scott's first appearance in print: "The Mystery of the Raymond Mortgage" (an Edgar Allan Poe–like mystery) published in *St. Paul Academy Now & Then*.

1911

Scott attends Newman boarding school in Hackensack, New Jersey.

1912

Scott's play *The Captured Shadow* is produced by an amateur theater group in St. Paul while he is home for the summer.

1913

Enters Princeton University.

1914

His first play for the Triangle Club, *Fie! Fie! Fi-Fi!*, tours during Christmas vacation; his poor grades prohibit him from traveling with the show. Home for Christmas, he meets Ginevra King and begins a two-year courtship.

1914–18

World War I; the United States enters the war in 1917.

1917

Eighteenth Amendment to the U.S. Constitution makes alcoholic beverages illegal (federal prohibition law goes into effect in 1919). Fitzgerald leaves Princeton and enters the army as a second lieutenant.

1918

March—Completes the first draft of *The Romantic Egoist* and submits it to Scribner's. (It will later be retitled *This Side of Paradise.*) July—Scott and Zelda meet in Montgomery, Alabama. Scribner's declines *The Romantic Egoist*; in October a revised version is also declined. November 11—World War I ends.

1919

Discharged from the army in February. *This Side of Paradise* is accepted by Scribner's in September.

1920

Fitzgerald publishes *This Side of Paradise* and marries Zelda Sayre. Sinclair Lewis publishes *Main Street.* Women are given the right to vote by constitutional amendment. "Red scare" leads to arrest of twenty-seven hundred American Communists.

1921

May/July—Fitzgeralds visit England, France, and Italy. October—Their daughter, Scottie, is born in Minnesota.

1922

Fitzgerald publishes *The Beautiful and Damned.* James Joyce publishes *Ulysses*; T.S. Eliot publishes *The Waste Land.* The Fitzgeralds move to Long Island, New York.

1923

Fitzgerald's play *The Vegetable* fails in Atlantic City. Hitler writes *Mein Kampf.*

1924

The Fitzgeralds leave for Europe in April, visiting Paris and the French Riviera. They move to Rome for the winter.

1925

Fitzgerald publishes *The Great Gatsby*. The family moves to Paris, where they meet Ernest Hemingway, among others.

1926

Ernest Hemingway publishes *The Sun Also Rises*. The Fitzgeralds move to the Riviera. In December, they return to America.

1928

After a brief stint in Hollywood and a year in Delaware, the family visits Europe from April until September, when they return to Delaware.

1929

The Fitzgeralds are in Europe again, having been there over six months when the stock market crashes in America on October 29. William Faulkner publishes *The Sound and the Fury*.

1929–37

Great Depression in the United States, following the stock market crash of 1929.

1930

Zelda suffers her first mental breakdown while in Paris; enters a Swiss clinic for treatment. Scott moves to Switzerland to be near the clinic. Zelda will remain in the clinic for fifteen months, eventually being diagnosed with schizophrenia.

1931

Zelda returns to Montgomery; Scott goes to Hollywood to work for MGM.

1932

Zelda's second breakdown; she enters a clinic in Baltimore for four months.

1933

Eighteenth Amendment repealed (see 1917). President Franklin Roosevelt introduces the "New Deal," programs intended to end the depression.

1934

Fitzgerald publishes *Tender Is the Night*. Zelda's third breakdown; she returns to the Baltimore clinic.

1935

Italy invades Ethiopia. Fitzgerald begins writing "The Crack-Up," a collection of essays discussing his ordeals.

1936–39

Spanish Civil War.

1937

Japan invades China. Fitzgerald, deeply in debt, returns to Hollywood. For the next eighteen months, he receives $1000 to $1500 per week as a screenwriter, although he receives only one screen credit (for his work on *Three Comrades*).

1938

Germany invades Austria. MGM does not renew Scott's contract.

1939

John Steinbeck publishes *The Grapes of Wrath*. Scott takes freelance jobs for various Hollywood studios. He begins work on *The Last Tycoon*.

1939–45

World War II. The United States enters the war in 1941, after the December 7 Japanese attack on Pearl Harbor.

1940

December 20—Fitzgerald dies.

FOR FURTHER RESEARCH

BIOGRAPHIES

Matthew J. Bruccoli, *Some Sort of Epic Grandeur: The Life of F. Scott Fitzgerald.* New York: Harcourt Brace Jovanovich, 1981.

Scott Donaldson, *Fool for Love: A Biography of F. Scott Fitzgerald.* New York: Delta, 1983.

William F. Goldhurst, *F. Scott Fitzgerald and His Contemporaries.* New York: World, 1963.

John J. Koblas, *F. Scott Fitzgerald in Minnesota: His Home and Haunts.* St. Paul: Minnesota Historical Society Press, 1978.

André Le Vot, *F. Scott Fitzgerald: A Biography.* Translated by William Byron. New York: Doubleday, 1983.

Sara Mayfield, *Exiles from Paradise.* New York: Delacorte Press, 1971.

Jeffrey Meyers, *Scott Fitzgerald: A Biography.* New York: HarperCollins, 1994.

Nancy Milford, *Zelda.* New York: Harper & Row, 1970.

Arthur Mizener, *The Far Side of Paradise: A Biography of F. Scott Fitzgerald.* Boston: Houghton Mifflin, 1951.

——, *Scott Fitzgerald and His World.* New York: Putnam, 1972.

David Page and Jack Koblas, *F. Scott Fitzgerald in Minnesota: Toward the Summit.* St. Cloud, MN: North Star Press of St. Cloud, 1996.

Henry Dan Piper, *F. Scott Fitzgerald: A Critical Portrait.* New York: Holt, Rinehart & Winston, 1965.

Charles E. Shain, *F. Scott Fitzgerald.* University of Minnesota Pamphlets on American Writers, No. 15. Minneapolis: University of Minnesota, 1961. (Also available as Charles E. Shain, "F. Scott Fitzgerald," in William Van O'Connor, ed., *Seven Modern American Novelists: An Introduction.* Minneapolis: University of Minnesota Press, 1964.)

Andrew Turnbull, *Scott Fitzgerald.* New York: Scribner's, 1962.

CRITICISM

Jackson Bryer, *The Critical Reputation of F. Scott Fitzgerald.* Hamden, CT: Shoe String Press, 1967.

John F. Callahan, *The Illusions of a Nation: Myth and History in the Novels of F. Scott Fitzgerald.* Urbana: University of Illinois, 1972.

Robert Cowley and Malcolm Cowley, eds., *Fitzgerald and the Jazz Age.* New York: Scribner's, 1966.

Katie de Koster, *Readings on F. Scott Fitzgerald,* San Diego: Greenhaven Press, 1998.

Scott Donaldson, ed., *Critical Essays on F. Scott Fitzgerald's The Great Gatsby.* Boston: G.K. Hall, 1984.

Kenneth Eble, ed., *F. Scott Fitzgerald: A Collection of Criticism.* New York: McGraw-Hill, 1973.

A.E. Elmore, *"The Great Gatsby* as Well Wrought Urn," in Thomas Daniel Young, ed., *Modern American Fiction: Form and Function.* Baton Rouge: Louisiana State University Press, 1989.

Frederick J. Hoffman, ed., *The Great Gatsby: A Study.* New York: Scribner's, 1962.

Alfred Kazin, ed., *F. Scott Fitzgerald: The Man and His Work.* New York: World, 1951.

Richard D. Lehan, *F. Scott Fitzgerald and the Craft of Fiction.* Carbondale: Southern Illinois University, 1966.

Ernest H. Lockridge, ed., *Twentieth Century Interpretations of The Great Gatsby: A Collection of Critical Essays.* Englewood Cliffs, NJ: Prentice-Hall, 1968.

Robert Emmet Long, *The Achieving of The Great Gatsby.* Cranbury, NJ: Associated University Presses, 1979.

Arthur Mizener, "F. Scott Fitzgerald: *The Great Gatsby,*" in Wallace Stegner, ed., *The American Novel: From James Fenimore Cooper to William Faulkner.* New York: Basic Books, 1965.

Sergio Perosa, *The Art of F. Scott Fitzgerald.* Translated by Charles Matz and Sergio Perosa. Ann Arbor: University of Michigan Press, 1965.

Robert Sklar, *F. Scott Fitzgerald: The Last Laocoön.* New York: Oxford University Press, 1967.

Milton Stern, *The Golden Moment: The Novels of F. Scott Fitzgerald.* Urbana: University of Illinois, 1970.

Brian Way, *F. Scott Fitzgerald and the Art of Social Fiction.* New York: St. Martin's Press, 1980.

HISTORICAL OR LITERARY BACKGROUND

Frederick Lewis Allen, *Only Yesterday: An Informal History of the Nineteen-Twenties.* New York: Harper, 1931. Reprint, New York: Perennial Library, 1964.

Ralph K. Andrist, ed., *The American Heritage History of the 20's and 30's.* New York: American Heritage, 1970.

A. Scott Berg, *Max Perkins: Editor of Genius.* New York: E.P. Dutton, 1978.

Matthew J. Bruccoli, *Scott and Ernest: The Authority of Failure and the Authority of Success.* New York: Random House, 1978.

Paul Allen Carter, *The Twenties in America.* New York: Crowell, 1968.

———, *The Uncertain World of Normalcy: The 1920's.* New York: Pitman, 1971.

Malcolm Cowley, *Exile's Return: A Literary Odyssey of the 1920s.* New York: Norton, 1934. Revised and expanded edition, New York: Viking, 1951. Edition with introduction and notes by Donald W. Faulkner, New York: Penguin, 1994.

Lynn Dumenil, *The Modern Temper: American Culture and Society in the 1920s.* New York: Hill and Wang, 1995.

Ellis Wayne Hawley, *The Great War and the Search for a Modern Order: A History of the American People and Their Institutions, 1917–1933.* New York: St. Martin's, 1979.

Ernest Hemingway, *A Moveable Feast.* New York: Scribner's, 1964.

Joan Hoff-Wilson, ed., *The Twenties: The Critical Issues.* Boston: Little, Brown, 1972.

Ethan Mordden, *That Jazz! An Idiosyncratic Social History of the American Twenties.* New York: Putnam, 1978.

Richard Brandon Morris and James Woodress, eds., *Boom and Bust: 1920–1939.* New York: McGraw-Hill, 1976.

Michael E. Parrish, *Anxious Decades: America in Prosperity and Depression, 1920–1941.* New York: Norton, 1992.

Geoffrey Perrett, *America in the Twenties: A History.* New York: Simon & Schuster, 1982.

Milton Plesur, ed., *The 1920's: Problems and Paradoxes.* Boston: Allyn and Bacon, 1969.

Paul Sann, *The Lawless Decade: A Pictorial History of a Great American Transition, from the World War I Armistice and Prohibition to Repeal and the New Deal.* New York: Crown, 1957.

Arthur M. Schlesinger Jr., *The Crisis of the Old Order, 1919–1933.* Boston: Houghton Mifflin, 1957.

Elizabeth Stevenson, *Babbitts and Bohemians: The American 1920s.* New York: Macmillan, 1970.

Edmund Traverso, *The 1920's: Rhetoric and Reality.* Boston: D.C. Heath, 1964.

THE WORLD WIDE WEB

Websites on the internet tend to be ephemeral—here today, "not at this server" tomorrow. At this writing there are several interesting sites dedicated to Fitzgerald's work. One of these seems likely to remain available for some time to come: the Fitzgerald site at the University of South Carolina. USC has become the repository of the collection of eminent Fitzgerald scholar Matthew J. Bruccoli, and the university created an impressive website in anticipation of the one-hundredth anniversary of Fitzgerald's birth in 1996. New additions to the site appear on occasion, often bits of research by students. The USC Fitzgerald Centenary site can be accessed at this URL (internet address):
http://www.sc.edu/fitzgerald/index.html/

For an online look at one of Fitzgerald's earlier works, the complete text of *This Side of Paradise* can be found at Columbia University's Bartleby Library site, at the following URL (other works will probably be added over time):
http://www.columbia.edu/acis/bartleby/fitzgerald/

Works by F. Scott Fitzgerald

Novels

This Side of Paradise (1920)

The Beautiful and Damned (1922)

The Great Gatsby (1925)

Tender Is the Night (1934, A new edition "With the Author's Final Revisions," ed. by Malcolm Cowley, was published in 1948.)

Collected Works

Flappers and Philosophers (1920)

Six Tales of the Jazz Age (1922)

All the Sad Young Men (1926)

Taps at Reveille (1935)

Plays

Fie! Fie! Fi-Fi! (1914) A Musical Comedy in Two Acts Presented by the Princeton University Triangle Club. Plot and Lyrics by F. Scott Fitzgerald.

The Evil Eye (1915). A Musical Comedy in Two Acts Presented by the Princeton University Triangle Club. Lyrics by F. Scott Fitzgerald.

Safety First (1916). A Musical Comedy in Two Acts Presented by the Princeton University Triangle Club. Lyrics by F. Scott Fitzgerald.

The Vegetable, or, From President to Postman (1923)

Published Posthumously

The Last Tycoon (1941, unfinished), edited with an introduction by Edmund Wilson

The Crack-Up (1945). With Other Uncollected Pieces, Note-Books and Unpublished Letters. Edited by Edmund Wilson.

The Stories of F. Scott Fitzgerald (1951)

Afternoon of an Author (1957). A Selection of Uncollected Stories and Essays.

The Pat Hobby Stories (1962)

The Letters of F. Scott Fitzgerald (1963), edited by Andrew Turnbull

The Apprentice Fiction of Francis Scott Fitzgerald (1965), 1909–17, edited by John Kuehl

Bits of Paradise (1973, twenty-one stories by F. Scott and Zelda Fitzgerald), edited by Matthew J. Bruccoli

The Price Was High (1979), edited by Matthew J. Bruccoli

F. Scott Fitzgerald: A Life in Letters (1994), edited and annotated by Matthew J. Bruccoli

INDEX

Adams, Brooks, 107
Adams, Henry, 19, 110
  on American materialism, 104–105
Adams, James Truslow, 129
Aiken, Conrad, 74
Alger, Horatio, Jr., 108, 121, 128
All the Sad Young Men, 30
Ambassadors, The (James), 36
American, The (James), 104
American Dream
  concept of, 124–25
  Daisy as symbol of, 84
  Gatsby as tribute and indictment of, 103
  Jay Gatsby as end-product of, 108–109
  materialist vs. romantic version, 117–18
  and nativism, 123–24, 129–30
American Mercury, 41
American Scene, The (James), 104, 109
American Tragedy (Dreiser), 79
America's Race Heritage (Burr), 127
Amorous, Martin, 19
"An Author's Mother," 16
aristocracy
  vs. democracy, in 1920s literature, 78–79
  failure of, 57
Arnstein, Jules "Nicky," 45
Art of F. Scott Fitzgerald, The (Perosa), 19
Asbury, Herbert, 41
Auchincloss, Louis, 83
Awkward Age, The (James)
  structural similarities with *Gatsby*, 52–53

Babbitt (Lewis), 82
Baker, Carlos, 75
Baker, Jordan, 50, 86, 157
  and Nick, 168–69
Barzun, Jacques, 98
Beautiful and the Damned, The, 26–27, 68, 176, 177
  characters
    Anthony Patch, 35, 36, 175, 176
    Gloria Gilbert, 176
  wealth and class as issue in, 175
Becker, Mary Lamberton, 134
Bewley, Marius, 96, 116, 123, 124, 155
Big Money, The (Dos Passos), 76–77
Birkerts, Sven, 168

Bishop, John Peale, 15, 20
Bradbury, Malcolm, 141
Brooks, Van Wyck, 74
Bruccoli, Matthew J., 16, 117
  on "The Pierian Springs and the Last Straw," 21
Buckner, Park, 70

characters, 37, 135
  Daisy Fay Buchanan, 21, 38–39, 91
    as American Dream, 84
    characterization of, 84, 93, 99
    divided perspective on, 155–56
    the green light as symbol of, 62, 100
    love for Gatsby, 57
    Midwestern roots of, 69
    qualities of, 114–15
    relationship with Gatsby, 63–65
  Dan Cody, 37, 57, 128
    as surrogate father, 90–91
  Ella Kaye, 91
  ethical indifference of, 81
  George Wilson, 71, 80, 81, 95, 169
  Henry Gatz, 36, 39, 109
  Jay Gatsby, 84
    background of, 126
      reveals truth of, 66
      rumors about, 165
    and Tom Buchanan
      as antagonists, 101–102
      resemblance to, 109
    and Carraway
      Gatsby as creation of, 156–57
      Nick's response to dream, 158–60
        assumption of responsibility for, 161–62
      Nick's take on, 48–51
    as comic character, 54, 56
    death of, 101
    deific quality of, 63, 89
    early ambition of, 129
    ego-ideal of, 62
    as end-product of American Dream, 108–109
    as Fitzgerald's alter ego, 15
    as gangster dandy, 42
    grandiosity of, 64, 91
    isolation of, 86
    and life of illusion, 114
    as model of spiritual ascent, 87–88
    as mythic character, 98–99
    paradox of, 47–48

parallels with Myrtle Wilson, 167
parties of, 57, 58–59
relationship with Daisy, 63–65
as self-made man, 121
sense of entitlement of, 63–64
Meyer Wolfsheim, 44, 45
Nick's encounters with, 56
and racial nativism, 126
as racial stereotype, 127
as surrogate father, 90–91
as moral commentaries, 112–15
Myrtle Wilson, 35, 55, 95
parallels with Gatsby, 167
Nick Carraway, 34
as Fitzgerald's alter ego, 15
Gatsby as creation of, 156–57
middle-class voice of, 69
as mirror to Gatsby, 66–67
as moral and compositional
center, 150–51
moral growth of, 112–13
reliability as narrator, 61
response to Daisy, 93
response to Gatsby's dream, 158–60
assumption of responsibility for,
161–62
understanding of Jay Gatsby,
48–51, 86
use of paraphrase, 159–60
as reflection of Fitzgerald's worldview, 118–19
T.J. Eckleburg
eyes of, 80, 92, 163, 171
religion-business theme in, 82
symbolism of, 81
Tom Buchanan, 21
and Gatsby, as antagonists,
101–102
hypocrisy of, 57
Midwestern roots of, 69
provinciality of, 39
shallowness of, 114
Chicago Daily Tribune, 25
Civilization in the United States, 74, 82
Clark, Edwin, 133
Coles, Robert, 111
*Connecticut Yankee in King Arthur's
Court, A* (Twain), 105
Conrad, Joseph, 161, 179
Coolidge, Calvin, 82, 122
Cowley, Malcolm, 30, 73, 77, 145
"Crack-Up, The," 33, 141
crime
as business of Gatsby, 46
connection of foreigners with, 125
in 1920s, 41–42
racketeer as last great folk hero, 38

real world influence on characters,
43–47
cultural periods
Apollonian vs. Faustian, 107

"Dalrymple Goes Wrong," 174
Decker, Jeffrey Louis, 121
Decline of the West, The (Spengler), 107
Democracy in America (de
Tocqueville), 78
"Diamond as Big as the Ritz, The,"
177, 178
Dickens, Charles, 55
Donaldson, Scott, 139
Dos Passos, John, 68, 75, 76
Dreiser, Theodore, 79
Durr, Virginia Foster, 23

Education of Henry Adams, The
(Adams), 104
Eliot, T.S., 77, 118
Elmer Gantry (Lewis), 75, 82
Emerson, Ralph Waldo, 87
Epic of America, The (Adams), 130
Exile's Return (Cowley), 73

Faulkner, William, 68, 76
Fay, Sigourney Webster, 19
*Fictional Technique of F. Scott
Fitzgerald* (Miller), 166
Fitzgerald, Edward (father), 16, 17, 18
Fitzgerald, F. Scott, 137
army life of, 22–23
bifurcated vision of, 148–49
childhood of, 16–18
courtship of Zelda Sayre, 23–25
creation of genteel romantic
heroine, 176
death of, 31
and Hemingway, 29
in Hollywood, 30
as novelist of immersion, 141
at Princeton, 19–22
pursuit of Ginevra King, 20–21
on reviewers, 138–39
self-understanding as goal of, 171
Spenglerian influence on, 106–107
young men in early work of, 68
Fitzgerald, Frances Scott (daughter), 25
Fitzgerald, Mary McQuillan (mother),
16, 17, 18
Fitzgerald, Zelda Sayre (wife), 23
death of, 31
engagement to Scott, 24
as model for Daisy, 115, 116
schizophrenia of, 25, 28, 30
Flappers and Philosophers, 26

"Four Fists, The," 175
Franklin, Benjamin, 121, 129
F. Scott Fitzgerald and the Craft of Fiction (Lehan), 109
Fussell, Edwin, 123, 124

Goldhurst, William, 73
Great Gatsby, The
  class differences in, 69
  East-West dichotomy in, 36–37, 40, 69
  fairy-tale elements in, 70–71, 100–101
  Fitzgerald's comic genius in, 60
  good vs. evil in, 71
  mythical nature of, 83–84, 98–99
    myth vs. history, 88–90
  narrative framework of, 166–67
  narrative sense of, 164–65
  as novel of new insights of old ideas, 173–74
  popularity of, 29, 139
  quest of romantic dream as theme in, 34
  scenic construction of, 52–54
  sense of absurd in, 55
  Spenglerian influence in, 107–108
  Zelda's influence on, 28

"Head and Shoulders," 25
Heart of Darkness (Conrad), 161
Hemingway, Ernest, 28, 29, 68, 143, 144, 145
Hofstadter, Richard, 89
Hopper, Edward, 85

Incorporation of America, The (Trachtenberg), 90
"Intellectual Life, The" (Stearns), 74
In the American Grain (Williams), 122
irony, 152
  in Fitzgerald's romantic dream, 35–36
Islands in the Stream (Hemingway), 144

James, Henry, 36, 54, 70
  on American materialism, 104
  compared with Fitzgerald, 52, 71, 109, 134
Jazz Age, 31
  affluence during, 116
  Daisy as symbol of, 100
  see also 1920s
Jefferson, Thomas, 97
"Jelly Bean, The," 176
Joyce, James, 179

Keats, John, 179
King, Ginevra, 20, 173

as model for Daisy, 115–16
Kohlberg, Lawrence, 113

Lardner, Ring, 74, 75, 76
Last Tycoon, The, 146
  Irving Thalberg as inspiration for, 31
Law of Civilization and Decay, The (Adams), 107
Lehan, Richard, 104
Leslie, Shane, 19
Le Vot, André, 29
Lewis, Sinclair, 75, 82
Lid, R.W., 163
Lippmann, Walter, 82
"Literary Life, The" (Brooks), 74
Long, Robert Emmet, 68
Lord Jim (Conrad), 161
Lorimer, George Horace, 122
Lynn, David H., 154

Main Street (Lewis), 76
Malraux, André, 172
Manhattan Transfer (Dos Passos), 69
Man's Hope (Malraux), 172
materialism, 104, 108
McAdams, Tony, 111
Mencken, H.L., 74, 78, 175
  on character of Gatsby, 54
  on Fitzgerald's versatility, 174
Michaelis, 169
Mitchell, Giles, 61
Mizener, Arthur, 15, 19, 85
  on Fitzgerald's use of narrator, 170
  on Zelda's affair, 28
Moby-Dick (Melville), 88, 168
Mumford, Lewis, 74
Myers, Alonzo, 23
"Myths for Materialists" (Barzun), 98

narrative sense of, 164–65
nativism, 122, 123, 130
  rising sentiment of, 125
Nietzsche, Friedrich, 175
nineteen-twenties
  business-of-religion phenomenon in, 82
  Fitzgerald's vision of, 70
  literary community of, 73–75
  literature of
    help shaped the period, 79–80
    significance of automobile in, 76–77
    variations in dominant motifs of, 79
  nativist and racist trends in, 122–23, 125–28, 130
Nordicism, 122

nostalgia, 65, 110, 153
  as common character trait, 92
  Fitzgerald's, for Jazz Age, 31
  in Gatsby's romantic dream, 37

"Offshore Pirate, The," 175, 178
Ornstein, Robert, 33
owl-eyed man, 59, 108, 163
  symbolism of, 81

Parker, Dorothy, 28
"Passing of the Gangster, The"
  (Asbury), 41
Pauly, Thomas H., 41
Perkins, Maxwell, 25, 27, 29, 117, 139,
  166
Petronius, 59
  influence on Fitzgerald, 60
"Pierian Springs and the Last Straw,
  The," 21
Plath, Sylvia, 70
Portrait of a Lady, The (James), 36, 71
Preface to Morals, A (Lippmann), 82
Prohibition
  connection of foreigners with, 125–26
  Jay Gatsby as product of, 51
  and rise of the gangster, 42, 43

Rascoe, Burton, 25, 133
Remus, George, 43
"Rich Boy, The," 35
Rising Tide of Color, The (Stoddard),
  108
"Romantic Egoist, The," 22
Rowe, Joyce A., 87

Sartoris (Faulkner), 69, 76
Saturday Evening Post
  Fitzgerald sells first story to, 25
  nativism expressed by, 122
Saturday Review
  on mystery of Jay Gatsby, 48
Satyricon, The (Petronius), 58, 59
Sayre, Zelda. *See* Fitzgerald, Zelda
  Sayre
Scarlet Letter, The (Hawthorne), 83,
  86, 158
"Scott Fitzgerald's Criticism of Amer-
  ica" (Bewley), 123
Scribner's Publishing Co., 19, 29
Sklar, Robert, 172
Smith, J. Thorne, 82
Spengler, Oswald, 106–107, 108
Spingarn, J.E., 74
Stearns, Harold, 74
Sun Also Rises, The (Hemingway), 28,
  29, 145, 147
"Swastika Holding Company," 124, 127

symbolism
  Dutch sailors, 106
    Gatsby as spiritual descendant of, 37
    link with nativism, 122
  eyes, 59, 80, 92, 108, 163, 171
    religion-business theme in, 82
    symbolism of, 81
  the green light, 35, 37
    as symbol of Daisy, 62

Tales of the Jazz Age, 27, 178
Taylor, Douglas, 147
Tender Is the Night, 30, 142, 144, 145,
  155
themes
  decline of the West, 106
  East-West dichotomy, 36–37, 40, 69,
    93–95, 114
  materialism vs. idealism, 104–105
  quest of romantic dream, 34
  as reflection of Fitzgerald's world-
    view, 118–19
  religion as business, 82
  suffusion of the material by the
    ideal, 143
  wealth and class, 174–75
"There Are Smiles" (Lardner), 76
This Side of Paradise, 22, 25, 36, 133,
  142, 174, 177
  characters
    Amory Blaine, 36, 174, 175, 177
    Rosalind, Ginevra King as model
      for, 21
  wealth and class as issue in, 174
Tocqueville, Alexis de, 78
Trachtenberg, Alan, 90
Trilling, Lionel, 123
Trimalchio, 58, 59, 60, 170
Turner, Frederick Jackson, 128
Turn of the Screw (James), 134
Twain, Mark, 105
"Two for a Cent," 175

"Unspeakable Egg, The," 175

Valley of Ashes, 80, 107, 171
Vegetable, The, 27, 29

Waste Land, The (Eliot), 77, 118
  motif in *The Great Gatsby*, 80
Way, Brian, 52
Wharton, Edith, 54, 56
Why Europe Leaves Home (Roberts),
  122
Williams, William Carlos, 122
Wilson, Edmund, 20, 24, 107, 117
Winesburg, Ohio (Anderson), 76
World Series of 1919, fixing of, 44, 45